OSGi Service Platform, Core Specification
Release 4, Version 4.2

OSGi Service Platform
Core Specification

Release 4, Version 4.2
June 2009

OSGi Alliance / aQute Publishing

Publisher

aQute Publishing
9c, Avenue St. Drézéry
34160 Beaulieu
FRANCE
http://www.aQute.biz

ISBN 978-90-79350-04-9   aQute Publishing

Legal Notice

The publisher is not responsible for he use which might be made of the following information.

Trademarks

OSGi™ is a trademark, registered trademark, or service mark of the OSGi Alliance in the US and other countries. Java is a trademark, registered trademark, or service mark of Sun Microsystems, Inc. in the US and other countries. All other trademarks, registered trademarks, or service marks used in this document are the property of their respective owners and are hereby recognized.

Feedback

This specification can be downloaded from the OSGi Alliance web site:

    http://www.osgi.org

Comments about this specification can be mailed to:

    speccomments@mail.osgi.org

Disclaimer

This is a reprinted copy of the OSGi Service Platform Core Specification, Release 4, Version 4.2. To fit the book size, this document had to be reformatted. In the unlikely case of any discrepancies between the original document and this book, the original document overrides this book. The original document can be downloaded from http://www.osgi.org

OSGi Specification License, Version 1.0

The OSGi Alliance ("OSGi Alliance") hereby grants you a fully-paid, non-exclusive, non-transferable, worldwide, limited license (without the right to sublicense), under the OSGi Alliance's applicable intellectual property rights to view, download, and reproduce the OSGi Specification ("Specification") which follows this License Agreement ("Agreement"). You are not authorized to create any derivative work of the Specification. The OSGi Alliance also grants you a perpetual, non-exclusive, worldwide, fully paid-up, royalty free, limited license (without the right to sublicense) under any applicable copyrights, to create and/or distribute an implementation of the Specification that: (i) fully implements the Specification including all its required interfaces and functionality; (ii) does not modify, subset, superset or otherwise extend the OSGi Name Space, or include any public or protected packages, classes, Java interfaces, fields or methods within the OSGi Name Space other than those required and authorized by the Specification. An implementation that does not satisfy limitations (i)-(ii) is not considered an implementation of the Specification, does not receive the benefits of this license, and must not be described as an implementation of the Specification. An implementation of the Specification must not claim to be a compliant implementation of the Specification unless it passes the OSGi Alliance Compliance Tests for the Specification in accordance with OSGi Alliance processes. "OSGi Name Space" shall mean the public class or interface declarations whose names begin with "org.osgi" or any recognized successors or replacements thereof.

THE SPECIFICATION IS PROVIDED "AS IS," AND THE OSGi ALLIANCE, ITS MEMBERS AND ANY OTHER AUTHORS MAKE NO REPRESENTATIONS OR WARRANTIES, EXPRESS OR IMPLIED, INCLUDING, BUT NOT LIMITED TO, WARRANTIES OF MERCHANTABILITY, FITNESS FOR A PARTICULAR PURPOSE, NON-INFRINGEMENT, OR TITLE; THAT THE CONTENTS OF THE SPECIFICATION ARE SUITABLE FOR ANY PURPOSE; NOR THAT THE IMPLEMENTATION OF SUCH CONTENTS WILL NOT INFRINGE ANY THIRD PARTY PATENTS, COPYRIGHTS, TRADEMARKS OR OTHER RIGHTS. THE OSGi ALLIANCE, ITS MEMBERS AND ANY OTHER AUTHORS WILL NOT BE LIABLE FOR ANY DIRECT, INDIRECT, SPECIAL, INCIDENTAL OR CONSEQUENTIAL DAMAGES ARISING OUT OF ANY USE OF THE SPECIFICATION OR THE PERFORMANCE OR IMPLEMENTATION OF THE CONTENTS THEREOF.

The name and trademarks of the OSGi Alliance or any other Authors may NOT be used in any manner, including advertising or publicity pertaining to the Specification or its contents without specific, written prior permission. Title to copyright in the Specification will at all times remain with the Authors.

No other rights are granted by implication, estoppel or otherwise.

Table Of Contents

1 Introduction

The OSGi™ Alliance was founded in March 1999. Its mission is to create open specifications for the network delivery of managed services to local networks and devices. The OSGi organization is the leading standard for next-generation Internet services to homes, cars, mobile phones, desktops, small offices, and other environments.

The OSGi Service Platform specification delivers an open, common architecture for service providers, developers, software vendors, gateway operators and equipment vendors to develop, deploy and manage services in a coordinated fashion. It enables an entirely new category of smart devices due to its flexible and managed deployment of services. OSGi specifications target set-top boxes, service gateways, cable modems, consumer electronics, PCs, industrial computers, cars, mobile phones, and more. Devices that implement the OSGi specifications will enable service providers like telcos, cable operators, utilities, and others to deliver differentiated and valuable services over their networks.

This is the fourth release of the OSGi Service Platform specification developed by representatives from OSGi member companies. The OSGi Service Platform Release 4 mostly extends the existing APIs into new areas. The few modifications to existing APIs are backward compatible so that applications for previous releases should run unmodified on Release 4 Frameworks. The built-in version management mechanisms allow bundles written for the new release to adapt to the old Framework implementations, if necessary.

1.1 OSGi Framework Overview

The Framework forms the core of the OSGi Service Platform Specifications. It provides a general-purpose, secure, and managed Java framework that supports the deployment of extensible and downloadable applications known as *bundles*.

OSGi-compliant devices can download and install OSGi bundles, and remove them when they are no longer required. The Framework manages the installation and update of bundles in an OSGi environment in a dynamic and scalable fashion. To achieve this, it manages the dependencies between bundles and services in detail.

It provides the bundle developer with the resources necessary to take advantage of Java's platform independence and dynamic code-loading capability in order to easily develop services for small-memory devices that can be deployed on a large scale.

The functionality of the Framework is divided in the following layers:

- Security Layer
- Module Layer
- Life Cycle Layer
- Service Layer
- Actual Services

This layering is depicted in Figure 1.1.

Figure 1.1   *Layering*

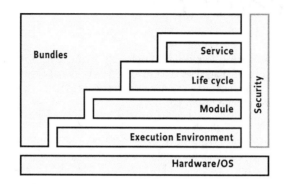

The Security Layer is based on Java 2 security but adds a number of constraints and fills in some of the blanks that standard Java leaves open. It defines a secure packaging format as well as the runtime interaction with the Java 2 security layer. The Security Layer is described in *Security Layer* on page 9.

The Module Layer defines a modularization model for Java. It addresses some of the shortcomings of Java's deployment model. The modularization layer has strict rules for sharing Java packages between bundles or hiding packages from other bundles. The Module Layer can be used without the life cycle and Service Layer. The Life Cycle Layer provides an API to manage the *bundles* in the Module Layer, while the Service Layer provides a communication model for the bundles. The Module Layer is described in *Module Layer* on page 23.

The Life Cycle Layer provides a life cycle API to bundles. This API provides a runtime model for bundles. It defines how bundles are started and stopped as well as how bundles are installed, updated and uninstalled. Additionally, it provides a comprehensive event API to allow a management bundle to control the operations of the service platform. The Life Cycle Layer requires the Module Layer but the Security Layer is optional. A more extensive description of the Life Cycle layer can be found at *Life Cycle Layer* on page 73

The Service Layer provides a dynamic, concise and consistent programming model for Java bundle developers, simplifying the development and deployment of service bundles by de-coupling the service's specification (Java interface) from its implementations. This model allows bundle developers to bind to services only using their interface specifications. The selection of a specific implementation, optimized for a specific need or from a specific vendor, can thus be deferred to run-time.

A consistent programming model helps bundle developers cope with scalability issues in many different dimensions – critical because the Framework is intended to run on a variety of devices whose differing hardware characteristics may affect many aspects of a service implementation. Consistent interfaces insure that the software components can be mixed and matched and still result in stable systems.

The Framework allows bundles to select an available implementation at run-time through the Framework service registry. Bundles register new services, receive notifications about the state of services, or look up existing services to adapt to the current capabilities of the device. This aspect of the Framework makes an installed bundle extensible after deployment: new bundles can be installed for added features or existing bundles can be modified and updated without requiring the system to be restarted.

The Service Layer is described in *Service Layer* on page 105.

The interactions between the layers is depicted in Figure 1.2.

Figure 1.2   *Interactions between layers*

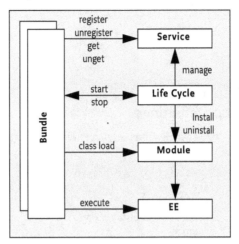

1.2   **Reader Level**

This specification is written for the following audiences:

*   Application developers
*   Framework and system service developers (system developers)
*   Architects

The OSGi Specifications assume that the reader has at least one year of practical experience in writing Java programs. Experience with embedded systems and server environments is a plus. Application developers must be aware that the OSGi environment is significantly more dynamic than traditional desktop or server environments.

System developers require a *very* deep understanding of Java. At least three years of Java coding experience in a system environment is recommended. A Framework implementation will use areas of Java that are not normally encountered in traditional applications. Detailed understanding is required of class loaders, garbage collection, Java 2 security, and Java native library loading.

Architects should focus on the introduction of each subject. This introduction contains a general overview of the subject, the requirements that influenced its design, and a short description of its operation as well as the entities that are used. The introductory sections require knowledge of Java concepts like classes and interfaces, but should not require coding experience.

Most of these specifications are equally applicable to application developers and system developers.

1.3   **Conventions and Terms**

1.3.1   **Typography**

A fixed width, non-serif typeface (sample) indicates the term is a Java package, class, interface, or member name. Text written in this typeface is always related to coding.

Emphasis (*sample*) is used the first time an important concept is introduced. Its explanation usually follows directly after the introduction.

When an example contains a line that must be broken into multiple lines, the « character is used. Spaces must be ignored in this case. For example:

```
http://www.acme.com/sp/ «
file?abc=12
```

is equivalent to:

```
http://www.acme.com/sp/file?abc=12
```

1.3.2   General Syntax Definitions

In many cases in these specifications, a syntax must be described. This syntax is based on the following symbols:

```
*               Repetition of the previous element zero or
                more times, e.g. ( ',' element ) *
+               Repetition one or more times
?               Previous element is optional
( ... )         Grouping
'...'           Literal
|               Or
[...]           Set (one of)
..              list, e.g. 1..5 is the list 1 2 3 4 5
<...>           Externally defined token
```

The following tokens are pre defined and used throughout the specifications:

```
digit          ::= [0..9]
alpha          ::= [a..zA..Z]
alphanum       ::= alpha | digit
token          ::= ( alphanum | '_' | '-' )+
number         ::= digit+
jletter        ::= <see [5] Lexical Structure Java Language for
                      JavaLetter>
jletterordigit::= <See [5] Lexical Structure Java Language for
                      JavaLetterOrDigit >

qname          ::= /* See [5] Lexical Structure Java Language for
                      fully qualified class names */
identifier     ::= jletter jletterordigit *
extended       ::= ( alphanum | '_' | '-' | '.' )+
quoted-string::= '"' ( [^"\#x0D#x0A#x00] | '\"'|'\\')* '"'
argument       ::= extended  | quoted-string
parameter      ::= directive | attribute
directive      ::= token ':=' argument
attribute      ::= token '=' argument

unique-name    ::= identifier ( '.' identifier )*
symbolic-name  ::= token('.'token)*
package-name   ::= unique-name

path           ::= path-unquoted | ('"' path-unquoted '"')
path-unquoted::= path-sep | path-sep? path-element
                    (path-sep path-element)*
path-element   ::= [^/"\#x0D#x0A#x00]+
path-sep       ::= '/'
```

Whitespaces between terminals are ignored unless specifically noted. Any value that contains a space, a comma, semi-colon, colon, equal sign or any other character that is part of a terminal in the grammar must be quoted.

1.3.3   Object Oriented Terminology

Concepts like classes, interfaces, objects, and services are distinct but subtly different. For example, "LogService" could mean an instance of the class LogService, could refer to the class LogService, or could indicate the functionality of the overall Log Service. Experts usually understand the meaning from the context, but this understanding requires mental effort. To highlight these subtle differences, the following conventions are used.

When the class is intended, its name is spelled exactly as in the Java source code and displayed in a fixed-width typeface: for example, the "HttpService class", "a method in the HttpContext class" or "a javax.servlet.Servlet object". A class name is used in its fully qualified form, like javax.servlet.Servlet, when the package is not obvious from the context, nor is it in one of the well known java packages like java.lang, java.io, java.util and java.net. Otherwise, the package is omitted like in String.

In many cases, a type can be used as a scalar but also a collection of that type or an array of that type. In those cases, a simple + will be suffixed to the type. For example String+, indicates that a String, a String[], and a Collection<String> are all valid forms.

Exception and permission classes are not followed by the word "object". Readability is improved when the "object" suffix is avoided. For example, "to throw a Security Exception" and to "to have File Permission" is more readable then "to have a FilePermission object".

Permissions can further be qualified with their actions. ServicePermission[com.acme.*, GET|REGISTER] means a ServicePermission with the action GET and REGISTER for all service names starting with com.acme. A ServicePermission[Producer|Consumer, REGISTER] means the ServicePermission for the Producer or Consumer class with REGISTER action.

When discussing functionality of a class rather than the implementation details, the class name is written as normal text. This convention is often used when discussing services. For example, "the User Admin service" is more readable.

Some services have the word "Service" embedded in their class name. In those cases, the word "service" is only used once but is written with an upper case S. For example, "the Log Service performs".

Service objects are registered with the OSGi Framework. Registration consists of the service object, a set of properties, and a list of classes and interfaces implemented by this service object. The classes and interfaces are used for type safety *and* naming. Therefore, it is said that a service object is registered *under* a class/interface. For example, "This service object is registered under PermissionAdmin."

1.3.4   Diagrams

The diagrams in this document illustrate the specification and are not normative. Their purpose is to provide a high-level overview on a single page. The following paragraphs describe the symbols and conventions used in these diagrams.

Classes or interfaces are depicted as rectangles, as in Figure 1.3. Interfaces are indicated with the qualifier <<interface>> as the first line. The name of the class/interface is indicated in bold when it is part of the specification. Implementation classes are sometimes shown to demonstrate a possible implementation. Implementation class names are shown in plain text. In certain cases class names are abbreviated. This is indicated by ending the abbreviation with a period.

Figure 1.3   *Class and interface symbol*

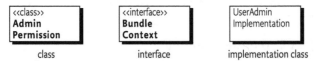

If an interface or class is used as a service object, it will have a black triangle in the bottom right corner.

Figure 1.4   *Service symbol*

Service are crucial interaction elements and they can occur many times in diagrams describing services. Therefore, an alternative service symbol is the triangle. Triangles can be connected in different ways, representing different meanings:

- *Point* – Connections to the point of a triangle indicate the registration. This makes the point of the triangle point to the object that receives the method calls from the service users.
- *Straight Side* – Connections to the straight side indicate service clients. Clients call the methods of the service.
- *Angled Side* – The angled side is reserved for service listeners.

Figure 1.5   *Alternative Service symbol*

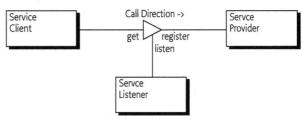

Inheritance (the extends or implements keyword in Java class definitions) is indicated with an arrow. Figure 1.6 shows that the AdminPermission class implements or extends the Permission class.

Figure 1.6   *Inheritance (implements or extends) symbol*

Relations are depicted with a line. The cardinality of the relation is given explicitly when relevant. Figure 1.7 shows that each (1) BundleContext object is related to 0 or more BundleListener objects, and that each BundleListener object is related to a single BundleContext object. Relations usually have some description associated with them. This description should be read from left to right and top to bottom, and includes the classes on both sides. For example: "A BundleContext object delivers bundle events to zero or more BundleListener objects."

Figure 1.7   *Relations symbol*

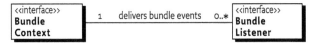

Associations are depicted with a dashed line. Associations are between classes, and an association can be placed on a relation. For example, "every ServiceRegistration object has an associated ServiceReference object." This association does not have to be a hard relationship, but could be derived in some way.

When a relationship is qualified by a name or an object, it is indicated by drawing a dotted line perpendicular to the relation and connecting this line to a class box or a description. Figure 1.8 shows that the relationship between a UserAdmin class and a Role class is qualified by a name. Such an association is usually implemented with a Dictionary or Map object.

Figure 1.8   *Associations symbol*

Bundles are entities that are visible in normal application programming. For example, when a bundle is stopped, all its services will be unregistered. Therefore, the classes/interfaces that are grouped in bundles are shown on a grey rectangle as is shown in Figure 1.9.

Figure 1.9   *Bundles*

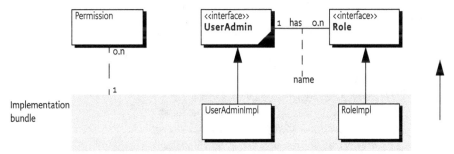

1.3.5   Key Words

This specification consistently uses the words *may, should,* and *must.* Their meaning is well-defined in [1] *Bradner, S., Key words for use in RFCs to Indicate Requirement Levels.* A summary follows.

- *must* – An absolute requirement. Both the Framework implementation and bundles have obligations that are required to be fulfilled to conform to this specification.
- *should* – Recommended. It is strongly recommended to follow the description, but reasons may exist to deviate from this recommendation.
- *may* or *can* – Optional. Implementations must still be interoperable when these items are not implemented.

1.4   Version Information

This document specifies OSGi Service Platform Core Specification, Release 4. This specification is backward compatible to releases 1, 2, and 3.

All Security, Module, Life Cycle and Service Layers are part of the Framework Specification

Components in this specification have their own specification version, independent of the document release number. The following table summarizes the packages and specification versions for the different subjects.

When a component is represented in a bundle, a version is needed in the declaration of the Import-Package or Export-Package manifest headers.

Table 1.1   *Packages and versions OSGi Service Platform, Release 4, Version 4.2*

Item	Package	Version
Framework Specification (all layers)	org.osgi.framework	Version 1.5
Framework Launching	org.osgi.framework.launch	Version 1.0
9 Conditional Permission Admin Specification	org.osgi.service.condpermission-admin	Version 1.1
7 Package Admin Service Specification	org.osgi.service.packageadmin	Version 1.2
10 Permission Admin Service Specification	org.osgi.service.permissionadmin	Version 1.2
8 Start Level Service Specification	org.osgi.service.startlevel	Version 1.1
11 URL Handlers Service Specification	org.osgi.service.url	Version 1.0
12 Service Hooks Specification	org.osgi.framework.hooks.service	Version 1.0

1.5   References

[1]   *Bradner, S., Key words for use in RFCs to Indicate Requirement Levels*
       http://www.ietf.org/rfc/rfc2119.txt, March 1997.

[2]   *OSGi Service Gateway Specification 1.0, May 2000*
       http://www.osgi.org/resources/spec_download.asp

[3]   *OSGi Service Platform, Release 2, October 2001*
       http://www.osgi.org/resources/spec_download.asp

[4]   *OSGi Service Platform, Release 3, March 2003*
       http://www.osgi.org/resources/spec_download.asp

[5]   *Lexical Structure Java Language*
       http://java.sun.com/docs/books/jls/second_edition/html/lexical.doc.html

2 Security Layer

Version 1.5

2.1 Introduction

The OSGi Security Layer is an optional layer that underlies the OSGi Service Platform. The layer is based on the Java 2 security architecture. It provides the infrastructure to deploy and manage applications that must run in fine-grained controlled environments.

2.1.1 Essentials

- *Fine-grained* – The control of applications running in an OSGi Framework must allow for detailed control of those applications.
- *Manageable* – The security layer itself does not define an API to control the applications. The management of the security layer is left to the life cycle layer.
- *Optional* – The security layer is optional.

2.2 Security Overview

The Framework security model is based on the Java 2 specification. If security checks are performed, they must be done according to [8] *Java 2 Security Architecture*. It is assumed that the reader is familiar with this specification. The security layer is optional, see *Optional Security* on page 9.

2.2.1 Code Authentication

The OSGi Service Platform can authenticate code in the following ways:

- By location
- By signer

At higher layers there are defined services that can manage the permissions that are associated with the authenticated unit of code. These services are:

- *Permission Admin service* – Manages the permission based on full location strings.
- *Conditional Permission Admin service* – Manages the permissions based on a comprehensive conditional model, where the conditions can test for location or signer.

For signing, this requires the JAR files to be signed; this is described in *Digitally Signed JAR Files* on page 10.

2.2.2 Optional Security

The Java platform on which the Framework runs must provide the Java Security APIs necessary for Java 2 permissions. On resource-constrained platforms, these Java Security APIs may be stubs that allow the bundle classes to be loaded and executed, but the stubs never actually perform the security checks. The behavior of these stubs must be as follows:

- checkPermission – Return without throwing a SecurityException.
- checkGuard – Return without throwing a SecurityException.
- implies – Return true.

This behavior allows code to run as if all bundles have AllPermission.

2.3 Digitally Signed JAR Files

This section defines in detail how JAR files must be signed. This section therefore overlaps with the different JAR file specifications that are part of the different versions of Java. The reason for this duplication is that there are many aspects left as optional or not well-defined in these specifications. A reference was therefore insufficient.

Digitally signing is a security feature that verifies the following:

- Authenticates the signer
- Ensures that the content has not been modified after it was signed by the principal.

In an OSGi Framework, the principals that signed a JAR become associated with that JAR. This association is then used to:

- Grant permissions to a JAR based on the authenticated principal
- Target a set of bundles by principal for a permission to operate on or with those bundles

For example, an Operator can grant the ACME company the right to use networking on their devices. The ACME company can then use networking in every bundle they digitally sign and deploy on the Operator's device. Also, a specific bundle can be granted permission to only manage the life cycle of bundles that are signed by the ACME company.

Signing provides a powerful delegation model. It allows an Operator to grant a restricted set of permissions to a company, after which the company can create JARs that can use those permissions, without requiring any intervention of, or communication with, the Operator for each particular JAR. This delegation model is shown graphically in Figure 2.10.

Figure 2.10   *Delegation model*

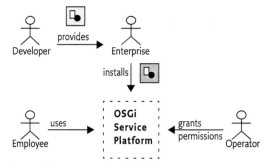

Digital signing is based on *public key cryptography*. Public key cryptography uses a system where there are two mathematically related keys: a public and a private key. The public key is shared with the world and can be dispersed freely, usually in the form of a certificate. The private key must be kept a secret.

Messages signed with the private key can only be verified correctly with the public key. This can be used to authenticate the signer of a message (assuming the public key is trusted, this is discussed in *Certificates* on page 13).

The digital signing process used is based on Java 2 JAR signing. The process of signing is repeated, restricted and augmented here to improve the inter-operability of OSGi bundles.

2.3.1 JAR Structure and Manifest

A JAR can be signed by multiple signers. Each signer must store two resources in the JAR file. These resources are:

- A signature instruction resource that has a similar format like the Manifest. It must have a .SF extension. This file provides digests for the complete manifest file.
- A PKCS#7 resource that contains the digital signature of the signature instruction resource. See [16] *Public Key Cryptography Standard #7* for information about its format.

These JAR file signing resources must be placed in the META-INF directory. For signing, the META-INF directory is special because files in there are not signed in the normal way. These signing resources must come directly after the MANIFEST.MF file, and before *any* other resources in a JAR stream. If this is not the case, then a Framework should not accept the signatures and must treat the bundle as unsigned. This ordering is important because it allows the receiver of the JAR file to stream the contents without buffering. All the security information is available before any resources are loaded. This model is shown in Figure 2.11.

Figure 2.11   *Signer files in JAR*

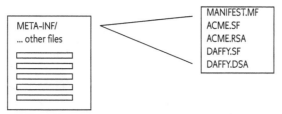

The signature instruction resource contains digests of the Manifest resource, not the actual resource data itself. A digest is a one way function that computes a value from the bytes of a resource in such a way that it is very difficult to create a set of bytes that matches that digest value.

The JAR Manifest must therefore contain one or more digests of the actual resources. These digests must be placed in their name section of the manifest. The name of the digest header is constructed with its algorithm followed by -Digest. An example is the SHA1-Digest. It is recommended that OSGi Framework implementations support the following digest algorithms.

- *MD5* – Message Digest 5, an improved version of MD4. It generates a 128-bit hash. It is described at page 436 in [12] *RFC 1321 The MD5 Message-Digest Algorithm.*
- *SHA1* – An improved version of SHA, delivers a 160 bit hash. It is defined in [11] *Secure Hash Algorithm 1.*

The hash must be encoded with a Base 64 encoding. Base 64 encoding is defined in [13] *RFC 1421 Privacy Enhancement for Internet Electronic Mail.*

For example, a manifest could look like:

```
Manifest-Version: 1.0
Bundle-Name: DisplayManifest
↵
Name: x/A.class
SHA1-Digest: RJpDp+igoJ1kxs8CSFeDtMbMq78=
↵
Name: x/B.class
SHA1-Digest: 3EuIPcx414w2QfFSXSZEBfLgKYA=
↵
```

Graphically this looks like Figure 2.12.

Figure 2.12   *Signer files in JAR*

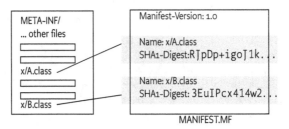

OSGi JARs must be signed by one or more signers that sign all resources except the ones in the META-INF directory; the default behavior of the jarsigner tool. This is a restriction with respect to standard Java JAR signing; there is no partial signing for an OSGi JAR. The OSGi specification only supports fully signed bundles. The reason for this restriction is because partially signing can break the protection of private packages. It also simplifies the security API because all code of a bundle is using the same protection domain.

Signature files in nested JAR files (For example JARs on the Bundle-ClassPath) must be ignored. These nested JAR files must share the same protection domain as their containing bundle. They must be treated as if their resources were stored directly in the outer JAR.

Each signature is based on two resources. The first file is the signature instruction file; this file must have a file name with an extension .SF. A signature file has the same syntax as the manifest, except that it starts with Signature-Version: 1.0 instead of Manifest-Version: 1.0.

The only relevant part of the signature resource is the digest of the Manifest resource. The name of the header must be the name algorithm (e.g. SHA1) followed by -Digest-Manifest. For example:

```
Signature-Version: 1.0
SHA1-Digest-Manifest: RJpDp+igoJ1kxs8CSFeDtMbMq78=
MD5-Digest-Manifest: IIsI6HranRNHMY27SK8M5qMunR4=
```

The signature resource can contain name sections as well. However, these name sections should be ignored.

If there are multiple signers, then their signature instruction resources can be identical if they use the same digest algorithms. However, each signer must still have its own signature instruction file. That is, it is not allowed to share the signature resource between signers.

The indirection of the signature instruction files digests is depicted in Figure 2.13 for two signers: ACME and DAFFY.

Figure 2.13   *Manifest, signature instruction files and digests in JAR*

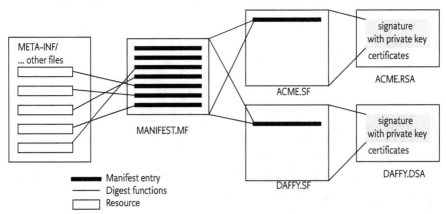

2.3.2   Java JAR File Restrictions

OSGi bundles are always valid JAR files. However, there are a few restrictions that apply to bundles that do not apply to JAR files.

- Bundles do not support partially signed bundles. The manifest must contain name sections for all resources but should not have entries for resources in the META-INF directory. Signed entries in the META-INF directory must be verified. Sub directories of META-INF must be treated like any other JAR directory.
- The name sections in the signature files are ignored. Only the Manifest digest is used.

2.3.3   Valid Signature

A bundle can be signed with a *signature* by multiple signers. A signature contains a pair of a signature file, with a SF extension and a PKCS#7 resource that has the same name as the signature file but with either an RSA or DSA extension.

Such a signature is valid when:

- The signature file has an entry for the META-INF/MANIFEST.MF resource.
- The manifest entry must contain an SHA1 and/or MD5 digest for the complete manifest.
- All listed digests match the manifest.
- The PCKS#7 resource is a valid signature (either signed using RSA or DSA as indicated by the extension) for the signature resource.

For a complete bundle to be validly signed it is necessary that all signatures are valid. That is, if one of the signatures is invalid, the whole bundle must be treated as unsigned.

2.3.4   Signing Algorithms

Several different available algorithms can perform digital signing. OSGi Framework implementations should support the following algorithms:

- *DSA* – The Digital Signature Algorithm. This standard is defined in [14] *DSA*. This is a USA government standard for Digital Signature Standard. The signature resource name must have an extension of .DSA.
- *RSA* – Rivest, Shamir and Adleman. A public key algorithm that is very popular. It is defined in [15] *RSA*. The extension of the signature resource name must be .RSA.

The signature files for RSA and DSA are stored in a PCKS#7 format. This is a format that has a structure as defined in [16] *Public Key Cryptography Standard #7*. The PKCS#7 standard provides access to the algorithm specific signing information as well as the certificate with the public key of the signer. The verification algorithm uses the public key to verify that:

- The digital signature matches the signature instruction resource.
- The signature was created with the private key associated with the certificate.

The complete signing structure is shown in Figure 2.13.

2.3.5   Certificates

A certificate is a general term for a signed document containing a name and public key information. Such a certificate can take many forms but the OSGi JAR signing is based on the X.509 certificate format. It has been around for many years and is part of the OSI group of standards. X.509 is defined in [7] *X.509 Certificates*.

An X.509 certificate contains the following elements:

- *Subject Name* – The subject name is a unique identifier for the object being certified. In the case of a person this might include the name, nationality and e-mail address, the organization, and the department within that organization. This identifier is a Distinguished Name, which is defined in *Distinguished Names* on page 15.

• *Issuer Name* – The Issuer name is a Distinguished Name for the principal that signed this certificate.

• *Certificate Extensions* – A certificate can also include pictures, codification of fingerprints, passport number, and other extensions.

• *Public Key Information* – A public key can be used with an encryption technique that requires its private counterpart to decrypt, and vice versa. The public key can be shared freely, the private key must be kept secret. The public key information specifies an algorithm identifier (such as DSA or RSA) and the subject's public key.

• *Validity* – A Certificate can be valid for only a limited time.

• *Certifying Authority Signature* – The Certificate Authority signs the first elements and thereby adds credibility to the certificate. The receiver of a certificate can check the signature against a set of trusted certifying authorities. If the receiver trusts that certifying authority, it can trust the statement that the certificate makes.

The structure of a certificate is depicted in Figure 2.14.

Figure 2.14   *Structure of a certificate*

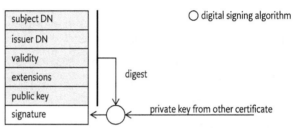

Certificates can be freely dispersed; they do not contain any secret information. Therefore, the PKCS#7 resource contains the signing certificate. It cannot be trusted at face value because the certificate is carried in the bundle itself. A perpetrator can easily create its own certificate with any content. The receiver can only verify that the certificate was signed by the owner of the public key (the issuer) and that it has not been tampered with. However, before the statement in the certificate can be trusted, it is necessary to authenticate the certificate itself. It is therefore necessary to establish a *trust model*.

One trust model, supported but not required by the OSGi specifications, is placing the signing certificate in a repository. Any certificate in this repository is treated as trusted by default. However, placing all possible certificates in this repository does not scale well. In an open model, a device would have to contain hundreds of thousands of certificates. The management of the certificates could easily become overwhelming.

The solution is to sign a certificate by another certificate, and this process can be repeated several times. This delegation process forms a *chain of certificates*. All certificates for this chain are carried in the PKCS#7 file: if one of those certificates can be found in the trusted repository, the other dependent ones can be trusted, on the condition that all the certificates are valid. This model scales very well because only a few certificates of trusted signers need to be maintained. This is the model used in web browsers, as depicted in Figure 2.15.

Figure 2.15   *Certificate authorities fan out*

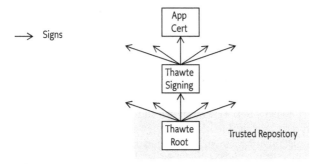

This specification does not specify access to the trusted repository. It is implementation specific how this repository is populated and maintained.

2.3.6   **Distinguished Names**

An X.509 name is a *Distinguished Name* (DN). A DN is a highly structured name, officially identifying a node in an hierarchical name space. The DN concept was developed for the X.500 directory service which envisioned a world wide name space managed by PTTs. Today, the DN is used as an identifier in a local name space, as in a name space designed by an Operator. For example, given a name space that looks like Figure 2.16, the DN identifying Bugs looks like:

    cn=Bug, o=ACME, c=US

Figure 2.16   *Country, Company, Person based name space.*

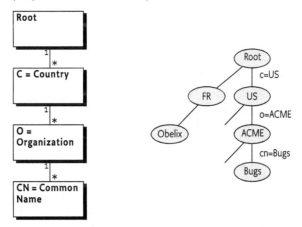

The traversal of the name space is *reversed* from the order in the DN, the first part specifies the least significant but most specific part. That is, the order of the attribute assertions is significant. Two DNs with the same attributes but different order are different DNs.

In the example, a node is searched in the root that has an attribute c (countryName) with a value that is US. This node is searched for a child that has an attribute o (organizationName) with a value of ACME. And the ACME node is searched for a child node with an attribute cn (commonName) that has a value "Bugs Bunny".

The tree based model is the official definition of a DN from the X.500 standards. However, in practice today, many DNs contain attributes that have no relation to a tree. For example, many DNs contain comments and copyrights in the ou (organizationalUnit) attribute.

The DN from an X.509 certificate is expressed in a binary structure defined by ASN.1 (a type language defined by ISO). However, the Distinguished Name is often used in interaction with humans. Sometimes, users of a system have to acknowledge the use of a certificate or an employee of an Operator must grant permissions based on a Distinguished Name of a customer. It is therefore paramount that the Distinguished Name has a good human readable string representation. The expressiveness of the ASN.1 type language makes this non-trivial. This specification only uses DN strings as defined in [6] *RFC 2253* with a number of extensions that are specified by the javax.security.auth.x500.X500Principal class in CANONICAL form.

However, the complexity of the encoding/decoding is caused by the use of rarely used types and features (binary data, multi-valued RDNs, foreign alphabets, and attributes that have special matching rules). These features must be supported by a compliant implementation but should be avoided by users. In practice, these features are rarely used today.

The format of a string DN is as follows:

```
dn          ::= rdn ( ',' rdn ) *
rdn         ::= attribute ( '+' attribute ) *
attribute   ::= name '=' value
name        ::= readable | oid
oid         ::= number ( '.' number ) *    // See 1.3.2
readable    ::= <see attribute table>
value       ::= <escaped string>
```

Spaces before and after the separators are ignored, spaces inside a value are significant but multiple embedded spaces are collapsed into a single space. Wildcard characters ('*' \u002A) are not allowed in a value part. The following characters must be escaped with a back slash:

```
comma         ','   \u002C
plus          '+'   \u002B
double quote  '"'   \u0022
back slash    '\'   \u005C
less then     '<'   \u003C
greater then  '>'   \u003E
semicolon     ';'   \u003B
```

Backslashes must already be escaped in Java strings, requiring 2 backslashes in Java source code. For example:

```
DN:             cn = Bugs Bunny, o = ACME++, C=US
Canonical form: cn=bugs bunny,o=acme\+\+,c=us
Java String:    "cn=Bugs Bunny,o=ACME\\+\\+,c=US"
```

The full unicode character set is available and can be used in DNs. String objects must be normalized and put in canonical form before being compared.

```
DN:             cn = Bugs Bunny, o = Ð Þ, C=US
Canonical form: cn=bugs bunny,o=đ þ,c=us
Java String:    "cn = Bugs Bunny, o = Ð Þ, C=US"
```

The names of attributes (attributes types as they are also called) are actually translated into an Object IDentifier (OID). An OID is a dotted decimal number, like 2.5.4.3 for the cn (commonName) attribute name. It is therefore not possible to use any attribute name because the implementation must know the aliasing as well as the comparison rules. Therefore only the attributes that are listed in the following table are allowed (in short or long form):

```
commonName      cn     2.5.4.3 ITU X.520
surName         sn     2.5.4.4
countryName     c      2.5.4.6
localityName    l      2.5.4.7
```

```
stateOrProvinceName       st          2.5.4.8
organizationName          o           2.5.4.10
organizationalUnitName    ou          2.5.4.11
title                                 2.5.4.12
givenName                             2.5.4.42
initials                              2.5.4.43
generationQualifier                   2.5.4.44
dnQualifier                           2.5.4.46

streetAddress             street      RFC 2256
domainComponent           dc          RFC 1274
userid                    uid         RFC 1274/2798?
emailAddress                          RFC 2985
serialNumber                          RFC 2985
```

The following DN:

```
2.5.4.3=Bugs Bunny,organizationName=ACME,2.5.4.6=US
```

Is therefore identical to:

```
cn=Bugs Bunny,o=ACME,c=US
```

The attribute types officially define a matching rule, potentially allowing cases sensitive and case insensitive. The attributes in the previous list all match case insensitive. Therefore, an OSGi DN must not depend on case sensitivity.

The X.500 standard supports multi-valued RDNs, however, their use is not recommended. See [18] *Understanding and Deploying LDAP Directory Services* for the rationale of this recommendation. Multi-valued RDNs separate their constituents with a plus sign ('+' \u002B). Their order is not significant. For example:

```
cn=Bugs Bunny+dc=x.com+title=Manager,o=ACME,c=US
```

Which is the same as

```
dc=x.com+cn=Bug Bunny+title=Manager, o=ACME, c=US"
```

2.3.7   Certificate Matching

Certificates are matched by their Subject DN. Before matching, DNs, they must first be put in canonical form according to the algorithm specified in javax.security.auth.x500.X500Principal.

DNs can also be compared using wildcards. A wildcard ('*' \u002A) replaces all possible values. Due to the structure of the DN, the comparison is more complicated than string-based wildcard matching.

A wildcard can stand for a number of RDNs, or the value of a single RDN. DNs with a wildcard must be canonicalized before they are compared. This means, among other things, that spaces must be ignored, except in values.

The format of a wildcard DN match is:

```
CertificateMatch::= dn-match ( ';' dn-match ) *
dn-match         ::= ( '*' | rdn-match )
                        ( ',' rdn-match ) * | '-'
rdn-match        ::= name '=' value-match
value-match      ::= '*' | value-star
value-star       ::= < value, requires escaped '*' and '-' >
```

The most simple case is a single wildcard; it must match any DN. A wildcard can also replace the first list of RDNs of a DN. The first RDNs are the least significant. Such lists of matched RDNs can be empty.

For example, a DN with a wildcard that matches all nodes descendant from the ACME node in Figure 2.16 on page 15, looks like:

```
*, o=ACME, c=US
```

This wildcard DN matches the following DNs:

```
cn = Bugs Bunny, o = ACME, c = US
ou = Carots, cn=Daffy Duck, o=ACME, c=US
street = 9C\, Avenue St. Drézéry, o=ACME, c=US
dc=www, dc=acme, dc=com, o=ACME, c=US
o=ACME, c=US
```

The following DNs must not match:

```
street = 9C\, Avenue St. Drézéry, o=ACME, c=FR
dc=www, dc=acme, dc=com, c=US
```

If a wildcard is used for a value of an RDN, the value must be exactly *. The wildcard must match any value, and no substring matching must be done. For example:

```
cn=*,o=ACME,c=*
```

This DN with wildcard must match the following DNs:

```
cn=Bugs Bunny,o=ACME,c=US
cn = Daffy Duck , o = ACME , c = US
cn=Road Runner, o=ACME, c=NL
```

But not:

```
o=ACME, c=NL
dc=acme.com, cn=Bugs Bunny, o=ACME, c=US
```

Both forms of wildcard usage can be combined in a single matching DN. For example, to match any DN that is from the ACME company worldwide, use:

```
*, o=ACME, c=*
```

Matching of a DN takes place in the context of a certificate. This certificate is part of a *certificate chain*, see *Certificates* on page 13. Each certificate has a Subject DN and an Issuer DN. The Issuer DN is the Subject DN used to sign the first certificate of the chain. DN matching can therefore be extended to match the signer. The semicolon (';' \u003B) must be used to separate DNs in a chain.

The following example matches a certificate signed by Tweety Inc. in the US.

```
* ; ou=S & V, o=Tweety Inc., c=US
```

The wildcard matches zero or one certificates,

however, sometimes it is necessary to match a longer chain. The minus sign ('-' \u002D) represents zero or more certificates, whereas the asterisk only represents a single certificate. For example, to match a certificate where the Tweety Inc. is in the certificate chain, use the following expression:

```
- ; *, o=Tweety Inc., c=US
```

The previous example matched if the Tweety Inc. certificate was trusted, or was signed by a trusted certificate. Certain certificates are trusted because they are known by the Framework, how they are known is implementation-defined.

2.4   Permissions

The OSGi Framework uses Java 2 permissions for securing bundles. Each bundle is associated with a set of permissions. During runtime, the permissions are queried when a permission is requested through the Security Manager. If a Framework uses postponed conditions, then it must install its own security manager, otherwise it can use any Security Manager.

The management of the bundle's permissions is handled through Conditional Permission Admin, Permission Admin, or another security agent.

2.4.1   Implied Permissions

Implied permissions are permissions that the framework grants a bundle without any specific action. These permissions are necessary for normal operation. For example, each bundle gets permissions to read, write, and delete the bundle persistent storage area. The complete list of implied permissions is as follows:

- File Permission for the bundle persistent storage area, for the READ, WRITE, and DELETE actions
- Property Permission with the READ action for org.osgi.framework.*
- Admin Permission with the RESOURCE, METADATA, CLASS, and CONTEXT actions for the bundle itself.

2.4.2   Filter Based Permissions

OSGi supports a number of permissions that are granted when the target of the permissions is related to a bundle. For example, Admin Permission can grant a bundle the permission to manage other bundles. This is expressed by using a *filter expression* for the *name* of the permission. When the permission is checked, the filter is evaluated with specific permission attributes as well as attributes that describe the bundle's identity. For example, a bundle can get permission to get all services registered by bundles coming from a specific location:

```
ServicePermission("(location=https://www.acme.com/*)", GET )
```

This provides a very powerful model because it allows operators to let a group of bundles closely collaborate without requiring ad hoc name spaces for services, packages, and bundles. Using the signer or location as the target for a permission, will allow the maintenance of the permission management to be significantly reduced. It is not necessary to configure for individual bundles: the signer or location is effectively used as a grouping mechanism.

The filter can contain the following keys:

- *id* – The bundle ID of a bundle. For example:

    (id=256)

- *location* – The location of a bundle. Filter wildcards for Strings are supported, allowing the value to specify a set of bundles. For example:

    (location=https://www.acme.com/download/*)

- *signer* – A Distinguished Name chain. See the *Certificate Matching* on page 17 for more information how Distinguished Names are matched. Wildcards in a DN are not matched according to the filter string rules, but according to the rules defined for a DN chain. The wildcard character ('*' or \u002a) must be escaped with a backslash ('\') to avoid being interpreted as a filter wildcard. For example:

    (signer=*,o=ACME,c=NL)

- *name* – The symbolic name of a bundle. Filter wildcards for Strings are supported allowing the value to specify a set of bundles. A single symbolic name may also map to a set of bundles. For example:

  (name=com. acme. *)

The name parameter of the permission can also be a single wildcard character ('*' or \u002a). In that case all bundles must match.

2.4.2.1   **Multiple Signers**

A bundle can be signed by multiple signers, in that case the signer will match against any of the signers' DN. Using multiple signers is both a feature as well as it is a possible threat. From a management perspective it is beneficial to be able to use signatures to handle the grouping. However, it could also be used to maliciously manage a trusted bundle.

For example a trusted bundle signed by T, could later have a signature added by an untrusted party U. This will grant the bundle the permissions of both T and U, which ordinarily is a desirable feature. However, If the permissions associated with signer U also allow the management of bundles signed by U, then U could unexpectedly gain the permission to manage this trusted bundle. For example, it could now start and stop this trusted bundle. This unexpected effect of becoming eligible to be managed should be carefully considered when multiple signers are used. The deny policies in Conditional Permission Admin can be used to prevent this case from causing harm.

2.5   Changes

- Introduced a section on permissions with filters.
- Added a summary of the implied permissions.
- Provided more details about what constitutes a valid signature.

2.6   References

[6]   *RFC 2253*
        http://www.ietf.org/rfc/rfc2253.txt

[7]   *X.509 Certificates*
        http://www.ietf.org/rfc/rfc2459.txt

[8]   *Java 2 Security Architecture*
        Version 1.2, Sun Microsystems, March 2002

[9]   *The Java 2 Package Versioning Specification*
        http://java.sun.com/j2se/1.4/docs/guide/versioning/index.html

[10]   *Manifest Format*
        http://java.sun.com/j2se/1.4/docs/guide/jar/jar.html#JAR%20Manifest

[11]   *Secure Hash Algorithm 1*
        http://csrc.nist.gov/publications/fips/fips180-2/fips180-2withchangenotice.pdf

[12]   *RFC 1321 The MD5 Message-Digest Algorithm*
        http://www.ietf.org/rfc/rfc1321.txt

[13]   *RFC 1421 Privacy Enhancement for Internet Electronic Mail*
        http://www.ietf.org/rfc/rfc1421.txt

[14]   *DSA*
        http://www.itl.nist.gov/fipspubs/fip186.htm

[15] *RSA*
http://www.ietf.org/rfc/rfc2313.txt which is superseded by
http://www.ietf.org/rfc/rfc2437.txt

[16] *Public Key Cryptography Standard #7*
http://www.rsasecurity.com/rsalabs/node.asp?id=2129

[17] *Unicode Normalization UAX # 15*
http://www.unicode.org/reports/tr15/

[18] *Understanding and Deploying LDAP Directory Services*
ISBN 1-57870-070-1

3   **Module Layer**

Version 1.5

3.1   **Introduction**

The standard Java platform provides only limited support for packaging, deploying, and validating Java-based applications and components. Because of this, many Java-based projects, such as JBoss and NetBeans, have resorted to creating custom module-oriented layers with specialized class loaders for packaging, deploying, and validating applications and components. The OSGi Framework provides a generic and standardized solution for Java modularization.

3.2   **Bundles**

The Framework defines a unit of modularization, called a bundle. A bundle is comprised of Java classes and other resources, which together can provide functions to end users. Bundles can share Java *packages* among an *exporter* bundle and an *importer* bundle in a well-defined way.

In the OSGi Service Platform, bundles are the only entities for deploying Java-based applications.

A bundle is deployed as a Java ARchive (JAR) file. JAR files are used to store applications and their resources in a standard ZIP-based file format. This format is defined by [27] *Zip File Format*. Bundles normally share the Java Archive extension of .jar. However, there is a special MIME type reserved for OSGi bundles that can be used to distinguish bundles from normal JAR files. This MIME type is:

    application/vnd.osgi.bundle

The type is defined in [34] *OSGi IANA Mime Type*.

A bundle is a JAR file that:

- Contains the resources necessary to provide some functionality. These resources may be class files for the Java programming language, as well as other data such as HTML files, help files, icons, and so on. A bundle JAR file can also embed additional JAR files that are available as resources and classes. This is however not recursive.
- Contains a manifest file describing the contents of the JAR file and providing information about the bundle. This file uses headers to specify information that the Framework needs to install correctly and activate a bundle. For example, it states dependencies on other resources, such as Java packages, that must be available to the bundle before it can run.
- Can contain optional documentation in the OSGI-OPT directory of the JAR file or one of its subdirectories. Any information in this directory is optional. For example, the OSGI-OPT directory is useful to store the source code of a bundle. Management systems may remove this information to save storage space in the OSGi Service Platform.

Once a bundle is started, its functionality is provided and services are exposed to other bundles installed in the OSGi Service Platform.

3.2.1   **Bundle Manifest Headers**

A bundle can carry descriptive information about itself in the manifest file that is contained in its JAR file under the name of META-INF/MANIFEST.MF.

The Framework defines OSGi manifest headers such as Export-Package and Bundle-ClassPath, which bundle developers use to supply descriptive information about a bundle. Manifest headers must strictly follow the rules for manifest headers as defined in [28] *Manifest Format*.

A Framework implementation must:

- Process the main section of the manifest. Individual sections of the manifest are only used during bundle signature verification.
- Ignore unrecognized manifest headers. The bundle developer can define additional manifest headers as needed.
- Ignore unknown attributes and directives.

All specified manifest headers are listed in the following sections. All headers are optional, unless specifically indicated.

3.2.1.1   **Bundle-ActivationPolicy: lazy**

The Bundle-ActivationPolicy specifies how the framework should activate the bundle once started. See *Activation Policies* on page 87.

3.2.1.2   **Bundle-Activator: com.acme.fw.Activator**

The Bundle-Activator header specifies the name of the class used to start and stop the bundle. See *Starting Bundles* on page 85.

3.2.1.3   **Bundle-Category: osgi, test, nursery**

The Bundle-Category header holds a comma-separated list of category names.

3.2.1.4   **Bundle-ClassPath: /jar/http.jar,.**

The Bundle-ClassPath header defines a comma-separated list of JAR file path names or directories (inside the bundle) containing classes and resources. The period ('.') specifies the root directory of the bundle's JAR. The period is also the default. See *Bundle Class Path* on page 46.

3.2.1.5   **Bundle-ContactAddress: 2400 Oswego Road, Austin, TX 74563**

The Bundle-ContactAddress header provides the contact address of the vendor.

3.2.1.6   **Bundle-Copyright: OSGi (c) 2002**

The Bundle-Copyright header contains the copyright specification for this bundle.

3.2.1.7   **Bundle-Description: Network Firewall**

The Bundle-Description header defines a short description of this bundle.

3.2.1.8   **Bundle-DocURL: http://www.acme.com/Firewall/doc**

The Bundle-DocURL headers must contain a URL pointing to documentation about this bundle.

3.2.1.9   **Bundle-Icon: /icons/acme-logo.png;size=64**

The optional Bundle-Icon header provides a list of URLs to icons representing this bundle in different sizes. The following attribute is permitted:

- size – (integer) Specifies the size of the icon in pixels horizontal. It is recommended to always include a 64x64 icon.

The URLs are interpreted as relative to the bundle. That is, if a URL with a scheme is provided, then this is taken as an absolute URL. Otherwise, the path points to an entry in the JAR file, taking any attached fragments into account. Implementations that want to use this header should at least support the Portable Network Graphics (PNG) format, see [36] *Portable Network Graphics (PNG) Specification (Second Edition)*.

3.2.1.10   **Bundle License: http://www.opensource.org/licenses/jabberpl.php**

The Bundle-License header provides an optional machine readable form of license information. The purpose of this header is to automate some of the license processing required by many organizations like for example license acceptance before a bundle is used. The header is structured to provide the use of unique license naming to merge acceptance requests, as well as links to human readable information about the included licenses. This header is purely informational for management agents and must not be processed by the OSGi Framework.

The syntax for this header is as follows:

```
Bundle-License ::= '<<EXTERNAL>>' |
                        ( license ( ',' license ) * )
license         ::= name ( ';' license-attr ) *
license-attr    ::= description | link
description     ::= 'description' '=' string
link            ::= 'link' '=' <url>
```

This header has the following attributes:

- name – Provides a globally unique name for this license, preferably world wide, but it should at least be unique with respect to the other clauses. The magic name <<EXTERNAL>> is used to indicate that this artifact does not contain any license information but that licensing information is provided in some other way. This is also the default contents of this header.
  Clients of this bundle can assume that licenses with the same name refer to the same license. This can for example be used to minimize the click through licenses. This name should be the canonical URL of the license, it must not be localized by the translator. This URL does not have to exist but must not be used for later versions of the license. It is recommended to use URLs from [37] *Open Source Initiative*. Other licenses should use the following structure, but this is not mandated:

  ```
  http://<domain-name>/licenses/
         <license-name>-<version>.<extension>
  ```

- description – (optional) Provide the description of the license. This is a short description that is usable in a list box on a UI to select more information about the license.
- link –(optional) Provide a URL to a page that defines or explains the license. If this link is absent, the name field is used for this purpose. The URL is relative to the root of the bundle. That is it is possible to refer to a file inside the bundle.

If the Bundle-License statement is absent, then this does not mean that the bundle is not licensed. Licensing could be handled outside the bundle and the <<EXTERNAL>> form should be assumed. This header is informational and may not have any legal bearing. Consult a lawyer before using this header to automate licensing processing.

3.2.1.11   **Bundle-Localization: OSGI-INF/l10n/bundle**

The Bundle-Localization header contains the location in the bundle where localization files can be found. The default value is OSGI-INF/l10n/bundle. Translations are by default therefore OSGI-INF/l10n/bundle_de.properties, OSGI-INF/l10n/bundle_nl.properties, etc. See *Manifest Localization* on page 59.

3.2.1.12   **Bundle-ManifestVersion: 2**

The Bundle-ManifestVersion header defines that the bundle follows the rules of this specification. The Bundle-ManifestVersion header determines whether the bundle follows the rules of this specification. It is 1 (the default) for Release 3 Bundles, 2 for Release 4 and later. Future version of the OSGi Service Platform can define higher numbers for this header.

3.2.1.13   **Bundle-Name: Firewall**
The Bundle-Name header defines a readable name for this bundle. This should be a short, human-readable name that can contain spaces.

3.2.1.14   **Bundle-NativeCode: /lib/http.DLL; osname = QNX; osversion = 3.1**
The Bundle-NativeCode header contains a specification of native code libraries contained in this bundle. See *Loading Native Code Libraries* on page 54.

3.2.1.15   **Bundle-RequiredExecutionEnvironment: CDC-1.0/Foundation-1.0**
The Bundle-RequiredExecutionEnvironment contains a comma-separated list of execution environments that must be present on the Service Platform. See *Execution Environment* on page 30.

3.2.1.16   **Bundle-SymbolicName: com.acme.daffy**
The Bundle-SymbolicName header specifies a non-localizable name for this bundle. The bundle symbolic name together with a version must identify a unique bundle. The bundle symbolic name should be based on the reverse domain name convention, see *Bundle-SymbolicName* on page 34. This header must be set.

3.2.1.17   **Bundle-UpdateLocation: http://www.acme.com/Firewall/bundle.jar**
The Bundle-UpdateLocation header specifies a URL where an update for this bundle should come from. If the bundle is updated, this location should be used, if present, to retrieve the updated JAR file.

3.2.1.18   **Bundle-Vendor: OSGi Alliance**
The Bundle-Vendor header contains a human-readable description of the bundle vendor.

3.2.1.19   **Bundle-Version: 1.1**
The Bundle-Version header specifies the version of this bundle. See *Version* on page 27. The default value is 0.0.0

3.2.1.20   **DynamicImport-Package: com.acme.plugin.***
The DynamicImport-Package header contains a comma-separated list of package names that should be dynamically imported when needed. See *Dynamic Import Package* on page 48.

3.2.1.21   **Export-Package: org.osgi.util.tracker;version=1.3**
The Export-Package header contains a declaration of exported packages. See *Export-Package* on page 36.

3.2.1.22   **Export-Service: org.osgi.service.log.LogService**
Deprecated.

3.2.1.23   **Fragment-Host: org.eclipse.swt; bundle-version="[3.0.0,4.0.0)"**
The Fragment-Host header defines the host bundles for this fragment. See *Fragment-Host* on page 64

3.2.1.24   **Import-Package: org.osgi.util.tracker,org.osgi.service.io;version=1.4**
The Import-Package header declares the imported packages for this bundle. See *Import-Package Header* on page 35.

3.2.1.25   **Import-Service: org.osgi.service.log.LogService**
Deprecated

3.2.1.26   **Require-Bundle: com.acme.chess**
The Require-Bundle header specifies that all exported packages from another bundle must be imported, effectively requiring the public interface of another bundle. See *Require-Bundle* on page 61

3.2.2   Custom Headers

The manifest an excellent place to provide metadata belonging to a bundle. This is true for the OSGi Alliance but it is also valid for other organizations. For historic reasons, the OSGi Alliance claims the default namespace, specifically headers that indicate OSGi related matters like names that contain Bundle, Import, Export, etc. Organizations that want to use headers that do not clash with OSGi Alliance defined names or bundle header names from other organizations should prefix custom headers with x-, for example x-LazyStart.

Organizations external to the OSGi can request header names in the OSGi namespace. The OSGi maintains a registry of such names at [35] *OSGi Header Name Space Registry*.

3.2.3   Header Value Syntax

Each Manifest header has its own syntax. In all descriptions, the syntax is defined with [29] *W3C EBNF*. These following sections define a number of commonly used tokens.

3.2.4   Common Header Syntax

Many Manifest header values share a common syntax. This syntax consists of:

```
header ::= clause ( ',' clause ) *
clause ::= path ( ';' path ) *
            ( ';' parameter ) *        // See 1.3.2
```

A parameter can be either a *directive* or an *attribute*. A directive is an instruction that has some implied semantics for the Framework. An attribute is used for matching and comparison purposes.

3.2.5   Version

Version specifications are used in several places. A version token has the following grammar:

```
version   ::=
    major( '.' minor ( '.' micro ( '.' qualifier )? )? )?
major     ::= number                     // See 1.3.2
minor     ::= number
micro     ::= number
qualifier ::= ( alphanum | '_' | '-' )+
```

A version token must not contain any white space. The default value for a version is 0.0.0.

3.2.6   Version Ranges

A version range describes a range of versions using a mathematical interval notation. See [31] *Mathematical Convention for Interval Notation*.

The syntax of a version range is:

```
version-range ::= interval | atleast
interval ::= ( '[' | '(' ) floor ',' ceiling ( ']' | ')' )
atleast ::= version
floor ::= version
ceiling ::= version
```

If a version range is specified as a single version, it must be interpreted as the range [version,∞). The default for a non-specified version range is 0, which maps to [0.0.0,∞).

Note that the use of a comma in the version range requires it to be enclosed in double quotes. For example:

```
Import-Package: com.acme.foo;version="[1.23, 2)",
    com.acme.bar;version="[4.0, 5.0)"
```

In the following table, for each specified range in the left-hand column, a version *x* is considered to be a member of the range if the predicate in the right-hand column is true.

Table 3.2   Examples of version ranges

Example	Predicate
[1.2.3, 4.5.6)	1.2.3 <= x < 4.5.6
[1.2.3, 4.5.6]	1.2.3 <= x <= 4.5.6
(1.2.3, 4.5.6)	1.2.3 < x < 4.5.6
(1.2.3, 4.5.6]	1.2.3 < x <= 4.5.6
1.2.3	1.2.3 <= x

3.2.7 Filter Syntax

The OSGi specifications use filter expressions extensively. Filter expressions allow for a concise description of a *constraint.*

The syntax of a filter string is based upon the string representation of LDAP search filters as defined in [23] *A String Representation of LDAP Search Filters.* It should be noted that RFC 2254: A String Representation of LDAP Search Filters supersedes RFC 1960, but only adds extensible matching and is not applicable to this OSGi Framework API.

The string representation of an LDAP search filter uses a prefix format and is defined by the following grammar:

```
filter       ::=  '(' filter-comp ')'
filter-comp  ::=  and | or | not | operation
and          ::=  '&' filter-list
or           ::=  '|' filter-list
not          ::=  '!' filter
filter-list  ::=  filter | filter filter-list
operation    ::=  simple | present | substring
simple       ::=  attr filter-type value
filter-type  ::=  equal | approx | greater-eq | less-eq
equal        ::=  '='
approx       ::=  '~='
greater-eq   ::=  '>='
less-eq      ::=  '<='
present      ::=  attr '=*'
substring    ::=  attr '=' initial any final
initial      ::=  () | value
any          ::=  '*' star-value
star-value   ::=  () | value '*' star-value
final        ::=  () | value
value        ::=  <see text>
attr         ::=  <see text>
```

attr is a string representing an attribute, or key, in the properties. Attribute names are not case sensitive; that is, cn and CN both refer to the same attribute. attr must not contain the characters '=', '>', '<', '~', '(' or ')'. attr may contain embedded spaces but leading and trailing spaces must be ignored.

value is a string representing the value, or part of one, which will be compared against a value in the filtered properties.

If value must contain one of the characters '\', '*', '(' or ')', then these characters should be preceded with the backslash ('\') character. Spaces are significant in value. Space characters are defined by Character.isWhiteSpace().

Although both the substring and present productions can produce the attr=∗ construct, this construct is used only to denote a presence filter.

The substring production only works for attributes that are of type String, Collection of String or String[]. In all other cases the result must be false.

The evaluation of the approximate match ('-=') filter type is implementation specific but should at least ignore case and white space differences. Codes such as soundex or other smart *closeness* comparisons may be used.

Values specified in the filter are compared to values in the properties against which the filter is evaluated. The comparison of these values is not straightforward. Strings compare differently than numbers, and it is also possible for a property to have multiple values. Property keys must always be String objects so that a case insensitive attr can be used to obtain the property value.

The object class of the property's value defines the comparison type. The properties values should be of the following types:

Figure 3.17   *Primary property types*

```
type       ::= scalar | collection | array
scalar     ::= String | Integer | Long | Float
                   | Double | Byte | Short
                   | Character | Boolean
primitive  ::= int | long | float | double | byte
                   | short | char | boolean
array      ::= ‹Array of primitive›
                   | ‹Array of scalar›
collection ::= ‹Collection of scalar›
```

The following rules apply for comparison:

- *String* – Use String comparison
- *Integer, Long, Float, Double, Byte, Short, Character objects and primitives* – Use numerical comparison
- *Boolean objects* – Use comparison defined by Boolean.valueOf(v).booleanValue().
- *Array or Collection elements* – Comparison is determined by the object type of the element

Array and Collection elements may be a mix of scalar types. Array and Collection elements may also be null.

If the type of the property value is not one of the above types, and the type has a constructor taking a single String argument, then the Framework must construct an object to compare with the property value by passing value to the single String argument constructor according to the following comparison rules:

- *Comparable objects* – Comparison through the Comparable interface
- *Other objects* – Equality comparison

If none of the above comparison rules apply, then the result of the comparison is false.

A filter matches a property with multiple values if it matches at least one of those values.

For example:

```
Dictionary dict = new Hashtable();
dict.put( "cn", new String[] { "a", "b", "c" } );
```

The dict will match against a filter with (cn=a) as well as (cn=b).

Service properties are often defined to take a type, a collection of that type, or an array of that type. In those cases, a simple + will be suffixed to the type name. For example String+, indicates that a String, a String[], and a Collection<String> are all valid forms.

3.3 Execution Environment

A bundle that is restricted to one or more execution environments must carry a header in its manifest file to indicate this dependency. This header is Bundle-RequiredExecutionEnvironment. The syntax of this header is a list of comma-separated names of execution environments.

```
Bundle-RequiredExecutionEnvironment ::=
    ee-name ( ',' ee-name )*

ee-name ::= <defined execution environment name>
```

For example:

```
Bundle-RequiredExecutionEnvironment: CDC-1.0/Foundation-1.0,
    OSGi/Minimum-1.1
```

If a bundle includes this header in the manifest then the bundle must only use methods with signatures that are contained within a proper subset of all mentioned execution environments. Bundles should list all (known) execution environments on which it can run the bundle.

A bundle can only resolve if the framework is running on a VM which implements one of the listed required execution environments. Frameworks should recognize that the current VM can implement multiple execution environments. For example, Java 6 is backward compatible with Java 5 and a bundle requiring the Java 6 execution environment must resolve on a Java 6 VM. The Bundle-RequiredExecutionEnvironment header can not hinder a bundle from being successfully installed.

3.3.1 Naming of Execution Environments

Execution environments require a proper name so that:

- A bundle can require that a Framework provides a certain execution environment before it is resolved.
- To provide information about which execution environments a Framework provides.

Execution environment names consist of any set of characters except white space characters and the comma character (' ,', or \u002C). The OSGi Alliance has defined a number of execution environments.

The naming scheme further uses J2ME configuration and profile names. There is no clear definition for this naming scheme but similar names are used in different specifications.

The J2ME scheme uses a configuration and a profile name to designate an execution environment. The OSGi Alliance naming combines those two names into a single execution environment name.

There already exist a number of Execution Environments from J2ME that are likely available in Service Platform Servers. The value for the execution environment header must be compatible with these specifications.

A J2ME CLDC execution environment name is a combination of a configuration and a profile name. In CLDC, these are two different system properties. These properties are:

```
microedition.configuration
microedition.profiles
```

For example, Foundation Profile has an execution environment name of CDC-1.0/Foundation-1.0. The structure of the name obeys the following rules:

```
ee-name = [ <configuration> '-' <version> '/' ]
            <profile> '-' <version>
```

Configuration and profile names are defined by the JCP or OSGi Alliance. If an execution environment does not have a configuration or profile, the profile part is the name identifying the execution environment. These guidelines are not normative.

Table 3.3 on page 31, contains a number of examples of the most common execution environments.

Table 3.3   *Sample EE names*

Name	Description
CDC-1.1/Foundation-1.1	Equal to J2ME Foundation Profile
OSGi/Minimum-1.2	OSGi EE that is a minimal set that allows the implementation of an OSGi Framework.
J2SE-1.2	Java 2 SE 1.2.x
J2SE-1.3	Java 2 SE 1.3.x
J2SE-1.4	Java 2 SE 1.4.x
J2SE-1.5	Java 2 SE 1.5.x
JavaSE-1.6	Java SE 1.6.x
CDC-1.1/PersonalBasis-1.1	J2ME Personal Basis Profile
CDC-1.1/PersonalJava-1.1	J2ME Personal Java Profile

The org.osgi.framework.executionenvironment property from BundleContext.get-Property(String) must contain a comma-separated list of execution environment names implemented by the Framework. This property is defined as *volatile*. A Framework implementation must not cache this information because bundles may change this system property at any time. The purpose of this volatility is testing and possible extension of the execution environments at run-time.

3.4 Class Loading Architecture

Many bundles can share a single virtual machine (VM). Within this VM, bundles can hide packages and classes from other bundles, as well as share packages with other bundles.

The key mechanism to hide and share packages is the Java *class loader* that loads classes from a subset of the bundle-space using well-defined rules. Each bundle has a single class loader. That class loader forms a class loading delegation network with other bundles as shown in Figure 3.18.

Figure 3.18   *Class Loader Delegation model*

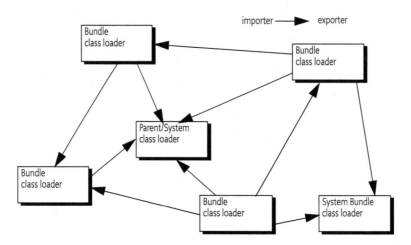

The class loader can load classes and resources from:

- *Boot class path* – The boot class path contains the java.* packages and its implementation packages.
- *Framework class path* – The Framework usually has a separate class loader for the Framework implementation classes as well as key service interface classes.
- *Bundle Space* – The bundle space consists of the JAR file that is associated with the bundle, plus any additional JAR that are closely tied to the bundle, like *fragments*, see *Fragment Bundles* on page 63.

A *class space* is then all classes reachable from a given bundle's class loader. Thus, a class space for a given bundle can contain classes from:

- The parent class loader (normally java.* packages from the boot class path)
- Imported packages
- Required bundles
- The bundle's class path (*private packages*)
- Attached fragments

A class space must be consistent, such that it *never* contains two classes with the same fully quali-fied name (to prevent Class Cast Exceptions). However, separate class spaces in an OSGi Platform may contain classes with the same fully qualified name. The modularization layer supports a model where multiple versions of the same class are loaded in the same VM.

Figure 3.19   *Class Space*

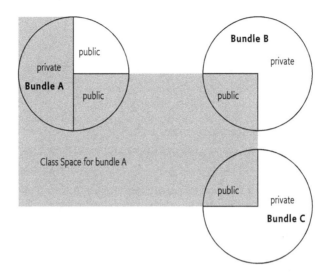

Class Space for bundle A

The Framework therefore has a number of responsibilities related to class loading. Before a bundle is used, it must resolve the constraints that a set of bundles place on the sharing of packages. Then select the best possibilities to create a *wiring*. See *Resolving Process* on page 45 for further information. The runtime aspects are described in *Runtime Class Loading* on page 46.

3.4.1   Resolving

The Framework must *resolve* bundles. Resolving is the process where importers are *wired* to exporters. Resolving is a process of satisfying constraints. This process must take place before any code from a bundle can be loaded or executed

A *wire* is an actual connection between an *exporter* and an *importer*, which are both bundles. A wire is associated with a number of constraints that are defined by its importer's and exporter's manifest headers. A *valid* wire is a wire that has satisfied all its constraints. Figure 3.20 depicts the class structure of the wiring model.

Figure 3.20   *Example class structure of wiring*

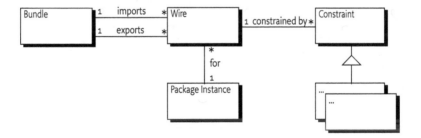

3.5   Resolving Metadata

The following sections define the manifest headers that provide the metadata for the resolver.

3.5.1   Bundle-ManifestVersion

A bundle manifest must express the version of the OSGi manifest header syntax in the Bundle-ManifestVersion header. Bundles exploiting this version of the Framework specification (or later) must specify this header. The syntax of this header is as follows:

```
Bundle-ManifestVersion ::= number     // See 1.3.2
```

The Framework version 1.3 (or later) bundle manifest version must be '2'. Bundle manifests written to previous specifications' manifest syntax are taken to have a bundle manifest version of '1', although there is no way to express this in such manifests. Therefore, any other value than '2' for this header is invalid unless the Framework explicitly supports such a later version.

OSGi Framework implementations should support bundle manifests without a Bundle-Manifest-Version header and assume Framework 1.2 compatibility at the appropriate places.

Version 2 bundle manifests must specify the bundle symbolic name. They need not specify the bundle version since this version header has a default value.

3.5.2   Bundle-SymbolicName

The Bundle-SymbolicName manifest header is a mandatory header. The bundle symbolic name and bundle version allow a bundle to be uniquely identified in the Framework. That is, a bundle with a given symbolic name and version is treated as equal to another bundle with the same (case sensitive) symbolic name and exact version.

The installation of a bundle with a Bundle-SymbolicName and Bundle-Version identical to an existing bundle must fail.

A bundle gets its unique Bundle-SymbolicName from the developer (The Bundle-Name manifest header provides a human-readable name for a bundle and is therefore not replaced by this header).

The Bundle-SymbolicName manifest header must conform to the following syntax:

```
Bundle-SymbolicName ::= symbolic-name
                   ( ';' parameter ) *    // See 1.3.2
```

The framework must recognize the following directives for the Bundle-SymbolicName header:

- singleton – Indicates that the bundle can only have a single version resolved. A value of true indicates that the bundle is a *singleton bundle*. The default value is false. The Framework must resolve at most one bundle when multiple versions of a singleton bundle with the same symbolic name are installed. Singleton bundles do not affect the resolution of non-singleton bundles with the same symbolic name.

- fragment-attachment – Defines how fragments are allowed to be attached, see the fragments in *Fragment Bundles* on page 63. The following values are valid for this directive:
  - always – Fragments can attach at any time while the host is resolved or during the process of resolving.
  - never – No fragments are allowed.
  - resolve-time – Fragments must only be attached during resolving.

For example:

```
Bundle-SymbolicName: com.acme.foo;singleton:=true
```

3.5.3   Bundle-Version

Bundle-Version is an optional header; the default value is 0.0.0.

```
Bundle-Version ::= version  // See 3.2.5
```

If the minor or micro version components are not specified, they have a default value of 0. If the qualifier component is not specified, it has a default value of the empty string ("").

Versions are comparable. Their comparison is done numerically and sequentially on the major, minor, and micro components and lastly using the String class compareTo method for the qualifier.

A version is considered equal to another version if the major, minor, micro, and the qualifier components are equal (using String method compareTo).

Example:

```
Bundle-Version: 22.3.58.build-345678
```

3.5.4   Import-Package Header

The Import-Package header defines the constraints on the imports of shared packages. The syntax of the Import-Package header is:

```
Import-Package ::= import ( ',' import )*
import ::= package-names ( ';' parameter )*
package-names ::= package-name
                   ( ';' package-name )* // See 1.3.2
```

The header allows many packages to be imported. An *import definition* is the description of a single package for a bundle. The syntax permits multiple package names, separated by semi-colons, to be described in a short form.

Import package directives are:

- resolution – Indicates that the packages must be resolved if the value is mandatory, which is the default. If mandatory packages cannot be resolved, then the bundle must fail to resolve. A value of optional indicates that the packages are optional. See *Optional Packages* on page 39.

The developer can specify arbitrary matching attributes. See *Attribute Matching* on page 42. The following arbitrary matching attributes are predefined:

- version – A version-range to select the exporter's package version. The syntax must follow *Version Ranges* on page 27. For more information on version selection, see *Version Matching* on page 38. If this attribute is not specified, it is assumed to be [0.0.0, ∞).

- specification-version – This attribute is an alias of the version attribute only to ease migration from earlier versions. If the version attribute is present, the values must be equal.

- bundle-symbolic-name – The bundle symbolic name of the exporting bundle. In the case of a fragment bundle, this will be the host bundle's symbolic name.

- bundle-version – A version-range to select the bundle version of the exporting bundle. The default value is [0.0.0, ∞). See *Version Matching* on page 38. In the case of a fragment bundle, the version is from the host bundle.

In order to be allowed to import a package (except for packages starting with java.), a bundle must have PackagePermission[<package-name>, IMPORT]. See PackagePermission for more information.

An error aborts an installation or update when:

- A directive or attribute appears multiple times, or
- There are multiple import definitions for the same package, or
- The version and specification-version attributes do not match.

Example of a correct definition:

```
Import-Package: com.acme.foo;com.acme.bar;
     version="[1.23,1.24]";
```

```
                              resolution:=mandatory
```

3.5.5   Export-Package

The syntax of the Export-Package header is similar to the Import-Package header; only the directives and attributes are different.

```
Export-Package  ::= export ( ',' export )*
export          ::= package-names ( ';' parameter )*
package-names   ::= package-name            // See 1.3.2
                         ( ';' package-name )*
```

The header allows many packages to be exported. An *export definition* is the description of a single package export for a bundle. The syntax permits the declaration of multiple packages in one clause by separating the package names with a semi-colon. Multiple export definitions for the same package are allowed for example, when different attributes are needed for different importers.

Export directives are:

*   uses – A comma-separated list of package names that are used by the exported package. Note that the use of a comma in the value requires it to be enclosed in double quotes. If this exported package is chosen as an export, then the resolver must ensure that importers of this package wire to the same versions of the package in this list. See *Package Constraints* on page 40.
*   mandatory - A comma-separated list of attribute names. Note that the use of a comma in the value requires it to be enclosed in double quotes. A bundle importing the package must specify the mandatory attributes, with a value that matches, to resolve to the exported package. See *Mandatory Attributes* on page 42.
*   include – A comma-separated list of class names that must be visible to an importer. Note that the use of a comma in the value requires it to be enclosed in double quotes. For class filtering, see *Class Filtering* on page 43.
*   exclude -A comma-separated list of class names that must be invisible to an importer. Note that the use of a comma in the value requires it to be enclosed in double quotes. For class filtering, see *Class Filtering* on page 43.

The following attribute is part of this specification:

*   version – The version of the named packages with syntax as defined in *Version* on page 27. It defines the version of the associated packages. The default value is 0.0.0.

*   specification-version – An alias for the version attribute only to ease migration from earlier versions. If the version attribute is present, the values must be equal.

Additionally, arbitrary matching attributes may be specified. See *Attribute Matching* on page 42.

The Framework will automatically associate each package export definition with the following attributes:

*   bundle-symbolic-name – The bundle symbolic name of the exporting bundle. In the case of a fragment bundle, this is the host bundle's symbolic name.
*   bundle-version – The bundle version of the exporting bundle. In the case of a fragment bundle, this is the host bundle's version.

An installation or update must be aborted when any of the following conditions is true:

*   a directive or attribute appears multiple times
*   the bundle-symbolic-name or bundle-version attribute is specified in the Export-Package header.

An export definition does not imply an automatic import definition. A bundle that exports a package and does not import that package will get that package via its bundle class path. Such an exported only package can be used by other bundles, but the exporting bundle does not accept a substitution for this package from another bundle.

In order to export a package, a bundle must have PackagePermission[<package>, EXPORTONLY].

Example:

```
Export-Package: com.acme.foo;com.acme.bar;version=1.23
```

3.5.6   Exporting and Importing a Package

Exporting a package does not imply the import of that same package (in Release 3, an export did imply an import). The reason for this separation is that it enables a bundle to provide a package to other bundles without having to take into account that the exported package could be *substituted* by the resolver with the same package from another bundle. This is a common case when an application consists of a set of closely intertwined bundles where implementation packages are provided to other bundles.

The substitution of packages is crucial for the inter-operability of bundles. In Java, bundles can only inter-operate when they use the same class loaders for the same classes. Therefore, two bundles that both export the same package, but do not import it, cannot share objects from that package. This is very important for a collaboration mechanism like the Service Layer. Bundles can only use the same service objects if their classes and interfaces come from the same class loaders.

Bundles should therefore import their exported packages, allowing the resolver to substitute packages that contain interfaces and other shared types. The import should be as unconstrained as possible to allow the resolver maximum flexibility. The imported and exported packages on a bundle are independent, that is, there is no requirement that the imported package matches the related exported package. It is valid to export package p, version 2, and import package p version 1.

3.5.7   Interpretation of Legacy Bundles

Bundles that are not marked with a Bundle-ManifestVersion that equals 2 or more must treat the headers according the definitions in the Release 3. More specifically, the Framework must map the Release 3 headers to the appropriate Release 4 headers:

*   *Import-Package* – An import definition must change the specification-version attribute to the version attribute. An import definition without a specification version needs no replacement since the default version value of 0.0.0 gives the same semantics as Release 3.
*   *Export-Package* – An export definition must change the specification-version attribute to the version attribute. The export definition must be appended with the uses directive. The uses directive must contain all imported and exported packages for the given bundle. Additionally, if there is no import definition for this package, then an import definition for this package with the given version must be added.
*   *DynamicImport-Package* – A dynamic import definition is unmodified.

A bundle manifest which mixes legacy syntax with bundle manifest version 2 syntax is in error and must cause the containing bundle to fail to install.

The specification-version attribute is a deprecated synonym for the version attribute in bundle manifest version 2 headers.

3.6   Constraint Solving

The OSGi Framework package resolver provides a number of mechanisms to match imports to exports. The following sections describe these mechanisms in detail.

3.6.1   Diagrams and Syntax

Wires create a graph of nodes. Both the wires as well as nodes (bundles) carry a significant amount of information. In the next sections, the following conventions are used to explain the many details.

Bundles are named A, B, C,... That is, uppercase characters starting from the character A. Packages are named p, q, r, s, t,... In other words, lower case characters starting from p. If a version is important, it is indicated with a dash followed by the version: q-1.0. The syntax A.p means the package definition (either import or export) of package p by bundle A.

Import definitions are graphically shown by a white box. Export definitions are displayed with a black box. Packages that are not exported or imported are called private packages. They are indicated with diagonal lines.

Bundles are a set of connected boxes. Constraints are written on the wires, which are represented by lines.

Figure 3.21   *Legend of wiring instance diagrams, and example*

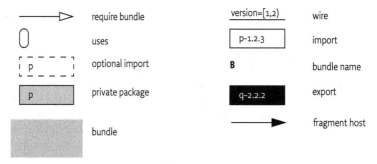

For example:

```
A: Import-Package: p; version="[1,2)"
   Export-Package: q; version=2.2.2; uses:=p
   Require-Bundle: C
B: Export-Package: p; version=1.5.1
C: Export-Package: r
```

Figure 3.22 shows the same setup graphically.

Figure 3.22   *Example bundle diagram*

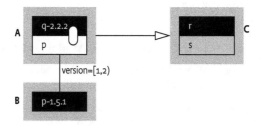

3.6.2   Version Matching

Version constraints are a mechanism whereby an import definition can declare a precise version or a version range for matching an export definition.

Version ranges encode the assumptions about compatibility. This specification does not define any compatibility policy; the policy decision is left to the importer that specifies a version range. A version range embeds such a policy.

However, the most common version compatibility policies are:

- major – An incompatible update
- minor – A backward compatible update
- micro – A change that does not affect the interface: for example, a bug fix

An import definition must specify a version range as the value for its version attribute, and the exporter must specify a version as the value for its version attribute. Matching is done with the rules for version range matches as described in *Version Ranges* on page 27.

For example, the following import and export definition resolve correctly because the version range in the import definition matches the version in the export definition:

```
A: Import-Package: p; version="[1,2)"
B: Export-Package: p; version=1.5.1
```

Figure 3.23 graphically shows how a constraint can exclude an exporter.

Figure 3.23   *Version Constrained*

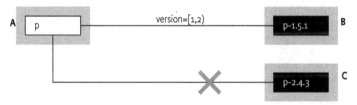

3.6.3   Optional Packages

A bundle can indicate that it does not require a package to resolve correctly, but it may use the package if it is available. For example, logging is important, but the absence of a log service should not prevent a bundle from running.

Optional imports can be specified in the following ways:

- *Dynamic Imports* – The DynamicImport-Package header is intended to look for an exported package when that package is needed. The key use case for dynamic import is the Class forName method when a bundle does not know in advance the class name it may be requested to load.
- *Resolution Directive* – The resolution directive on an import definition specifying the value optional. A bundle may successfully resolve if a suitable optional package is not present.

The key difference between these two mechanisms is when the wires are made. An attempt is made to establish a wire for a dynamic import every time there is an attempt to load a class in that package, whereas the wire for a resolution optional package may only be established when the bundle is resolved.

The resolution directive of the import definition can take the value mandatory or optional.

- mandatory – (Default) Indicates that the package must be wired for the bundle to resolve.
- optional – Indicates that the importing bundle may resolve without the package being wired. If the package is not wired, the class loading will treat this package as if it is not imported.

The following example will resolve even though bundle B does not provide the correct version (the package will *not* be available to the code when bundle A is resolved).

```
A: Import-Package: p;
```

```
            resolution:=optional;
            version=1.6
    B: Export-Package: p;
            q;
            version=1.5.0
```

Figure 3.24   *Optional import*

The implementation of a bundle that uses optional packages must be prepared to handle the fact that the packages may not be available: that is, an exception can be thrown when there is a reference to a class from a missing package. This can be prevented by including a fallback package on the bundle's classpath. When an optional package cannot be resolved, any attempts by the bundle to load classes from it will follow normal bundle class loading search order as if the import never existed. It will load it from the bundle's class path or in the end through dynamic class loading when set for that bundle and package.

3.6.4   Package Constraints

Classes can depend on classes in other packages. For example, when they extend classes from another package, or these other classes appear in method signatures. It can therefore be said that a package *uses* other packages. These inter-package dependencies are modeled with the uses directive on the Export-Package header.

For example, org.osgi.service.http depends on the package javax.servlet because it is used in the API. The export definition of the org.osgi.service.http must therefore contain the uses directive with the javax.servlet package as its value.

Class space consistency can only be ensured if a bundle has only one exporter for each package.

For example, the Http Service implementation requires servlets to extend the javax.servlet.http.HttpServlet base class. If the Http Service bundle would import version 2.4 and the client bundle would import version 2.1 then a class cast exception is bound to happen. This is depicted in Figure 3.25.

Figure 3.25   *Uses directive in B, forces A to use javax.servlet from D*

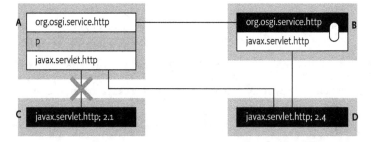

If a bundle imports a package from an exporter then the export definition of that package can imply constraints on a number of other packages through the uses directive. The uses directive lists the packages that the exporter depends upon and therefore constrains the resolver for imports. These constraints ensure that a set of bundles share the same class loader for the same package.

When an importer imports a package with implied constraints, the resolver must wire the import to the exporter implied by the constraint. This exporter may in turn imply additional constraints, and so on. The act of wiring a single import of a package to an exporter can therefore imply a large set of constraints. The term *implied package constraints* refers to the complete set of constraints constructed from recursively traversing the wires. Implied package constraints are not automatic imports; rather, implied package constraints only constrain how an import definition must be resolved.

For example, in Figure 3.26, bundle A imports package p. Assume this import definition is wired to bundle B. Due to the uses directive (the ellipse symbols indicates the uses directive) this implies a constraint on package q.

Further, assuming that the import for package q is wired to bundle C, then this implies a constraint on the import of package r and s. Continuing, assuming C.s and C.r are wired to bundle D and E respectively. These bundles both add package t to the set of implied packages for bundle A.

Figure 3.26   *Implied Packages*

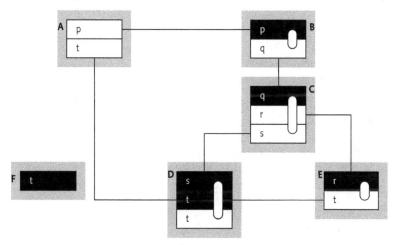

To maintain class space consistency, the Framework must ensure that none of its bundle imports conflicts with any of that bundle's implied packages.

For the example, this means that the Framework must ensure that the import definition of A.t is wired to package D.t. Wiring this import definition to package F.t violates the class space consistency. This violation occurs because bundle A could be confronted with objects with the same class name but from the class loaders of bundle D and F. This would potentially create ClassCastExceptions. Alternatively, if all bundles are wired to F.t, then the problem also goes away.

Another scenario with this case is depicted in Figure 3.25. Bundle A imports the Http Service classes from bundle B. Bundle B has grouped the org.osgi.service.http and the javax.servlet and bundle A is therefore constrained to wire javax.servlet to the same exporter as bundle B.

As an example of a situation where the uses directive makes resolving impossible consider the following setup that is correctly resolved:

```
A: Import-Package: q; version="[1.0,1.0]"
   Export-Package: p; uses:="q,r", r
B: Export-Package: q; version=1.0
C: Export-Package: q; version=2.0
```

These specific constraints can be resolved because the import A.q can be wired to the export B.q but not C.q due to the version constraint.

Adding a bundle D will now not be possible:

```
D: Import-Package: p, q; version=2.0
```

Package D.p must be wired to package A.p because bundle A is the only exporter. However, this implies the use of package q due the uses directive in the package A.q import. Package A.q is wired to B.q-1.0. However, import package D.q requires version 2.0 and can therefore not be resolved without violating the class space constraint.

This scenario is depicted in Figure 3.27.

Figure 3.27   *Uses directive and resolving*

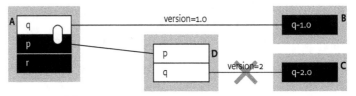

3.6.5   Attribute Matching

Attribute matching is a generic mechanism to allow the importer and exporter to influence the matching process in a declarative way. In order for an import definition to be resolved to an export definition, the values of the attributes specified by the import definition must match the values of the attributes of the export definition. By default, a match is not prevented if the export definition contains attributes that do not occur in the import definition. The mandatory directive in the export definition can reverse this by listing all attributes that the Framework must match in the import definition. Any attributes specified in the DynamicImport-Package is ignored during the resolve phase but can influence runtime class loading.

For example, the following statements will match.

```
A: Import-Package: com.acme.foo; company=ACME
B: Export-Package: com.acme.foo;
        company="ACME";
        security=false
```

Attribute values are compared string wise except for the version and bundle-version attributes which use version range comparisons. Leading and trailing white space in attribute values must be ignored.

3.6.6   Mandatory Attributes

There are two types of attributes: *mandatory* and *optional.* Mandatory attributes must be specified in the import definition to match. Optional attributes are ignored when they are not referenced by the importer. Attributes are optional by default.

The exporter can specify mandatory attributes with the mandatory directive in the export definition. This directive contains a comma-separated list of attribute names that must be specified by the importer to match.

For example, the following import definition must not match the export definition because security is a mandatory attribute:

```
A: Import-Package: com.acme.foo; company=ACME

B: Export-Package: com.acme.foo;
        company="ACME";
        security=false;
```

```
mandatory:=security
```

3.6.7   Class Filtering

An exporter can limit the visibility of the classes in a package with the include and exclude direc-tives on the export definition. The value of each of these directives is a comma-separated list of class names. Note that the use of a comma in the value requires it to be enclosed in double quotes.

Class names must not include their package name and do not end with .class. That is, the class com.acme.foo.Daffy is named Daffy in either list. The class name can include multiple wildcards ('*').

The default for the include directive is '*' (wildcard matching all names), and for the exclude direc-tive, so that no classes or resources are excluded, an empty list that matches no names. If include or exclude directive are specified, the corresponding default is overridden.

A class is only visible if it is:

- Matched with an entry in the included list, *and*
- Not matched with an entry in the excluded list.

In all other cases, loading or finding fails, and a Class Not Found Exception is thrown for a class load. The ordering of include and exclude is not significant.

The following example shows an export statement, and a list of files with their visibility status.

```
Export-Package: com.acme.foo; include:="Qux*,BarImpl";
        exclude:=QuxImpl

com/acme/foo
    QuxFoo          visible
    QuxBar          visible
    QuxImpl         excluded
    BarImpl         visible
```

Care must be taken when using filters. For example, a new version of a module that is intended to be backward compatible with an earlier version should not filter out classes or resources that were not filtered out by the earlier version. In addition, when modularizing existing code, filtering out classes or resources from an exported package may break users of the package.

For example, packages defined by standard bodies often require an implementation class in the standardized package to have package access to the specification classes.

```
package org.acme.open;
public class Specified {
    static Specified implementation;
    public void foo() { implementation.foo(); }
}

package org.acme.open;
public class Implementation {
    public void initialize(Specified implementation) {
        Specified.implementation = implementation;
    }
}
```

The Implementation class must not be available to external bundles because it allows the implementation to be set. By excluding the Implementation class, only the exporting bundle can see this class. The export definition for this header could look like:

```
Export-Package: org.acme.open; exclude:=Implementation
```

3.6.8   Provider Selection

Provider selection allows the importer to select which bundles can be considered as exporters. Provider selection is used when there is no specification contract between the importer and the exporter. The importer tightly couples itself to a specific exporter, typically the bundle that was used for testing. To make the wiring less brittle, the importer can optionally specify a range of bundle versions that will match.

An importer can select an exporter with the import attributes bundle-symbolic-name and bundle-version. The Framework automatically provides these attributes for each export definition. These attributes must not be specified in an export definition.

The export definition bundle-symbolic-name attribute will contain the bundle symbolic name as specified in the Bundle-SymbolicName header without any parameters. The export definition bundle-version attribute is set to the value of the Bundle-Version header or its default of 0.0.0 when absent.

The bundle-symbolic-name is matched as an attribute. The bundle-version attribute is matched using the version range rules as defined in *Version Ranges* on page 27. The import definition must be a version range and the export definition is a version.

For example, the following definitions will match:

```
A: Bundle-SymbolicName: A
   Import-Package: com.acme.foo;
       bundle-symbolic-name=B;
       bundle-version="[1.41,2.0.0)"

B: Bundle-SymbolicName: B
   Bundle-Version: 1.41
   Export-Package: com.acme.foo
```

The following statements will not match because B does not specify a version and thus defaults to 0.0.0:

```
A: Bundle-SymbolicName: A
   Import-Package: com.acme.foo;
       bundle-symbolic-name=B;
       bundle-version="[1.41,2.0.0)"

B: Bundle-SymbolicName: B
   Export-Package: com.acme.foo;version=1.42
```

Selecting an exporter by symbolic name can result in brittleness because of hard coupling of the package to the bundle. For example, if the exporter eventually needs to be refactored into multiple separate bundles, all importers must be changed. Other arbitrary matching attributes do not have this disadvantage as they can be specified independently of the exporting bundle.

The brittleness problem of the bundle symbolic name in bundle refactoring can be partly overcome by writing a façade bundle using the same bundle symbolic name as the original bundle.

3.7 Resolving Process

Resolving is the process that creates a wiring between bundles. Constraints on the wires are statically defined by:

- The required execution environments
- Native code
- Import and export packages (the DynamicImport-Package header is ignored in this phase)
- Required bundles, which import all exported packages from a bundle as defined in *Requiring Bundles* on page 60.
- Fragments, which provide their contents and definitions to the host as defined in *Fragment Bundles* on page 63

A bundle can only be resolved when a number of constraints are satisfied:

- *Execution Environment* – The underlying VM implements at least one of the execution environments listed in the Bundle-RequiredExecutionEnvironment header. See *Execution Environment* on page 30.
- *Native code* – The native code dependencies specified in the Bundle-NativeCode header must be resolved. See *Loading Native Code Libraries* on page 54.

The resolving process is then a constraint-solving algorithm that can be described in terms of requirements on wiring relations. The resolving process is an iterative process that searches through the solution space.

If a module has both import and export definitions for the *same* package, then the Framework needs to decide which to choose.

It must first try to resolve the overlapping import definition. The following outcomes are possible:

- *External* – If this resolves to an export statement in another bundle, then the overlapping export definition in this bundle is discarded.
- *Internal* – If it is resolved to an export statement in this module, then the overlapping import definition in this module is discarded.
- *Unresolved* – There is no matching export definition. This is however a developer error because it means the overlapping export definition of the bundle is not compatible with the overlapping import definition.

A bundle can be resolved if the following conditions are met:

- All its mandatory imports are wired
- All its mandatory required bundles are available and their exports wired

A wire is only created when the following conditions are met:

- The importer's version range matches the exporter's version. See *Version Matching* on page 38.
- The importer specifies all mandatory attributes from the exporter. See *Mandatory Attributes* on page 42.
- All the importer's attributes match the attributes of the corresponding exporter. See *Attribute Matching* on page 42
- Implied packages referring to the same package as the wire are wired to the same exporter. See *Package Constraints* on page 40.
- The wire is connected to a valid exporter.

The following list defines the preferences, if multiple choices are possible, in order of decreasing priority:

- A resolved exporter must be preferred over an unresolved exporter.
- An exporter with a higher version is preferred over an exporter with a lower version.
- An exporter with a lower bundle ID is preferred over a bundle with a higher ID.

3.8   Runtime Class Loading

Each bundle installed in the Framework must not have an associated class loader until after it is resolved. After a bundle is resolved, the Framework must create one class loader for each bundle that is not a fragment. The framework may delay creation of the class loader until it is actually needed.

One class loader per bundle allows all resources within a bundle to have package level access to all other resources in the bundle within the same package. This class loader provides each bundle with its own name space, to avoid name conflicts, and allows resource sharing with other bundles.

This class loader must use the wiring as calculated in the resolving process to find the appropriate exporters. If a class is not found in the imports, additional headers in the manifest can control the searching of classes and resources in additional places.

The following sections define the factors that influence the runtime class loading and then define the exact search order the Framework must follow when a class or resource is loaded.

3.8.1   Bundle Class Path

JAR, ZIP, directories, etc. are called *containers*. Containers contain *entries* organized in hierarchical paths. In runtime, an entry from a bundle can actually come from different containers because of attached fragments. The order in which an entry can be found is significant because it can shadow other entries. For a bundle, the search order for a named entry is:

- First the container of the (host) bundle
- Then the (optional) fragment containers in ascending id order

This search order is called the *entry path*. A *resource* (or class) is not loaded via the entry path, but it is loaded through the *bundle class path*. The bundle class path provides an additional indirection on top of the entry path. It defines an ordered list of *container paths*. Each container path can be found on the entry path.

The dot ('.' \u002E) container path is a synonym for '/' or the root of a container. The dot is the default value for a bundle or fragment if no Bundle-ClassPath header is specified.

The Bundle-ClassPath manifest header must conform to the following syntax:

```
Bundle-ClassPath::=  entry ( ',' entry )*
entry            ::= target ( ';' target )*
                     ( ';' parameter ) *
target           ::= path | '.'           // See 1.3.2
```

The Framework must ignore any unrecognized parameters.

The content of the *effective* bundle class path is constructed from the bundle's Bundle-Classpath header, concatenated with the Bundle-Classpath headers of any fragments, in ascending bundle id order. The effective Bundle-Classpath is calculated during resolve time, however, a dynamically attached fragment can append elements at the end if the Framework supports dynamically attached fragments.

An element from the bundle's Bundle-ClassPath header refers to the first match when searched through the entry path, while a fragment's Bundle-ClassPath can refer only to an entry in its own container.

An example can illustrate this:

```
A: Bundle-Classpath: .,resource.jar
B: Fragment-Host: A
```

The previous example uses an effective bundle class path of:

/, resource.jar, B:/

The first element / is the root of a container. The bundle always has a root and can therefore always be found in the (host) bundle. The second element is first looked up in the host bundle's container, and if not found, the entry is looked up in the container of B. The Framework must use the first entry that matches. The last element in the effective bundle class path is the / from fragment B; the / is the default because there is no Bundle-ClassPath specified. However, a fragment can only refer to an internal entry. This dot therefore refers to the root of the container of fragment B. Assuming, fragment B contains an entry for resource.jar and bundle A does not, then the search order must be:

A: /
B: resource.jar
B: /

The Framework must ignore a container path in the bundle class-path if the container cannot be located when it is needed, which can happen at any time after the bundle is resolved. However, the Framework should publish a Framework Event of type INFO once with an appropriate message for each entry that cannot be located at all.

An entry on the Bundle-ClassPath can refer to a directory in the container. However, it is not always possible to establish the directory's existence. For example, directories can be omitted in JAR/ZIP files. In such a case, a Framework must probe the directory to see if any resources can be found in this directory. That is, even if the directory construct is absent in the container, if resources can be found assuming this directory, than it must still be chosen for the Bundle-ClassPath.

A host bundle can allow a fragment to insert code ahead of its own code by naming a container in its Bundle-Classpath that will be provided by a fragment. Fragments can never unilaterally insert code ahead of their host's bundle class path. The following example illustrates the possibilities of the bundle class path in more detail:

```
A:  Bundle-SymbolicName: A
    Bundle-ClassPath: /, required.jar, optional, default.jar
    content ...
    required.jar
    default.jar
B:  Bundle-SymbolicName: B
    Bundle-ClassPath: fragment.jar
    Fragment-Host: A
    content ...
    optional/
        content ...
    fragment.jar
```

The names of the bundle class path elements indicate their intention. The required.jar is a container that provides mandatory functionality, it is packaged in bundle A. The optional container is a directory containing optional classes, and the default.jar is a JAR entry with backup code. In this example, the effective bundle class path is:

A: /
A: required.jar
B: optional
A: default.jar
B: fragment.jar

This will expand to the following (logical) search order for a resource X.class:

A: /X.class
A: required.jar!X.class
B: optional/X.class

```
A: default.jar!X.class
B: fragment.jar!X.class
```

The exclamation mark (!) indicates a load from a JAR resource.

3.8.2 Dynamic Import Package

Dynamic imports are matched to export definitions (to form package wirings) during class loading, and therefore do not affect module resolution. Dynamic imports apply only to packages for which no wire has been established and no definition could be found in any other way. Dynamic import is used as last resort.

```
DynamicImport-Package ::= dynamic-description
          ( ',' dynamic-description )*
dynamic-description::= wildcard-names ( ';' parameter )*
wildcard-names     ::= wildcard-name ( ';' wildcard-name )*
wildcard-name      ::= package-name
       | ( package-name '.*' )   // See 1.3.2
       | '*'
```

No directives are architected by the Framework for DynamicImport-Package. Arbitrary matching attributes may be specified. The following arbitrary matching attributes are architected by the Framework:

- version -- A version range to select the version of an export definition. The default value is 0.0.0 .
- bundle-symbolic-name – The bundle symbolic name of the exporting bundle.
- bundle-version – a version range to select the bundle version of the exporting bundle. The default value is 0.0.0.

Packages may be named explicitly or by using wild-carded expressions such as org.foo.* and *. The wildcard can stand for any suffix, including multiple sub-packages. If a wildcard is used, then the package identified by the prefix must *not* be included. That is, org.foo.* will include all sub-packages of org.foo but it must not include package org.foo itself.

Dynamic imports must be searched in the order in which they are specified. The order is particularly important when package names with wildcards are used. The order will then determine the order in which matching occurs. This means that the more specific package specifications should appear before the broader specifications. For example, the following DynamicImport-Package header indicates a preference for packages supplied by ACME:

```
DynamicImport-Package: *;vendor=acme, *
```

If multiple packages need to be dynamically imported with identical parameters, the syntax permits a list of packages, separated by semicolons, to be specified before the parameters.

During class loading, the package of the class being loaded is compared against the specified list of (possibly wild-carded) package names. Each matching package name is used in turn to attempt to wire to an export using the same rules as Import-Package. If a wiring attempt is successful (taking any uses constraints into account), the search is forwarded to the exporter's class loader where class loading continues. The wiring must not subsequently be modified, even if the class cannot be loaded. This implies that once a package is dynamically resolved, subsequent attempts to load classes or resources from that package are treated as normal imports.

In order for a DynamicImport-Package to be resolved to an export statement, all attributes of the dynamic import definition must match the attributes of the export statement. All mandatory arbitrary attributes (as specified by the exporter, see *Mandatory Attributes* on page 42) must be specified in the dynamic import definition and match.

Once a wire is established, any uses constraints from the exporter must be obeyed for further dynamic imports.

Dynamic imports are very similar to optional packages, see *Optional Packages* on page 39, but differ in the fact that they are handled after the bundle is resolved.

3.8.3 Parent Delegation

The Framework must always delegate any package that starts with java. to the parent class loader.

Certain Java virtual machines, also SUN's VMs, appear to make the erroneous assumption that the delegation to the parent class loader always occurs. This implicit assumption of strictly hierarchical class loader delegation can result in NoClassDefFoundErrors. This happens if the virtual machine implementation expects to find its own implementation classes from any arbitrary class loader, requiring that packages loaded from the boot class loader not be restricted to only the java.* packages.

Other packages that must be loaded from the boot class loader can therefore be specified with the System property:

```
org.osgi.framework.bootdelegation
```

This property must contain a list with the following format:

```
org.osgi.framework.bootdelegation ::= boot-description
        ( ',' boot-description )*
boot-description::= package-name                    // See 1.3.2
        | ( package-name '.*' )
        | '*'
```

The .* wildcard means deep matching, that is, com.acme.*, matches any sub-package of package com.acme, however, it does not match com.acme. Packages that match this list must be loaded from the parent class loader. The java.* prefix is always implied; it does not have to be specified.

The single wildcard means that the Framework must always delegate to the parent class loader first, which is the same as the Release 3 behavior. For example, when running on a SUN JVM, it may be necessary to specify a value like:

```
org.osgi.framework.bootdelegation=sun.*,com.sun.*
```

With such a property value, the Framework must delegate all java.*, sun.*, and com.sun.* packages to the parent class loader.

3.8.4 Overall Search Order

Frameworks must adhere to the following rules for class or resource loading. When a bundle's class loader is requested to load a class or find a resource, the search must be performed in the following order:

1 If the class or resource is in a java.* package, the request is delegated to the parent class loader; otherwise, the search continues with the next step. If the request is delegated to the parent class loader and the class or resource is not found, then the search terminates and the request fails.
2 If the class or resource is from a package included in the boot delegation list (org.osgi.framework.bootdelegation), then the request is delegated to the parent class loader. If the class or resource is found there, the search ends.
3 If the class or resource is in a package that is imported using Import-Package or was imported dynamically in a previous load, then the request is delegated to the exporting bundle's class loader; otherwise the search continues with the next step. If the request is delegated to an exporting class loader and the class or resource is not found, then the search terminates and the request fails.
4 If the class or resource is in a package that is imported from one or more other bundles using Require-Bundle, the request is delegated to the class loaders of the other bundles, in the order in which they are specified in this bundle's manifest. This entails a depth-first strategy; all required

    bundles are searched before the bundle classpath is used. If the class or resource is not found, then the search continues with the next step.

5   Search the bundle's embedded classpath, see *Bundle Class Path* on page 46. If the class or resource is not found, then continue with the next step.

6   If the class or resource is in a package that is exported by the bundle or the package is imported by the bundle (using Import-Package or Require-Bundle), then the search ends and the class or resource is not found.

7   Otherwise, if the class or resource is in a package that is imported using DynamicImport-Package, then a dynamic import of the package is now attempted. An exporter must conform to any implied package constraints. If an appropriate exporter is found, a wire is established so that future loads of the package are handled in Step 3. If a dynamic wire is not established, then the request fails.

8   If the dynamic import of the package is established, the request is delegated to the exporting bundle's class loader. If the request is delegated to an exporting class loader and the class or resource is not found, then the search terminates and the request fails.

When delegating to another bundle class loader, the delegated request enters this algorithm at Step 4.

The following non-normative flow chart illustrates the search order described above:

Figure 3.28   *Flow chart for class loading (non-normative)*

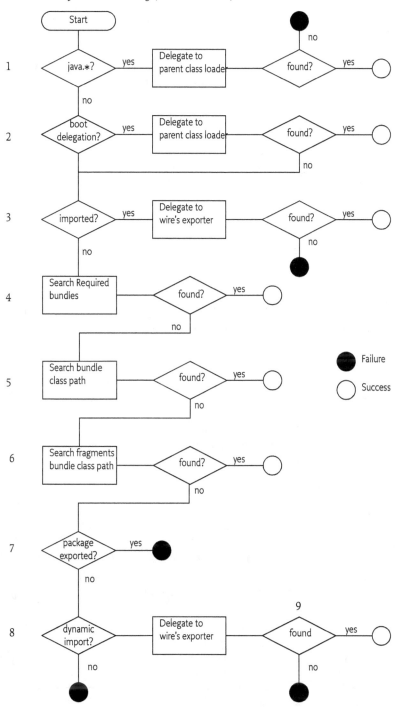

3.8.5   Parent Class Loader

The set of implicitly imported packages are all java.* packages, since these packages are required by the Java runtime, and using multiple versions at the same time is not easy. For example, all objects must extend the same Object class.

A bundle must not declare imports or exports for java.* packages; doing so is an error and any such bundle must fail to install. All other packages available through the parent class loader must be hidden from executing bundles.

However, the Framework must explicitly export relevant packages from the parent class loader. The system property

    org.osgi.framework.system.packages

contains the export packages descriptions for the system bundle. This property employs the standard Export-Package manifest header syntax:

    org.osgi.framework.system.packages ::= package-description (',' package-
    description)*

Some classes on the boot class path assume that they can use any class loader to load other classes on the boot class path, which is not true for a bundle class loader. Framework implementations should attempt to load these classes from the boot class path.

The system bundle (bundle ID zero) is used to export non-java.* packages from the parent class loader. Export definitions from the system bundle are treated like normal exports, meaning that they can have version numbers, and are used to resolve import definitions as part of the normal bundle resolving process. Other bundles may provide alternative implementations of the same packages.

The set of export definitions for the parent class loader can either be set by this property or calculated by the Framework. The export definitions must have the implementation specific bundle symbolic name and version value of the system bundle.

Exposing packages from the parent class loader in this fashion must also take into account any uses directives of the underlying packages. For example, the definition of javax.crypto.spec must declare its usage of javax.crypto.interfaces and javax.crypto.

3.8.6   Resource Loading

A resource in a bundle can be accessed through the class loader of that bundle but it can also be accessed with the getResource, getEntry or findEntries methods. All these methods return a URL object or an Enumeration object of URL objects. The URLs are called *bundle entry URLs*. The schemes for the URLs returned by these methods can differ and are implementation dependent.

Bundle entry URLs are normally created by the Framework, however, in certain cases bundles need to manipulate the URL to find related resources. The Framework is therefore required to ensure that:

- Bundle entry URLs must be hierarchical (See [32] *Uniform Resource Identifiers URI: Generic Syntax*)
- Usable as a context for constructing another URL.
- The java.net.URLStreamHandler class used for a bundle entry URL must be available to the java.net.URL class to setup a URL that uses the protocol scheme defined by the Framework.
- The getPath method for a bundle entry URL must return an absolute path (a path that starts with '/') to a resource or entry in a bundle. For example, the URL returned from getEntry("myimages/test.gif") must have a path of /myimages/test.gif.

For example, a class can take a URL to an index.html bundle resource and map URLs in this resource to other files in the same JAR directory.

    public class BundleResource implements HttpContext {

```
    URL root;   // to index.html in bundle
    URL getResource( String resource ) {
        return new URL( root, resource );
    }
    ...
}
```

3.8.7   Bundle Cycles

Multiple required bundles can export the same package. Bundles which export the same package involved in a require bundle cycle can lead to lookup cycles when searching for classes and resources from the package. Consider the following definitions:

```
A: Require-Bundle: B, C
C: Require-Bundle: D
```

These definitions are depicted in Figure 3.29.

Figure 3.29   *Depth First search with Require Bundle*

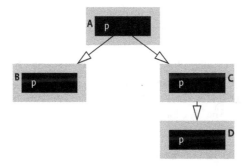

Each of the bundles exports the package p. In this example, bundle A requires bundle B, and bundle C requires bundle D. When bundle A loads a class or resource from package p, then the required bundle search order is the following: B, D, C, A. This is a depth first search order because required bundles are searched before the bundle classpath is searched (see step 4). The required bundles are searched in the order that they appear in the Require-Bundle header. The depth first search order can introduce endless search cycles if the dependency graph has a cycle in it.

Using the previous setup, a cycle can be introduced if bundle D requires bundle A as depicted in Figure 3.30.

```
D: Require-Bundle: A
```

Figure 3.30   *Cycles*

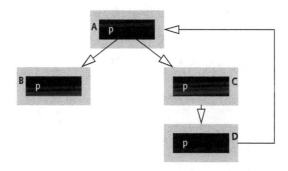

When the class loader for bundle A loads a class or resource from package p then the bundle search order would be the following: B, B, B,... if cycles were not taken into account.

Since a cycle was introduced each time bundle D is reached the search will recurs back to A and start over. The framework must prevent such dependency cycles from causing endless recursive lookups.

To avoid endless looping, the Framework must mark each bundle upon first visiting it and not explore the required bundles of a previously visited bundle. Using the visited pattern on the dependency graph above will result in the following bundle search order: B, D, C, A.

3.8.8 Code Executed Before Started

Packages exported from a bundle are exposed to other bundles as soon as the bundle has been resolved. This condition could mean that another bundle could call methods in an exported package *before* the bundle exporting the package is started.

3.8.9 Finding an Object's Bundle

The Package Admin service has a method getBundle(Class) that can provide the bundle of a specific class. In a well written OSGi bundle this should suffice. However, there are legacy scenarios where a bundle is required in code that has no access to a Bundle Context, and thereby cannot get the Package Admin service.

For this reasons, the framework provides the following methods:

- *Framework Util* – Through the FrameworkUtil class with the getBundle(Class) method. The framework provides this method to allow code to find the bundle of an object without having the permission to get the class loader. The method returns null when the class does not originate from a bundle.
- *Class Loader* – An OSGi framework must ensure that the class loader of a class that comes from a bundle implements the BundleReference interface. This allows legacy code to find an object's bundle by getting its class loader and casting it to a BundleReference object, which provides access to the Bundle. However, this requires the code to have the permission to access the class loader. The following code fragment shows how to obtain a Bundle object from any object.

```
ClassLoader cl = target.getClassLoader();
if ( cl instanceof BundleReference ) {
   BundleReference ref = (BundleReference) cl;
   Bundle b = ref.getBundle();
   ...
}
```

In an OSGi system, not all objects belong to the framework. It is therefore possible to get hold of a class loader that does not implement the BundleReference interface, for example the boot class path loader.

3.9 Loading Native Code Libraries

Dependency on native code is expressed in the Bundle-NativeCode header. The framework must verify this header and satisfy its dependencies before it attempts to resolve the bundle. However, a bundle can be installed without an exception if the header is properly formatted according to its syntax. If the header contains invalid information, or can not be satisfied, errors will be reported during resolving.

A Java VM has a special way of handling native code. When a class loaded by a bundle's class loader attempts to load a native library, by calling System.loadLibrary, the findLibrary method of the bundle's class loader must be called to return the file path in which the Framework has made the requested native library available. The parameter to the findLibrary method is the name of the library in operating system independent form, like http. The bundle class loader can use the mapLibraryName method from the VM to map this name to an operating system dependent name, like libhttp.so.

The bundle's class loader must attempt to find the native library by examining the selected native code clauses, if any, of the bundle associated with the class loader and each attached fragment. Fragments are examined in ascending bundle ID order. If the library is not referenced in any of the selected native code clauses then null must be returned which allows the parent class loader to search for the native library.

The bundle must have the required RuntimePermission[loadLibrary. <library name>] in order to load native code in the OSGi Service Platform.

The Bundle-NativeCode manifest header must conform to the following syntax:

```
Bundle-NativeCode  ::= nativecode
      ( ',' nativecode )* ( ',' optional) ?
nativecode           ::= path ( ';' path )*     // See 1.3.2
                     ( ';' parameter )+
optional             ::= '*'
```

When locating a path in a bundle the Framework must attempt to locate the path relative to the root of the bundle that contains the corresponding native code clause in its manifest header.

The following attributes are architected:

- osname – Name of the operating system. The value of this attribute must be the name of the operating system upon which the native libraries run. A number of canonical names are defined in *Environment Properties* on page 94.
- osversion – The operating system version. The value of this attribute must be a version range as defined in *Version Ranges* on page 27.
- processor – The processor architecture. The value of this attribute must be the name of the processor architecture upon which the native libraries run. see *Environment Properties* on page 94.
- language – The ISO code for a language. The value of this attribute must be the name of the language for which the native libraries have been localized.
- selection-filter – A selection filter. The value of this attribute must be a filter expression that indicates if the native code clause should be selected or not.

The following is a typical example of a native code declaration in a bundle's manifest:

```
Bundle-NativeCode: lib/http.dll ; lib/zlib.dll ;
     osname = Windows95 ;
     osname = Windows98 ;
     osname = WindowsNT ;
     processor = x86 ;
     selection-filter=
        "(com.acme.windowing=win32)";
     language = en ;
     language = se ,
   lib/solaris/libhttp.so ;
     osname = Solaris ;
     osname = SunOS ;
     processor = sparc,
   lib/linux/libhttp.so ;
```

```
osname = Linux ;
processor = mips;
selection-filter
  = "(com.acme.windowing=gtk)"
```

If multiple native code libraries need to be installed on one platform, they must all be specified in the same clause for that platform.

If a Bundle-NativeCode clause contains duplicate parameter entries, the corresponding values must be OR'ed together. This feature must be carefully used because the result is not always obvious. This is highlighted by the following example:

```
// The effect of this header has probably
// not the intended effect!
Bundle-NativeCode: lib/http.DLL ;
   osname = Windows95 ;
   osversion = "3.1" ;
   osname = WindowsXP ;
   osversion = "5.1" ;
   processor = x86
```

The above example implies that the native library will load on Windows XP 3.1 and later, which was probably not intended. The single clause should be split in two clauses:

```
Bundle-NativeCode: lib/http.DLL ;
    osname = Windows95 ;
    osversion = 3.1;
    processor = x86,
   lib/http.DLL ;
    osname = WindowsXP ;
    osversion = 5.1;
    processor = x86
```

Any paths specified in the matching clause must be present in the bundle or any of its attached fragments for a bundle to resolve. The framework must report a Bundle Exception with the NATIVECODE_ERROR as error code when the bundle can not be resolved due to a native code problem.

If the optional'*' is specified at the end of the Bundle-NativeCode manifest header, the bundle will still resolve even if the Bundle-NativeCode header has no matching clauses.

The following is a typical example of a native code declaration in a bundle's manifest with an optional clause:

```
Bundle-NativeCode: lib/win32/winxp/optimized.dll ;
    lib/win32/native.dll ;
    osname = WindowsXP ;
    processor = x86 ,
   lib/win32/native.dll ;
    osname = Windows95 ;
    osname = Windows98 ;
    osname = WindowsNT ;
    osname = Windows2000;
    processor = x86 ,
    *
```

3.9.1   **Native Code Algorithm**

In the description of this algorithm, [x] represents the value of the Framework property x and ~= represents the match operation. The match operation is a case insensitive comparison.

Certain properties can be aliased. In those cases, the manifest header should contain the generic name for that property but the Framework should attempt to include aliases when it matches. (See *Environment Properties* on page 94). If a property is not an alias, or has the wrong value, the Operator should set the appropriate system property to the generic name or to a valid value because Java System properties with this name override the Framework construction of these properties. For example, if the operating system returns version 2.4.2-kwt, the Operator should set the system property org.osgi.framework.os.version to 2.4.2.

The Framework must select the native code clause using the following algorithm:

1   Only select the native code clauses for which the following expressions all evaluate to true.
    - osname ~= [org.osgi.framework.os.name]
    - processor ~= [org.osgi.framework.processor]
    - osversion range includes [org.osgi.framework.os.version] or osversion is not specified
    - language ~= [org.osgi.framework.language] or language is not specified
    - selection-filter evaluates to true when using the values of the system properties or selection-filter is not specified
2   If no native clauses were selected in step 1, this algorithm is terminated and a BundleException is thrown if the optional clause is not present.
3   The selected clauses are now sorted in the following priority order:
    - osversion: floor of the osversion range in descending order,   osversion not specified
    - language: language specified, language not specified
    - Position in the Bundle-NativeCode manifest header: lexical left to right.
4   The first clause of the sorted clauses from step 3 must be used as the selected native code clause.

If a native code library in a selected native code clause cannot be found within the bundle then the bundle must fail to resolve. This is true even if the optional clause is specified. If the selected clause contains multiple libraries with the same base file name then only the lexically left most library with that base file name will be used. For example, if the selected clause contains the libraries lib1/http.dll; lib2/http.dll; lib3/foo.dll; a/b/c/http.dll then only http.dll in lib1 and foo.dll will be used.

If a selection filter is evaluated and its syntax is invalid, then the bundle must fail to resolve. If a selection filter is not evaluated (it may be in a native code clause where the osname or processor does not match), then the invalid filter must not cause the bundle to fail to resolve. This is also true even if the optional clause is specified.

Designing a bundle native code header can become quickly complicated when different operating systems, libraries, and languages are used. The best practice for designing the header is to place all parameters in a table. Every targeted environment is then a row in that table. See Table 3.4 for an example. This table makes it easier to detect missing combinations. This table is then mapped to

Table 3.4   Native code table

Libraries

Libraries	osname	osversion	processor	language	filter
nativecodewin32.dll, delta.dll	win32		x86	en	
nativecodegtk.so	linux		x86	en	(com.acme.windowing=gtk)
nativecodeqt.so	linux		x86	en	(com.acme.windowing=qt)

the Bundle-NativeCode header in the following code example.

```
Bundle-NativeCode: nativecodewin32.dll;
```

```
        delta.dll;
        osname=win32;
        processor=x86;
        language=en,
    nativecodegtk.so;
        osname=linux;
        processor=x86;
        language=en;
        selection-filter=
            "(com.acme.windowing=gtk)",
    nativecodeqt.so;
        osname=linux;
        processor=x86;
        language=en;
        selection-filter =
            "(com.acme.windowing=qt)"
```

3.9.2   **Considerations Using Native Libraries**

There are some restrictions on loading native libraries due to the nature of class loaders. In order to preserve name space separation in class loaders, only one class loader can load a native library as specified by an absolute path. Loading of a native library file by multiple class loaders (from multiple bundles, for example) will result in a linkage error.

Care should be taken to use multiple libraries with the same file name but in a different directory in the JAR. For example, foo/http.dll and bar/http.dll. The Framework must only use the first library and ignore later defined libraries with the same name. In the example, only foo/http.dll will be visible.

A native library is unloaded only when the class loader that loaded it has been garbage collected.

When a bundle is uninstalled or updated, any native libraries loaded by the bundle remain in memory until the bundle's class loader is garbage collected. The garbage collection will not happen until all references to objects in the bundle have been garbage collected, and all bundles importing packages from the updated or uninstalled bundle are refreshed. This implies that native libraries loaded from the system class loader always remain in memory because the system class loader is never garbage collected.

It is not uncommon that native code libraries have dependencies on other native code libraries. This specification does not support these dependencies, it is assumed that native libraries delivered in bundles should not rely on other native libraries.

3.10   Localization

A bundle contains a significant amount of information that is human-readable. Some of this information may require different translations depending on the user's language, country, and any special variant preferences, a.k.a. the *locale*. This section describes how a bundle can provide common translations for the manifest and other configuration resources depending on a locale.

Bundle localization entries share a common base name. To find a potential localization entry, an underscore ('_' \u005F) is added plus a number of suffixes, separated by another underscore, and finally appended with the suffix .properties . The suffixes are defined in java.util.Locale. The order for the suffixes this must be:

- language
- country
- variant

For example, the following files provide manifest translations for English, Dutch (Belgium and the Netherlands) and Swedish.

```
OSGI-INF/l10n/bundle_en.properties
OSGI-INF/l10n/bundle_nl_BE.properties
OSGI-INF/l10n/bundle_nl_NL.properties
OSGI-INF/l10n/bundle_sv.properties
```

The Framework searches for localization entries by appending suffixes to the localization base name according to a specified locale and finally appending the .properties suffix. If a translation is not found, the locale must be made more generic by first removing the variant, then the country and finally the language until an entry is found that contains a valid translation. For example, looking up a translation for the locale en_GB_welsh will search in the following order:

```
OSGI-INF/l10n/bundle_en_GB_welsh.properties
OSGI-INF/l10n/bundle_en_GB.properties
OSGI-INF/l10n/bundle_en.properties
OSGI-INF/l10n/bundle.properties
```

This allows localization files for more specific locales to override localizations from less specific localization files.

3.10.1 Finding Localization Entries

Localization entries can be contained in the bundle or delivered in fragments. The framework must search for localization entries using the following search rules based on the bundle type:

- fragment bundle – If the bundle is a *resolved* fragment, then the search for localization data must delegate to the attached host bundle with the highest version. If the fragment is not resolved, then the framework must search the fragment's JAR for the localization entry.
- other bundle – The framework must first search in the bundle's JAR for the localization entry. If the entry is not found and the bundle has fragments, then the attached fragment JARs must be searched for the localization entry.

The bundle's class loader is not used to search for localization entries. Only the contents of the bundle and its attached fragments are searched. The bundle will still be searched for localization entries even if dot ('.') is not in the bundle class path.

3.10.2 Manifest Localization

Localized values are stored in property resources within the bundle. The default base name of the bundle localization property files is OSGI-INF/l10n/bundle. The Bundle-Localization manifest header can be used to override the default base name for the localization files. This location is relative to the root of the bundle and bundle fragments.

A localization entry contains key/value entries for localized information. All headers in a bundle's manifest can be localized. However, the Framework must always use the non-localized versions of headers that have Framework semantics.

A localization key can be specified as the value of a bundle's manifest header using the following syntax:

```
header-value ::= '%' text
text ::= < any value which is both a valid manifest header value and a valid
property key name >
```

For example, consider the following bundle manifest entries:

```
Bundle-Name: %acme bundle
Bundle-Vendor: %acme corporation
Bundle-Description: %acme description
```

```
Bundle-Activator: com.acme.bundle.Activator
Acme-Defined-Header: %acme special header
```

User-defined headers can also be localized. Spaces in the localization keys are explicitly allowed.

The previous example manifest entries could be localized by the following entries in the manifest localization entry OSGI-INF/l10n/bundle.properties.

```
# bundle.properties
acme\ bundle=The ACME Bundle
acme\ corporation=The ACME Corporation
acme\ description=The ACME Bundle provides all of the ACME \ services
acme\ special header=user-defined Acme Data
```

The above manifest entries could also have French localizations in the manifest localization entry OSGI-INF/l10n/bundle_fr_FR.properties.

3.11   Bundle Validity

If the Bundle-ManifestVersion is not specified, then the bundle manifest version defaults to 1, and certain Release 4 syntax, such as a new manifest header, is ignored rather than causing an error. Release 3 bundles must be treated according to the R3 specification.

The following (non-exhaustive) list of errors causes a bundle to fail to install:

- Missing Bundle-SymbolicName.
- Duplicate attribute or duplicate directive (except in the Bundle-Native code clause).
- Multiple imports of a given package.
- Export or import of java.*.
- Export-Package with a mandatory attribute that is not defined.
- Installing a bundle that has the same symbolic name and version as an already installed bundle.
- Updating a bundle to a bundle that has the same symbolic name and version as another installed bundle.
- Any syntactic error (for example, improperly formatted version or bundle symbolic name, unrecognized directive value, etc.).
- Specification-version and version specified together (for the same package(s)) but with different values on manifest headers that treat them as synonyms. For example:
    ```
    Import-Package p; specification-version=1; version=2
    ```
    would fail to install, but:
    ```
    Import-Package p; specification-version=1, q; version=2
    ```
    would not be an error.
- The manifest lists a OSGI-INF/permission.perm file but no such file is present.
- Bundle-ManifestVersion value not equal to 2, unless the Framework specifically recognizes the semantics of a later release.
- Requiring the same bundle symbolic name more than once.

3.12   Requiring Bundles

The Framework supports a mechanism where bundles can be directly wired to other bundles. The following sections define the relevant headers and then discuss the possible scenarios. At the end, some of the (sometimes unexpected) consequences of using Require-Bundle are discussed.

3.12.1   ## Require-Bundle

The Require-Bundle manifest header contains a list of bundle symbolic names that need to be searched after the imports are searched but before the bundle's class path is searched. Fragment or extension bundles can not be required.

The framework must take *all* exported packages from a required bundle, including any packages exported by attached fragments, and wire these packages to the requiring bundle.

The Require-Bundle manifest header must conform to the following syntax:

```
Require-Bundle     ::= bundle-description
  ( ',' bundle-description )*
bundle-description ::= symbolic-name          // See 1.3.2
  (';' parameter )*
```

The following directives can be used in the Require-Bundle header:

- visibility – If the value is private (Default), then all visible packages from the required bundles are not re-exported. If the value is reexport then bundles that require this bundle will transitively have access to these required bundle's exported packages. That is, if bundle A requires bundle B, and bundle B requires bundle C with visibility:=reexport then bundle A will have access to all bundle C's exported packages as if bundle A had required bundle C.
- resolution – If the value is mandatory (default) then the required bundle must exist for this bundle to resolve. If the value is optional, the bundle will resolve even if the required bundle does not exist.

The following matching attribute is architected by the Framework:

- bundle-version – The value of this attribute is a version range to select the bundle version of the required bundle. See *Version Ranges* on page 27. The default value is [0.0.0,∞).

A specific symbolic name can only be required once, listing the same symbolic name multiple times must be regarded as an install error.

Requiring bundles must get wired to all exported packages of all their required bundles including exported packages from their attached fragments. This means that any mandatory attributes on these exports must be ignored. However, if a required bundle's exported package is substituted for an imported package, then the requiring bundles must get wired to the same exported package that the required bundle is wired to ensure class space consistency.

For example, assume that bundle A exports and imports package p and bundle B requires bundle A:

```
Bundle A
Export-Package: p;x=1;mandatory:=x
Import-Package: p

Bundle B
Require-Bundle: A
```

In this constellation, bundle B will get package p from the same source as bundle A. Bundle A can get the package from itself if it is chosen as an exporter for p, but it can also get the package from another bundle because it also imports it. In all cases, bundle B must use exactly the same exporter for package p as bundle A.

A given package may be available from more than one of the required bundles. Such packages are named *split packages* because they derive their contents from different bundles. If these different bundles provide the same classes unpredictable shadowing of classes can arise, see *Issues With Requiring Bundles* on page 62. However, split packages without shadowing are explicitly permitted.

For example, take the following setup:

```
A:   Require-Bundle: B
     Export-Package: p
B:   Export-Package: p;partial=true;mandatory:=partial
```

If bundle C imports package p, it will be wired to package A.p, however the contents will come from B.p › A.p. The mandatory attribute on bundle B's export definition ensures that bundle B is not accidentally selected as exporter for package p. Split packages have a number drawbacks that are discussed in *Issues With Requiring Bundles* on page 62.

Resources and classes from a split package must be searched in the order in which the required bundles are specified in the Require-Bundle header.

As an example, assume that a bundle requires a number of required bundles and a number of language resources (also bundles) that are optional.

```
Require-Bundle: com.acme.facade;visibility:=reexport,
  com.acme.bar.one;visibility:=reexport,
  com.acme.bar.two;visibility:=reexport,
  com.acme.bar._nl;visibility:=reexport;resolution:=optional,
  com.acme.bar._en;visibility:=reexport;resolution:=optional
```

A bundle may both import packages (via Import-Package) and require one or more bundles (via Require-Bundle), but if a package is imported via Import-Package, it is not also visible via Require-Bundle: Import-Package takes priority over Require-Bundle, and packages which are exported by a required bundle and imported via Import-Package must *not* be treated as split packages.

In order to be allowed to require a named bundle, the requiring bundle must have BundlePermission[<bundle symbolic name>, REQUIRE], where the bundle symbolic name is the name of the bundle that is required. The required bundle must be able to provide the bundle and must therefore have BundlePermission[<bundle symbolic name>, PROVIDE], where the name designates the requiring bundle. In the case a fragment bundle requires another bundle, the Bundle Permission must be checked against the fragment bundle's Protection Domain.

3.12.2   Split Package Compatibility

A package is a split package whenever there are multiple *sources* for the package; only bundles using the Require-Bundle header can have split packages.

A source is a bundle that provides the given package. Both the required bundles as well as the requiring bundle can act as a source. The required bundles and the requiring bundle can only contribute their exported packages.

Exported split packages from two bundles are compatible if the package sources for one are a subset of the other.

3.12.3   Issues With Requiring Bundles

The preferred way of wiring bundles is to use the Import-Package and Export-Package headers because they couple the importer and exporter to a much lesser extent. Bundles can be refactored to have a different package composition without causing other bundles to fail.

The Require-Bundle header provides a way for a bundle to bind to all the exports of another bundle, regardless of what those exports are. Though this can seem convenient at first, it has a number of drawbacks:

- *Split Packages* – Classes from the same package can come from different bundles with Require bundle, such a package is called a split package. Split packages have the following drawbacks:
  - *Completeness* – Split packages are open ended, it is difficult to guarantee that all the intended pieces of a split package have actually been included.

- *Ordering* – If the same classes are present in more than one required bundle, then the ordering of Require-Bundle is significant. A wrong ordering can cause hard to trace errors, similar to the traditional class path model of Java.
- *Performance* – A class must be searched in all providers when packages are split. This potentially increases the number of times that a ClassNotFoundException must be thrown which can potentially introduce a significant overhead.
- *Confusing* – It is easy to find a setup where there is lots of potential for confusion. For example, the following setup is non-intuitive.

```
A: Export-Package:  p; uses:=q
   Import-Package:  q
B: Export-Package:  q
C: Export-Package:  q
D: Require-Bundle:  B, C
   Import-Package:  p
```

Figure 3.31   *Split packages and package constraints*

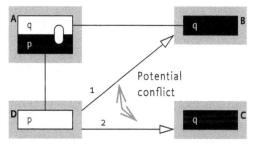

In this example, bundle D merges the split package q from bundles B and bundle C, however, importing package p from bundle A puts a uses constraint on package p for package q. This implies that bundle D can see the valid package q from bundle B but also the invalid package q from bundle C. This wiring is allowed because in almost all cases there will be no problem. However, the consistency can be violated in the rare case when package C.q contains classes that are also in package B.q.

- *Mutable Exports* – The feature of visibility:=reexport that the export signature of the requiring bundle can unexpectedly change depending on the export signature of the required bundle.
- *Shadowing* – The classes in the requiring bundle that are shadowed by those in a required bundle depend on the export signature of the required bundle and the classes the required bundle contains. (By contrast, Import-Package, except with resolution:=optional, shadows whole packages regardless of the exporter.)

3.13   **Fragment Bundles**

Fragments are bundles that can be *attached* to one or more *host bundles* by the Framework. Attaching is done as part of resolving: the Framework appends the relevant definitions of the fragment bundles to the host's definitions before the host is resolved. Fragments are therefore treated as part of the host, including any permitted headers; they must not have their own class loader though fragments must have their own Protection Domain.

Fragments can be attached to multiple hosts with the same symbolic name but different versions. If multiple fragments with the same symbolic name match the same host, then the Framework must only select one fragment, this must be the fragment with the highest version.

A key use case for fragments is providing translation files for different locales. This allows the translation files to be treated and shipped independently from the main application bundle.

When an attached fragment is updated, the content of the previous fragment must remain attached to its host bundles. The new content of the updated fragment must not be allowed to attach to the host bundles until the Framework is restarted or the host bundle is refreshed. During this time, an attached fragment will have two versions: the old version, attached to the old version of the host, and a new fragment bundle that can get attached to a new version or to a different host bundle.

In this case, the Package Admin service must return information only for the last version of the supplied bundles. In the previous described case, the getHosts method must return the host bundles of the *new* version of the fragment bundle, and the getFragments method must return the fragment bundles attached to the new version of the host bundle.

When attaching a fragment bundle to a host bundle the Framework must perform the following steps:

1 Append the import definitions for the Fragment bundle that do not *conflict* with an import definition of the host to the import definitions of the host bundle. A Fragment can provide an import statement for a private package of the host. The private package in the host is hidden in that case.
2 Append the Require-Bundle entries of the fragment bundle that do not conflict with a Require-Bundle entry of the host to the Require-Bundle entries of the host bundle.
3 Append the export definitions of a Fragment bundle to the export definitions of the host bundle unless the exact definition (directives and attributes must match) is already present in the host. Fragment bundles can therefore add additional exports for the same package name. The bundle-version attributes and bundle-symbolic-name attributes will reflect the host bundle.

A host and a fragment conflict when they cannot resolve to provide a consistent class space. If a conflict is found, the Fragment bundle is not attached to the host bundle.

A Fragment bundle must enter the resolved state only if it has been successfully attached to at least one host bundle.

During runtime, the fragment's JAR is searched after the host's bundle class path as described in *Fragments During Runtime* on page 65.

A Fragment bundle can not be required by another bundle with the Require-Bundle header.

3.13.1   Fragment-Host

The Fragment-Host manifest header links the fragment to its potential hosts. It must conform to the following syntax:

```
Fragment-Host        ::= bundle-description
bundle-description   ::= symbolic-name
                         ( ';' parameter ) * // See 1.3.2
```

The following directives are architected by the Framework for Fragment-Host:

• extension – Indicates this extension is a system or boot class path extension. It is only applicable when the Fragment-Host is the System Bundle. This is discussed in *Extension Bundles* on page 66. The following values are supported:
  • framework - The fragment bundle is a Framework extension bundle.
  • bootclasspath - The fragment bundle is a boot class path extension bundle.
  The fragment must be the bundle symbolic name of the implementation specific system bundle or the alias system.bundle. The Framework should fail to install an extension bundle when the bundle symbolic name is not referring to the system bundle.

The following attributes are architected by the Framework for Fragment-Host:

• bundle-version – The version range to select the the host bundle. If a range is used, then the fragment can attach to multiple hosts. See *Version Matching* on page 38. The default value is [0.0.0,∞).

When a fragment bundle is attached to a host bundle, it logically becomes part of it. All classes and resources within the fragment bundle must be loaded using the class loader (or Bunde object) of its host bundle. The fragment bundles of a host bundle must be attached to a host bundle in the order that the fragment bundles are installed, which is in ascending bundle ID order. If an error occurs during the attachment of a fragment bundle then the fragment bundle must not be attached to the host. A fragment bundle must enter the resolved state only if it has been successfully attached to one or more host bundles.

In order for a host bundle to allow fragments to attach, the host bundle must have BundlePermission[<bundle symbolic name>,HOST]. In order to be allowed to attach to a host bundle, a fragment bundle must have BundlePermission[<bundle symbolic name>,FRAGMENT].

3.13.2   Fragments During Runtime

All class or resource loading of a fragment is handled through the host's class loader or Bundle object, a fragment must never have its own class loader, it therefore fails the class and resource loading methods of the Bundle object. Fragment bundles are treated as if they are an intrinsic part of their hosts.

Though a fragment bundle does not have its own class loader, it still must have a separate Protection Domain when it is not an extension fragment. Each fragment can have its own permissions linked to the fragment bundle's location and signer.

A host bundle's class path is searched before a fragment's class path. This implies that packages can be split over the host and any of its fragments. Searching the fragments must be done in ascending bundle ID order. This is the order that the fragment bundles were installed.

Figure 3.32   *Resource/class searching with fragments*

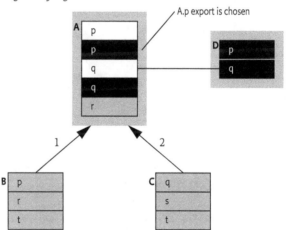

Figure 3.32 shows a setup with two fragments. Bundle B is installed before bundle C and both bundle B and bundle C attach to bundle A. The following table shows where different packages originate in this setup. Note that the order of the append (>) is significant.

In the example above, if package p had been imported from bundle D, the table would have looked quite different. Package p would have come from bundle D, and bundle A's own contents as well as the contents of bundle B would have been ignored.

If package q had bundle D, then the class path would have to be searched, and A.q would have consisted of A.q > C.q.

Table 3.5   *Effect of fragments on searching*

Package Requested	From	Remark
p	A.p › B.p	Bundle A exports package p, therefore, it will search its class path for p. This class path consists of the JAR and then its Fragment bundles.
q	D.q	The import does not handle split packages and package q is imported from bundle D. Therefore, C.q is not found.
r	A.r › B.r	Package r is not imported and therefore comes from the class path.
s	C.s	
t	B.t › C.t	

Fragments must remain attached to a host as long as the host remains resolved. When a host bundle becomes unresolved, then all its attached Fragment bundles must be detached from the host bundle. When a fragment bundle becomes unresolved the Framework must:

• Detach it from the host
• Re-resolve the host bundles
• Reattach the remaining attached fragment bundles.

A Fragment bundle can become unresolved by calling the `refreshPackages` method.

3.13.3 Illegal Manifest Header for Fragment Bundles

The following list contains the headers that must not be used in a fragment bundle:

• `Bundle-Activator`

3.14 Extension Bundles

Extension bundles can deliver optional parts of the Framework implementation or provide functionality that must reside on the boot class path. These packages cannot be provided by the normal import/export mechanisms.

Boot class path extensions are necessary because certain package implementations assume that they are on the boot class path or are required to be available to all clients. An example of a boot class path extension is an implementation of `java.sql` such as JSR 169. Boot class path extensions are not required to be implemented by a compliant framework.

Framework extensions are necessary to provide implementation aspects of the Framework. For example, a Framework vendor could supply the optional services like Permission Admin service and Start Level service with Framework extension bundles.

An extension bundle should use the bundle symbolic name of the implementation system bundle, or it can use the alias of the system bundle, which is `system.bundle`.

The following example uses the Fragment-Host manifest header to specify an extension bundle for a specific Framework implementation.

```
Fragment-Host: com.acme.impl.framework; extension:=framework
```

The following example uses the Fragment-Host manifest header to specify a boot class path extension bundle.

```
Fragment-Host: system.bundle; extension:=bootclasspath
```

The following steps describe the life cycle of an extension bundle:

1   When an extension bundle is installed it enters the INSTALLED state.
2   The extension bundle is allowed to enter the RESOLVED state at the Frameworks discretion, which can require a Framework re-launch.
3   If a RESOLVED extension bundle is refreshed then the Framework must shutdown; the host VM must terminate and framework must be re-launched.
4   When a RESOLVED extension bundle is updated or UNINSTALLED, it is not allowed to re-enter the RESOLVED state. If the extension bundle is refreshed then the Framework must shutdown; the host VM must terminate and framework must be re-launched.

It is valid to update an extension bundle to a bundle of another type. If the old extension bundle is resolved then it must be attached as a fragment to the system bundle. When this bundle is updated the old content of the bundle must remain attached to the system bundle until the system bundle is refreshed or the extension bundle is refreshed (using Package Admin service). This must initiate a VM and Framework restart. When the framework comes back up the new content of the bundle may be resolved.

All Bundle events should be dispatched for extension bundles as for ordinary bundles.

3.14.1   Illegal Manifest Headers for Extension Bundles

An extension bundle must throw a BundleException if it is installed or updated and it specifies any of the following headers.

- Import-Package
- Require-Bundle
- Bundle-NativeCode
- DynamicImport-Package
- Bundle-Activator

Both boot class path and framework extension bundles are permitted to specify an Export-Package header. Any exported packages specified by a framework extension bundle must be exported by the System Bundle when the extension bundle is resolved.

3.14.2   Class Path Treatment

A boot class path extension bundle's JAR file must be appended to the boot class path of the host VM. A framework extension bundle's JAR is appended to the class path of the Framework.

Extension bundles must be appended to their class path in the order in which the extension bundles are installed: that is, ascending bundle ID order.

How a framework configures itself or the boot class path to append the extension bundle's JAR is implementation specific. In some execution environments, it may be impossible to support extension bundles. In such environments, the Framework must throw a BundleException when such an extension bundle is installed. The resulting Bundle Exception must have a cause of type UnsupportedOperationException.

3.14.3   Optionality Boot Class Path Extension

This specification provides for one optional mechanism: the boot class path extension. The reason to make this mechanism optional is that it is not possible to implement this in a portable way. A compliant framework must set the following property to true or false depending on the implementation of the boot class path extension:

- org.osgi.supports.bootclasspath.extension

If the property is not set or the value is unrecognized, then the value defaults to false. A Framework that does not implement the bootclasspath extension must refuse to install or update a bundle that carries this option. It must then throw an exception at install or update time.

Additionally, frameworks must implement fragments, require bundle, and extensions. They must therefore set the following properties to true.

- org.osgi.supports.framework.requirebundle
- org.osgi.supports.framework.fragments
- org.osgi.supports.framework.extension

3.15 Security

3.15.1 Extension Bundles

In an environment that has Java 2 security enabled the Framework must perform an additional security check before allowing an extension bundle to be installed. In order for an extension bundle to successfully install, the Framework must check that the extension bundle has All Permissions assigned to it. This means that the permissions of an extension bundle must be setup before the extension bundle is installed.

AllPermission must be granted to extension bundles because they will be loaded under the Protection Domain of either the boot class path or the Framework implementation. Both of these Protection Domains have All Permissions granted to them. It must therefore not be allowed for an extension bundle to be installed unless it already has been granted AllPermissions.

The installer of an extension bundle must have AdminPermission[<extension bundle>, EXTENSIONLIFECYCLE] to install an extension bundle.

3.15.2 Bundle Permission

Most package sharing permissions are based on Package Permission. However, fragments and required bundles use the bundle symbolic name to handle sharing. The Bundle Permission is used to control this type of package sharing.

The name parameter of the Bundle Permission is a bundle symbolic name. The symbolic name is used as the identifier for the *target bundle*. A wild card ('.*' \u002E,\u002A) is permitted at the end of the name.

For example, if fragment bundle A attaches to its host bundle B then fragment bundle A requires BundlePermission("B", "fragment") so that A is permitted to target host bundle B. The direction of the actions is depicted in Figure 3.33.

Figure 3.33   *Permissions and bundle sharing*

The following actions are architected:

- provide – Permission to provide packages to the target bundle.
- require – Permission to require packages from the target bundle.
- host – Permission to attach to the target fragment bundle.
- fragment – Permission to attach as a fragment to the target host bundle.

When a fragment contains a Require-Bundle header, the Framework must check the permission against the domain of the fragment.

3.15.3   **Package Permission**

Bundles can only import and export packages for which they have the required permission. A PackagePermission must be valid across all versions of a package.

A PackagePermission has two parameters:

- The name, either the name of the target package (with a possible wildcard character at the end) or a filter expression that can verify the exporting bundle. A filter expression can test for the package name with the package.name key. A filter can only be used for an IMPORT action. Filters are described in *Filter Based Permissions* on page 19.
- The action, either IMPORT or EXPORTONLY.

For example, the following Package Permission permits to import any package from a bundle downloaded from ACME:

```
PackagePermission("(location=http://www.acme.com/*", IMPORT)
```

When a fragment adds imports and exports to the host, the framework must check the protection domain of the fragment and not of the related host.

3.15.4   **Resource Permissions**

A Framework must always give a bundle the RESOURCE, METADATA, and CLASS AdminPermission actions to access the resources contained within:

- Itself
- Any attached fragments
- Any resources from imported packages

A resource in a bundle may also be accessed by using certain methods on Bundle. The caller of these methods must have AdminPermission[bundle, RESOURCE].

If the caller does not have the necessary permission, a resource is not accessible and null must be returned. Otherwise, a URL object to the resource must be returned. These URLs are called *bundle resource URLs*. Once the URL object is returned, no further permission checks are performed when the contents of the resource are accessed. The URL object must use a scheme defined by the Framework implementation.

Bundle resource URLs are normally created by the Framework, however, in certain cases bundles need to manipulate the URL to find related resources. For example, a URL can be constructed to a resource that is in the same directory as a given resource.

URLs that are not constructed by the Framework must follow slightly different security rules due to the design of the java.net.URL class. Not all constructors of the URL class interact with the URL Stream Handler classes (the implementation specific part). Other constructors call at least the parseURL method in the URL Stream Handler where the security check can take place. This design makes it impossible for the Framework check the permissions during construction of a bundle resource URL.

The following constructors use the parseURL method and are therefore checked when a bundle resource URL is constructed.

```
URL(String spec)
URL(URL context, String spec)
URL(URL context, String spec, URLStreamHandler handler)
```

When one of these constructors is called for a bundle resource URL, the implementation of the Framework must check the caller for the necessary permissions in the parseURL method. If the caller does not have the necessary permissions then the parseURL method must throw a Security Exception. This will cause a Malformed URL Exception to be thrown by the URL constructor. If the caller has the necessary permissions, then the URL object is setup to access the bundle resource without further checks.

The following java.net.URL constructors do not call the parseURL method in the URL Stream Handler, making it impossible for the Framework to verify the permission during construction.

```
URL(String protocol, String host, int port, String file)
URL(String protocol, String host, int port, String file, URLStreamHandler
handler)
URL(String protocol, String host, String file)
```

Bundle resource URLs that are created with these constructors cannot perform the permission check during creation and must therefore delay the permission check. When the content of the URL is accessed, the Framework must throw a Security Exception if the caller does not have AdminPermission[bundle, RESOURCE] for the bundle referenced by the URL.

3.15.5   Permission Checks

Since multiple bundles can export permission classes with the same class name, the Framework must make sure that permission checks are performed using the correct class. For example, a bundle that calls the checkPermission method provides an instance of the Permission class:

```
void foo(String name) {
    checkPermission(new FooPermission(name, "foo"));
}
```

This class of this Permission instance comes from a particular source. Permissions can only be tested against instances that come from the same source.

Therefore, the Framework needs to look up permissions based on *class* rather than *class name*. When it needs to instantiate a permission it must use the class of the permission being checked to do the instantiation. This is a complication for Framework implementers; bundle programmers are not affected.

Consider the following example:

```
Bundle A
    Import-Package: p
    Export-Package: q
Bundle B
    Import-Package: p
```

- Bundle A uses a p.FooService. Usage of this class checks q.FooPermission whenever one of its methods is invoked.
- Bundle B has a FooPermission in its Protection Domain in a (Conditional) Permission Info object.
- Bundle B invokes a method in the FooService that was given by bundle A.
- The FooService calls the checkPermission method with a new FooPermission instance.
- The Framework must use a FooPermission object that is from the same class loader as the given FooPermission object before it can call the implies method. In this case, the FooPermission class comes from package A.q.

After the permission check, bundle B will have a FooPermission instantiated using a class from a package it does not import. It is therefore possible that the Framework has to instantiate multiple variations of the FooPermission class to satisfy the needs of different bundles.

3.16　Changes

- The Bundle-RequiredExecutionEnvironment is changed from an install time check to a resolve time check. See *Execution Environment* on page 30.
- Added the OSGi Mime type for bundles
- Added export for package r in example about uses, package r was visible in the picture but not in the text.
- Made the search path for localization entries more clear in *Finding Localization Entries* on page 59.
- Clarified that a requiring bundle must use the same exporter for a package as the required bundle in the case of import/export substitution and that mandatory attributes for exported packages are ignored. See *Require-Bundle* on page 61.
- Clarified that the import and export clauses for the same package are independent, see *Exporting and Importing a Package* on page 37.
- *Fragments During Runtime* on page 65 erroneously specified that resolve Bundles could unresolve a fragment.
- Defined how organizations can extend the set of manifest headers. See *Custom Headers* on page 27.
- Added a Bundle-Icon header, see *Bundle-Icon: /icons/acme-logo.png;size=64* on page 24.
- Clarified that optional packages that are not found are treated as private packages.
- Added filters to the Package Permission IMPORT.
- Allow fragments to attach to multiple hosts
- Rewritten Bundle-ClassPath section, see *Bundle Class Path* on page 46 for clarification. Removed step 6 in runtime loading because it contradicted the bundle class path section.

3.17　References

[19]　*The Standard for the Format of ARPA Internet Text Messages*
STD 11, RFC 822, UDEL, August 1982
http://www.ietf.org/rfc/rfc822.txt

[20]　*The Hypertext Transfer Protocol - HTTP/1.1*
RFC 2068 DEC, MIT/LCS, UC Irvine, January 1997
http://www.ietf.org/rfc/rfc2068.txt

[21]　*The Java 2 Platform API Specification*
Standard Edition, Version 1.3, Sun Microsystems
http://java.sun.com/j2se/1.4

[22]　*The Java Language Specification*
Second Edition, Sun Microsystems, 2000
http://java.sun.com/docs/books/jls/index.html

[23]　*A String Representation of LDAP Search Filters*
RFC 1960, UMich, 1996
http://www.ietf.org/rfc/rfc1960.txt

[24]　*The Java Security Architecture for JDK 1.2*
Version 1.0, Sun Microsystems, October 1998

[25]　*The Java 2 Package Versioning Specification*
http://java.sun.com/j2se/1.4/docs/guide/versioning/index.html

[26]　*Codes for the Representation of Names of Languages*
ISO 639, International Standards Organization
http://lcweb.loc.gov/standards/iso639-2/langhome.html

[27]　*Zip File Format*
The Zip file format as defined by the java.util.zip package.

[28]   *Manifest Format*
       http://java.sun.com/j2se/1.4/docs/guide/jar/jar.html#JAR%20Manifest

[29]   *W3C EBNF*
       http://www.w3c.org/TR/REC-xml#sec-notation

[30]   *Lexical Structure Java Language*
       http://java.sun.com/docs/books/jls/second_edition/html/lexical.doc.html

[31]   *Mathematical Convention for Interval Notation*
       http://planetmath.org/encyclopedia/Interval.html

[32]   *Uniform Resource Identifiers URI: Generic Syntax*
       RFC 2396
       http://www.ietf.org/rfc/rfc2396.txt

[33]   *Codes for the Representation of Names of Languages*
       ISO 639, International Standards Organization
       http://lcweb.loc.gov/standards/iso639-2/langhome.html

[34]   *OSGi IANA Mime Type*
       http://www.iana.org/assignments/media-types/application/vnd.osgi.bundle

[35]   *OSGi Header Name Space Registry*
       http://www.osgi.org/headers

[36]   *Portable Network Graphics (PNG) Specification (Second Edition)*
       http://www.w3.org/TR/2003/REC-PNG-20031110/

[37]   *Open Source Initiative*
       http://www.opensource.org/

4   Life Cycle Layer

Version 1.5

4.1   Introduction

The Life Cycle Layer provides an API to control the security and life cycle operations of bundles. The layer is based on the module and security layer.

4.1.1   Essentials

- *Complete* – The Life Cycle layer must implement an API that fully covers the installation, starting, stopping, updating, uninstallation, and monitoring of bundles.
- *Reflective* – The API must provide full insight into the actual state of the Framework.
- *Secure* – It must be possible to use the API in a secure environment using fine-grained permissions. However, security must be optional.
- *Manageable* – It must be possible to manage a Service Platform remotely.
- *Launching* – It must be able to launch an implementation of a framework in a standardized way.

4.1.2   Entities

- *Bundle* – Represents an installed bundle in the Framework.
- *Bundle Context* – A bundle's execution context within the Framework. The Framework passes this to a Bundle Activator when a bundle is started or stopped.
- *Bundle Activator* – An interface implemented by a class in a bundle that is used to start and stop that bundle.
- *Bundle Event* – An event that signals a life cycle operation on a bundle. This event is received via a (Synchronous) Bundle Listener.
- *Framework Event* – An event that signals an error or Framework state change. The event is received via a Framework Listener.
- *Bundle Listener* – A listener to Bundle Events.
- *Synchronous Bundle Listener* – A listener to synchronously delivered Bundle Events.
- *Framework Listener* – A listener to Framework events.
- *Bundle Exception* – An Exception thrown when Framework operations fail.
- *System Bundle* – A bundle that represents the Framework.
- *Framework* – An interface implemented by an object that represents the actual framework. It allows external management of a Framework.
- *Framework Factory* – An interface implemented by Framework providers that allows the creation of a framework object.

Figure 4.34   Class diagram org.osgi.framework *Life Cycle Layer*

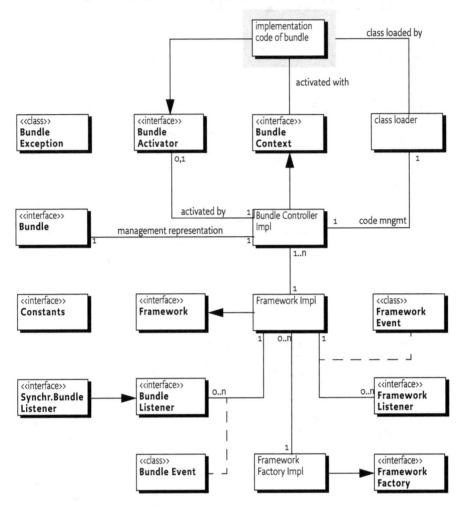

4.2   Frameworks

This section outlines how a *launcher* can launch a framework implementation and then manage it, regardless of the implementation type of the framework. This allows a launcher to embed an OSGi framework without having to provide code that differs between different implementations.

4.2.1   Launching and Controlling a Framework

Code that wants to use one of the OSGi Framework implementations must provide the chosen framework implementation on the class path, or create a special class loader that loads the code and resources from that implementation. How this is achieved, is outside this specification.

A framework implementation must provide a *factory* class. A factory class is an indirection to create a framework implementation object. The implementation factory class must implement the FrameworkFactory interface. The launcher can use the following ways to get this class name:

- Service Provider Configuration model, see *Java Service Provider Configuration Support* on page 82,
- Get it from some configuration and use Class.forName, or

- Hardcode the name.

The FrameworkFactory interface has a single method: newFramework(Map). The map provides the sole configuration properties for the framework object. The result of this method is a *framework object*, this object implements the Framework interface. The Framework interface extends the Bundle interface and adds methods to handle the issues unique to launching a framework. The framework object can be seen as the system bundle, though the framework object and the system bundle do not have to be identical, implementations are allowed to implement them in different objects.

Before the framework object can be used, the launcher must first *initialize* it by calling the init method. After initialization, the framework object can provide a valid Bundle Context and has registered any framework services, but any installed bundles must be in the INSTALLED state. The launcher can then configure the framework object by installing bundles, interacting with the framework services, or registering launcher services. The launcher can also start bundles, but these bundles will not be started until the framework object becomes ACTIVE.

After the framework object is properly configured, the launcher can *start* it by calling the start method. The framework object will become ACTIVE, and it will move the startlevel (if present) to the configured start level. This can then resolve and start any installed bundle. After a framework has become ACTIVE, it can be stopped from the framework object, or through the system bundle.

The launcher can wait for a framework object to be stopped with the waitForStop method. This method will block until the framework is completely stopped and return a Framework event indicating the cause of the stop. After the framework object has been shutdown, and the waitForStop method has returned, all installed bundles will be in the INSTALLED state. The same framework object can be re-initialized, and started again, any number of times.

The action diagram in Figure 4.35 shows a typical session. A new framework is created and initialized. The launcher then gets the Bundle Context, installs a bundle and starts the framework. It then gets a service, calls a method and then waits for the framework to stop. The service waits some time and calls stop on the System Bundle. The dotted lines indicate some non-specified interactions that are implementation dependent.

Figure 4.35   *Action Diagram for Framework Launching*

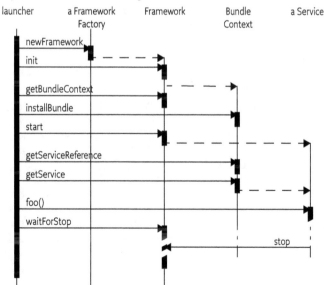

If security is enabled, then the launcher and the framework require All Permission. If All Permission is not available, then the framework must throw a Security Exception.

The following code shows how a framework can be launched.

```
void launch( String factoryName, File[] bundles )
       throws Exception {
  Map p = new HashMap();
  p.put( "org.osgi.framework.storage",
       System.getProperties("user.home")
     + File.separator+"osgi");

  FrameworkFactory factory =
     (FrameworkFactory) Class.forName( factoryName )
                             .newInstance();
  Framework framework = factory.newFramework(p);
  framework.init();

  BundleContext context = framework.getBundleContext();

  for ( File bundle : bundles )
     context.installBundle( bundle.toURL().toString() );

  framework.start()

  framework.waitForStop()
}
```

4.2.2 Launching Properties

The Map object given as a parameter to the newFramework method provides the initialization properties to the framework. This parameter may be null, in that case the framework must be started with reasonable defaults for the environment it is started in. For example, the framework should export the JRE packages as system packages and it should store its bundles in an appropriate place.

The properties Map may contain any properties for implementation specific values. However, the properties in Table 4 must be accepted by all conformant frameworks. The framework must not look in the System properties, the given Map is complete.

Table 4   *Framework Launching Properties*

org.osgi.framework.« bootdelegation	Set the boot delegation mask, see *Parent Delegation* on page 49.
org.osgi.framework.« bundle.parent	This property is used to specify what class loader is used for boot delegation. That is, java.* and the packages specified on the org.osgi.framework.bootdelegation. All other packages must be accessed through a wire. This property can have the following values: • boot – The boot class loader of the VM. This is the default. • app – The applicaton class loader • ext – The extension class loader • framework – The class loader of the framework

Table 4   *Framework Launching Properties*

org.osgi.framework.« command.execpermission	Specifies an optional OS specific command to set file permissions on a bundle's native code. This is required on some operating systems to use native libraries. For example, on a UNIX style OS you could have the following value:

> org.osgi.framework.command.execpermission=«
>   "chmod +rx ${abspath}"

The ${abspath} macro will be substituted for the actual file path.

org.osgi.framework.« executionenvironment	The current execution environment. If not set, the framework must provide an appropriate value. See *Execution Environment* on page 30. For example

> org.osgi.framework.executionenvironment =
>   J2SE-1.5

org.osgi.framework.language	The language used by the framework for the selection of native code. If not set, the framework must provide a value.
org.osgi.framework.library.« extensions	A comma separated list of additional library file extensions that must be used when searching for native code. If not set, then only the library name returned by System.mapLibraryName(String) will be used. This list of extensions is needed for certain operating systems which allow more than one extension for native libraries. For example, the AIX operating system allows library extensions of .a and .so, but System.mapLibraryName(String) will only return names with the .a extension. For example:

> org.osgi.framework.library.extensions= a,so,dll

org.osgi.framework.os.name	The name of the operating system as used in the native code clause. See *Environment Properties* on page 94 for more information. If not set, then the framework must provide a default value.
org.osgi.framework.os.version	The version of the operating system as used in the native code clause. See *Environment Properties* on page 94 for more information. If not set, then the framework must provide a default value.
org.osgi.framework.processor	The name of the processor as used in the native code clause. See *Environment Properties* on page 94 for more information. If not set, then the framework must provide a value.
org.osgi.framework.security	Specifies the type of security manager the framework must use. If not specified then the framework will not set the VM security manager. The following type is architected:

- osgi – Enables a security manager that supports all security aspects of the OSGi Release 4 specifications (including postponed conditions).

If specified, and there is a security manager already installed, then a SecurityException must be thrown when the Framework is initialized.

For example:

> org.osgi.framework.security = osgi

Table 4   *Framework Launching Properties*

org.osgi.framework.startlevel.« beginning	Specifies the beginning start level of the framework. See *Start Level Service Specification* on page 203 for more information. org.osgi.framework.startlevel.beginning = 3
org.osgi.framework.storage	A valid file path in the file system to a directory. If the specified directory does not exist then the framework must create the directory. If the specified path exists, but is not a directory, or if the framework fails to create the storage directory, then the framework initialization must fail with an exception being thrown. The framework is free to use this directory as it sees fit, for example, completely erase all files and directories in it. If this property is not set, it must use a reasonable platform default.
org.osgi.framework.storage.« clean	Specifies if and when the storage area for the framework should be cleaned. If no value is specified, the framework storage area will not be cleaned. The possible values is: • onFirstInit - The framework storage area will be cleaned before the Framework bundle is initialized for the first time. Subsequent inits, starts or updates of the Framework bundle will not result in cleaning the framework storage area. For example: org.osgi.framework.storage.clean = onFirstInit It could seem logical to provide delete on exit and clean at initialization. However, restrictions in common Java VM implementations make it impossible to provide this functionality reliably.
org.osgi.framework.system.« packages	The packages that should be exported from the System Bundle. If not set, the framework must provide a reasonable default for the current VM.
org.osgi.framework.system.« packages.extra	Packages specified in this property are added to the org.osgi.framework.system.packages property and therefore have the same syntax. This allows the configurator to only define the additional packages and leave the standard VM packages to be defined by the framework. For example: org.osgi.framework.system.packages.extra= org.acme.foo; version=1.2, org.acme.foo.impl

Table 4   *Framework Launching Properties*

org.osgi.framework.trust.« repositories	This property is used to configure trust repositories for the framework. The value is path of files.The file paths are separated by the pathSeparator defined in the File class. Each file path should point to a JKS key store. The framework will use the key stores as trust repositories to authenticate certificates of trusted signers. The key stores must only be used as read-only trust repositories to access public keys. The keystore must not have a password. For example:

org.osgi.framework.trust.repositories =
/var/trust/keystore.jks:~/.cert/certs.jks

org.osgi.framework.« windowsystem	Provide the name of the current window system. This can be used by the native code clause, *Native Code Algorithm* on page 57. If not set, the framework should provide a value that depends on the current environment.

All properties in this map will be available through the getProperty(String) method at BundleContext, unless they are overridden by the framework. See *Environment Properties* on page 94.

4.2.3   Life Cycle of a Framework

Once the frameworks is created, it must be in the INSTALLED state. In this state, the framework is not active and there is no valid Bundle Context. for the framework object From this point on, the framework object can go through its life cycle with the following methods.

- init – If the framework object is not active, then this method moves the framework object into the STARTING state.
- start – Ensure that the framework is in the ACTIVE state. This method can be called only on the framework because there are no bundles running yet.
- update – Stop the framework. This returns the Framework event STOPPED_UPDATE or STOPPED_BOOTCLASSPATH_MODIFIED to the waitForStop method and then restarts the framework to its previous state. The launcher should then take the appropriate action and then call the waitForStop method again or reboot the VM. The update method can be called on the framework or on the system bundle. If the framework is not active, this has no effect.
- stop – Move the framework into the RESOLVED state via the STOPPING state. This will return a Framework STOPPED event from the waitForStop method. The Framework's Bundle Context is no longer valid. The framework must be initialized again to get a new, valid Bundle Context. The stop method can be called on the framework or on the system bundle.
- uninstall – Must not be called, will throw an Exception when called.

Figure 4.36 on page 80 shows how the previous methods traverse the state diagram.

Figure 4.36   *State diagram Framework*

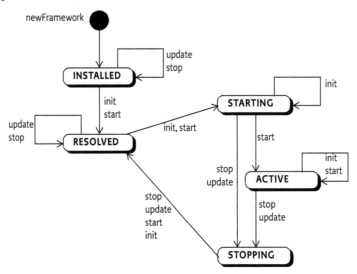

4.2.4   Initializing the Framework

Before the framework can be used, it must be *initialized.* Initialization is caused by the init method or implicitly the start method. An initialized framework is operational, but none of its bundles are active. This is reflected in the STARTING state. As long as the framework is in this state, new bundles can be installed without any installed code interfering. Existing bundles must all be in the INSTALLED state. In this state, the framework will run at start level 0.

A framework object can be initialized multiple times. After initialization:

- Event handling is enabled,
- The security manager is configured,
- Start level is set to 0,
- The framework object has a valid Bundle Context,
- Any installed bundle is in the INSTALLED state,
- Framework services are available,
- The framework state is STARTING

4.2.5   Starting the Framework

After the framework has been initialized, it can be started with the start method. This start method must be called on the framework object. The start method moves the framework into the ACTIVE state. If the framework was not initialized, it must be initialized first.

In the active state, all installed bundles previously recorded as being started must be started as described in the Bundle.start method. Any exceptions that occur during startup must be wrapped in a BundleException and then published as a Framework ERROR event. Bundles, and their different states, are discussed in *The Bundle Object* on page 83. If the Framework implements the optional Start Level specification, this behavior can be different. See *Start Level Service Specification* on page 203. Any bundles that specify an activation policy must be treated according to their activation policy, see *Activation Policies* on page 87.

After the system bundle enters the ACTIVE state, a Framework STARTED event is broadcast.

4.2.6   Stopping a Framework

Shutdown can be initiated by stopping the system bundle, covered in *The System Bundle* on page 97 or calling the stop method on the framework object. When the framework is shut down, it first enters the STOPPING state. All ACTIVE bundles are stopped as described in the Bundle.stop method, except that their persistently recorded start state is kept unchanged. Any exceptions that occur during shutdown must be wrapped in a BundleException and then published as a Framework event of type FrameworkEvent.ERROR. If the Framework implements the optional Start Level specification, this behavior can be different. See *Start Level Service Specification* on page 203. During the shutdown, bundles with a lazy policy must not be activated even when classes are loaded from them and they are not yet activated.

The framework then moves to start level 0, stops event handling and releases any resources (like threads, class loaders, etc.) it held. The framework then enters the RESOLVED state and destroys the Bundle Context. The last action is to notify any threads that are waiting in the waitForStop method. The Framework must be re-initialized if it needs to be used again.

After a framework object is stopped and in the resolved state, it can be initialized and started again. Framework implementations must ensure that holding on to a framework object does not consume significant resources.

4.2.7   Embedding a Framework

The launcher is not running as an OSGi bundle, it is a plain Java application. However, often this launcher needs to communicate with the bundles inside the framework. The launcher can use the Bundle Context of the framework object to get and register services. However, it must ensure that there is class compatibility between its objects and objects from the bundle. A framework will not automatically share packages between the launcher code and the bundles. Packages must be explicitly exported from the parent class loader. The org.osgi.framework.system.packages.extra is specifically designed to hold any application packages that needs to be shared between the OSGi bundles and the application. Packages in that property are added to the system packages of the framework, which are packages exported by the system bundle from its parent loader. Care should be taken to ensure that all these system packages are visible to the class loader that loaded the framework.

The OSGi Framework is running in a multi-threaded environment. After the framework is started, it will start bundles and these bundles will be activated. Activated bundles normally start background threads or react on events from other bundles. That is, after the start method returns, the framework has moved to the ACTIVE state and many bundles can be busy on different threads. At this point, the framework object can be stopped by the launcher through the framework object, or by a bundle through the System Bundle's stop method.

The waitForStop(long) method on the framework object is included to handle any launcher cleanup that is required after the framework has completely stopped. It blocks until the framework has been completely shutdown. It returns one of the following Framework events to indicate the reason for stopping:

- STOPPED – This framework object has been shutdown. It can be restarted.
- STOPPED_UPDATE – This Framework object has been updated. The framework will begin to restart. The framework will return to its state before it was updated, either ACTIVE or STARTING.
- STOPPED_BOOTCLASSPATH_MODIFIED – This framework object has been stopped because a boot class path extension bundle has been installed or updated. The VM must be restarted in order for the changed boot class path to take affect.
- ERROR – The Framework encountered an error while shutting down or an error has occurred that forced the framework to shutdown.
- WAIT_TIMEDOUT – This method has timed out and returned before this Framework has stopped.

4.2.8 Daemon Threads

A Java VM will automatically exit when there are only daemon threads running. This can create the situation where the VM exits when the Framework uses only daemon threads and all threads created by bundles are also daemon threads. A Framework must therefore ensure that the VM does not exit when there are still active bundles. One way to achieve this, is to keep at least one non-daemon thread alive at all times.

4.2.9 Java Service Provider Configuration Support

The Java Service Provider Configuration model, as described in [52] *Java Service Provider Configuration*, provides a way to obtain the name of the framework factory by reading a resource in the JAR. In this specification, it is assumed that the framework implementation is on the class path. The name is obtained by reading the content of the configuration resource with the path META-INF/services/org.osgi.framework.launch.FrameworkFactory.

For example, if the com.acme.osgi framework has a factory class com.acme.osgi.Factory, then it should have the following resource:

    META-INF/services/org.osgi.framework.launch.FrameworkFactory

And the contents should be:

    # ACME Impl. for OSGi framework
    com.acme.osgi.Factory

In contrast with the [52] *Java Service Provider Configuration*, there must only be one class name listed in the resource. However, launchers should be aware that the class path could contain multiple resources with the same name.

Java 6 has introduced the java.util.ServiceLoader class that simplifies creating objects through these types of factories. The following code assumes there is a framework implementation JAR on the class path:

```
ServiceLoader<FrameworkFactory> sl =
    ServiceLoader.load(FrameworkFactory.class);

Iterator<FrameworkFactory> it = sl.iterator();
if ( it.hasNext() ) {
    Framework fw = it.next().newFramework(null);
    ...
}
```

4.3 Bundles

A bundle represents a JAR file that is executed in an OSGi Framework. The class loading aspects of this concept were specified in the Module Layer. However, the Module Layer does not define how a bundle is installed, updated, and uninstalled. These life cycle operations are defined here.

The installation of a bundle can only be performed by another bundle or through implementation specific means (for example as a command line parameter of the Framework implementation).

A Bundle is started through its Bundle Activator. Its Bundle Activator is identified by the Bundle-Activator manifest header. The given class must implement the BundleActivator interface. This interface has a start and stop method that is used by the bundle programmer to register itself as listener and start any necessary threads. The stop method must clean up and stop any running threads.

Upon the activation of a bundle, it receives a Bundle Context. The Bundle Context interface's methods can roughly be divided in the following categories:

- *Information –* Access to information about the rest of the Framework.
- *Life Cycle –* The possibility to install other bundles.
- *Service Registry –* The service registry is discussed in *Service Layer* on page 105.

4.4 The Bundle Object

For each bundle installed in the OSGi Service Platform, there is an associated Bundle object. The Bundle object for a bundle can be used to manage the bundle's life cycle. This is usually done with a Management Agent, which is also a Bundle.

4.4.1 Bundle Identifiers

A bundle is identified by a number of names that vary in their scope:

- *Bundle identifier –* A long that is a Framework assigned unique identifier for the full lifetime of a bundle, even if it is updated or the Framework is restarted. Its purpose is to distinguish bundles in a Framework. Bundle identifiers are assigned in ascending order to bundles when they are installed. The method getBundleId() returns a bundle's identifier.
- *Bundle location –* A name assigned by the management agent (Operator) to a bundle during the installation. This string is normally interpreted as a URL to the JAR file but this is not mandatory. Within a particular Framework, a location must be unique. A location string uniquely identifies a bundle and must not change when a bundle is updated. The getLocation() method retrieves the location of a bundle.
- *Bundle Symbolic Name and Bundle Version–* A name and version assigned by the developer. The combination of Bundle Version and Bundle Symbolic Name is a globally unique identifier for a bundle. The getSymbolicName() method returns the assigned bundle name. The Bundle getVersion() method returns the version.

4.4.2 Bundle State

A bundle can be in one of the following states:

- INSTALLED – The bundle has been successfully installed.
- RESOLVED – All Java classes that the bundle needs are available. This state indicates that the bundle is either ready to be started or has stopped.
- STARTING – The bundle is being started, the BundleActivator.start method will be called, and this method has not yet returned. When the bundle has a lazy activation policy, the bundle will remain in the STARTING state until the bundle is activated. See *Activation Policies* on page 87 for more information.
- ACTIVE – The bundle has been successfully activated and is running; its Bundle Activator start method has been called and returned.
- STOPPING – The bundle is being stopped. The BundleActivator.stop method has been called but the stop method has not yet returned.
- UNINSTALLED – The bundle has been uninstalled. It cannot move into another state.

Figure 4.37   *State diagram Bundle*

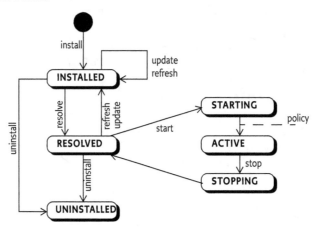

When a bundle is installed, it is stored in the persistent storage of the Framework and remains there until it is explicitly uninstalled. Whether a bundle has been started or stopped must be recorded in the persistent storage of the Framework. A bundle that has been persistently recorded as started must be started whenever the Framework starts until the bundle is explicitly stopped. The Start Level service influences the actual starting and stopping of bundles. See *Start Level Service Specification* on page 203.

The Bundle interface defines a getState() method for returning a bundle's state.

If this specification uses the term *active* to describe a state, then this includes the STARTING and STOPPING states.

Bundle states are expressed as a bit-mask though a bundle can only be in one state at any time. The following code sample can be used to determine if a bundle is in the STARTING, ACTIVE, or STOPPING state:

```
if ((b.getState() & (STARTING | ACTIVE | STOPPING) != 0)
    doActive()
```

4.4.3   Installing Bundles

The BundleContext interface, which is given to the Bundle Activator of a bundle, defines the following methods for installing a bundle:

- installBundle(String) – Installs a bundle from the specified location string (which should be a URL).
- installBundle(String,InputStream) – Installs a bundle from the specified InputStream object.

A bundle must be valid before it is installed, otherwise the install must fail. The validity of a bundle is discussed in *Bundle Validity* on page 60.

Every bundle is uniquely identified by its location string. If an installed bundle is using the specified location, the installBundle methods must return the Bundle object for that installed bundle and not install a new bundle.

The Framework must assign a unique bundle identifier that is higher than any previous bundle identifier.

The installation of a bundle in the Framework must be:

- *Persistent* – The bundle must remain installed across Framework and Java VM invocations until it is explicitly uninstalled.

- *Atomic* – The install method must completely install the bundle or, if the installation fails, the OSGi Service Platform must be left in the same state as it was in before the method was called.

Once a bundle has been installed, a Bundle object is created and all remaining life cycle operations must be performed upon this object. The returned Bundle object can be used to start, stop, update, and uninstall the bundle.

4.4.4 Resolving Bundles

A bundle can enter the RESOLVED state when the Framework has successfully resolved the bundle's dependencies as described in the manifest. These dependencies are described in *Resolving Process* on page 45.

4.4.5 Starting Bundles

A bundle can be *started* by calling one of the start methods on its Bundle object or the Framework can automatically start the bundle if the bundle is *ready* and the *autostart setting* of the bundle indicates that it must be started.

A bundle is *ready* if following conditions are all met:

- The bundle can be resolved
- If the optional Start Level service is used, then the bundle's start level is met.

Once a bundle is started, a bundle must be *activated*, see *Activation* on page 86, to give control to the bundle so that it can initialize. This activation can take place immediately (*eager activation*), or upon the first class load from the bundle (*lazy activation*). A started bundle may need to be automatically started again by the framework after a restart or changes in the start level. The framework therefore maintains a persistent *autostart setting* for each bundle. This autostart setting can have the following values:

- *Stopped* – The bundle should not be started.
- *Started with eager activation* – The bundle must be started once it is ready and it must then be eagerly activated.
- *Started with declared activation* – The bundle must be started once it is ready and it must then be activated according to its declared activation policy. See *Activation Policies* on page 87.

The Bundle interface defines the start(int) method for starting a bundle and controlling the autostart setting. The start(int) method takes an integer option, the following values have been defined for this option:

- 0 – Start the bundle with eager activation and set the autostart setting to *Started with eager activation*. If the bundle was already started with the lazy activation policy and is awaiting activation, then it must be activated immediately.
- START_TRANSIENT – Identical to 0 in behavior, however, the autostart setting must *not* be altered.
  If the bundle can not be started, for example, the bundle is not ready, then a Bundle Exception must be thrown.
- START_ACTIVATION_POLICY – Start the bundle using the activation policy declared in the manifest's Bundle-ActivationPolicy header and set the autostart setting to *Started with declared activation*.
- START_ACTIVATION_POLICY | START_TRANSIENT – Start the bundle with the bundle's declared activation policy but do not alter the autostart setting.

The Framework must attempt to resolve the bundle, if not already resolved, when trying to start the bundle. If the bundle fails to resolve, the start method must throw a BundleException. In this case, the bundle's autostart setting must still be set unless START_TRANSIENT is used.

When the start method returns without an exception, the state of the bundle will either be ACTIVE or STARTING, depending on the declared activation policy and whether it was used. If the start method throws an exception, then the bundle will not be in either of these states and the stop method will not be called for this Bundle Activator instance.

The start()method calls start(0).

The optional Start Level service influences the actual order of starting and stopping of bundles. See *Start Level Service Specification* on page 203. The Start Level service can also be used to query the autostart setting:

- isBundlePersistentlyStarted(Bundle) – false if the bundle's autostart setting indicates *Stopped*, otherwise true.
- isBundleActivationPolicyUsed(Bundle) – true if the bundle's autostart setting indicates that the activation policy declared in the manifest must be used. false if the bundle must be eagerly activated.

Fragment bundles can not be started and must cause a Bundle Exception when there is an attempt to start them.

4.4.6 Activation

A bundle is activated by calling its Bundle Activator object, if one exists. The BundleActivator interface defines methods that the Framework invokes when it starts and stops the bundle.

To inform the OSGi environment of the fully qualified class name serving as its Bundle Activator, a bundle developer must declare a Bundle-Activator manifest header in the bundle's manifest file. The Framework must instantiate a new object of this class and cast it to a BundleActivator instance. It must then call the BundleActivator.start method to start the bundle.

The following is an example of a Bundle-Activator manifest header:

```
Bundle-Activator: com.acme.Activator
```

A class acting as a Bundle Activator must implement the BundleActivator interface, be declared public, and have a public default constructor so an instance of it may be created with Class.newInstance.

Supplying a Bundle Activator is optional. For example, a library bundle that only exports a number of packages does not need to define a Bundle Activator. In addition, other mechanism exists to obtain control and get a Bundle Context, like for example the Service Component Runtime.

The BundleActivator interface defines these methods for starting and stopping a bundle:

- start(BundleContext) – This method can allocate resources that a bundle needs, start threads, register services, and more. If this method does not register any services, the bundle can register services it needs later: for example, in a callback or an external event, as long as it is in the ACTIVE state. If the start(BundleContext) method throws an exception, the Framework must mark the bundle as stopped and send out STOPPING and STOPPED events but it must not call the Bundle Activator stop(BundleContext) method. The start method must therefore be careful to clean up any resources it creates in the start method when it throws an exception.
- stop(BundleContext) – This method must undo all the actions of the BundleActivator.start(BundleContext) method. However, it is unnecessary to unregister services or Framework listeners, because they must be cleaned up by the Framework anyway. This method is only called when the bundle has reached the ACTIVE state. That is, when the start method has thrown exception, the stop method is never called for the same instance.

A Bundle Activator must be created when a Bundle is started, implying the creation of a class loader. For larger systems, this greedy strategy can significantly increase startup times and unnecessarily increase the memory footprint. Mechanisms such as the Service Component Runtime and activation policies can mitigate these problems.

Fragment bundles must not have a Bundle Activator specified.

4.4.6.1   **Activation Policies**

The activation of a bundle can also be deferred to a later time from its start using an *activation policy*. This policy is specified in the Bundle-ActivationPolicy header with the following syntax:

```
Bundle-ActivationPolicy ::= policy ( ';' directive )*
policy ::= 'lazy'
```

The only policy defined is the lazy activation policy. If no Bundle-ActivationPolicy header is specified, the bundle will use eager activation.

4.4.6.2   **Lazy Activation Policy**

A lazy activation policy indicates that the bundle, once started, must not be activated until a class is loaded from it; either during normal class loading or via the Bundle loadClass method. Resource loading does not trigger the activation. This change from the default eager activation policy is reflected in the state of the bundle and its events. When a bundle is started using a lazy activation policy, the following steps must be taken:

- A Bundle Context is created for the bundle.
- The bundle state is moved to the STARTING state.
- The LAZY_ACTIVATION event is fired.
- The system waits for a class load from the bundle to occur.
- The normal STARTING event is fired.
- The bundle is activated.
- The bundle state is moved to ACTIVE.
- The STARTED event is fired.

If the activation fails because the Bundle Activator start method has thrown an exception, the bundle must be stopped without calling the Bundle Activator stop method. These steps are pictured in a flow chart in Figure 4.38. This flow chart also shows the difference in activation policy of the normal eager activation and the lazy activation.

Figure 4.38   *Starting with eager activation versus lazy activation*

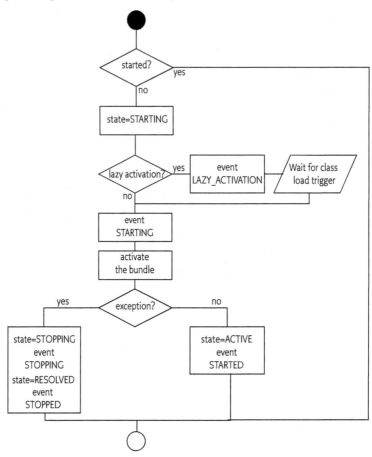

The lazy activation policy allows a Framework implementation to defer the creation of the bundle class loader and activation of the bundle until the bundle is first used; potentially saving resources and initialization time during startup.

By default, any class load can trigger the lazy activation, however, resource loads must not trigger the activation. The lazy activation policy can define which classes cause the activation with the following directives:

- include – A list of package names that must trigger the activation when a class is loaded from any of these packages. The default is all package names present in the bundle.
- exclude – A list of package names that must not trigger the activation of the bundle when a class is loaded from any of these packages. The default is no package names.

For example:

```
Bundle-ActivationPolicy: lazy;
    include:="com.acme.service.base,com.acme.service.help"
```

When a class load triggers the lazy activation, the Framework must first define the triggering class. This definition can trigger additional lazy activations. These activations must be deferred until all transitive class loads and defines have finished. Thereafter, the activations must be executed in the reverse order of detection. That is, the last detected activation must be executed first. Only after all deferred activations are finished must the class load that triggered the activation return with the loaded class. If an error occurs during this process, it should be reported as a Framework ERROR event. However, the class load must succeed normally. A bundle that fails its lazy activation should not be activated again until the framework is restarted or the bundle is explicitly started by calling the Bundle start method.

4.4.6.3   Restoring State After Refresh or Update

The operations Package Admin refreshPackage and the update methods can cause other bundles to be stopped. Started bundles can be in the ACTIVE state or waiting to be activated, depending on their activation policy. The following rules must be applied when restoring the state after an update or refresh:

- An ACTIVE or STARTING bundle must be started *transiently* after an update or refresh operation to not change its persistent autostart state.
- If the bundle was in the STARTING state due to lazy activation, the bundle's activation policy should be used when starting the bundle.

4.4.7   Stopping Bundles

The Bundle interface defines the stop(int) method for stopping a bundle. This calls the stop method when the bundle is in the ACTIVE state and sets the bundle's state to RESOLVED. The stop(int) takes an integer option. The following value has been defined for this option:

- 0 – If the bundle was activated, then deactivate the bundle and sets the autostart setting for this bundle to *Stopped*.
- STOP_TRANSIENT – If the bundle was activated, then deactivate the bundle. Does not alter the autostart setting for this bundle.

The stop() method calls stop(0).

The optional Start Level service influences the actual order of starting and stopping of bundles. See *Start Level Service Specification* on page 203.

Attempting to stop a Fragment bundle must result in a Bundle Exception.

4.4.8   Deactivation

The BundleActivator interface defines a stop(BundleContext) method, which is invoked by the Framework to stop a bundle. This method must release any resources allocated since activation. All threads associated with the stopping bundle should be stopped immediately. The threaded code may no longer use Framework-related objects (such as services and BundleContext objects) once the stop method returns.

If the stopping bundle had registered any services or Framework listeners during its lifetime, then the Framework must automatically unregister all registered services and Framework listeners when the bundle is stopped. It is therefore unnecessary from the Framework's point of view to unregister any services or Framework listeners in the stop method.

The Framework must guarantee that if a BundleActivator.start method has executed successfully, that same BundleActivator object must be called with its BundleActivator.stop method when the bundle is deactivated. After calling the stop method, that particular BundleActivator object must never be used again.

Packages exported by a stopped bundle continue to be available to other bundles. This continued export implies that other bundles can execute code from a stopped bundle, and the designer of a bundle should assure that this is not harmful. Exporting interfaces only is one way to prevent such unwanted execution when the bundle is not started. Generally, to ensure they cannot be executed, interfaces should not contain executable code.

4.4.9   ## Updating Bundles

The Bundle interface defines two methods for updating a bundle:

- update() – This method updates a bundle.
- update(InputStream) – This method updates a bundle from the specified InputStream object.

The update process supports migration from one version of a bundle to a newer version of the same bundle. The exports of an updated bundle must be immediately available to the Framework. If none of the old exports are used, then the old exports must be removed. Otherwise, all old exports must remain available for existing bundles and future resolves until the refreshPackages method is called or the Framework is restarted.

After the update operation is complete, the framework must attempt to move the bundle to the same state as it was before the operation taking the activation policy into account, without changing the autostart setting. This is described in more detail in *Restoring State After Refresh or Update* on page 89.

An updater of a bundle must have AdminPermission[<bundle>,LIFECYCLE] for both the installed bundle as well as the new bundle. The parameters of AdminPermission are explained in *Admin Permission* on page 101.

4.4.10   ## Uninstalling Bundles

The Bundle interface defines the uninstall() method for uninstalling a bundle from the Framework. This method causes the Framework to notify other bundles that the bundle is being uninstalled, and sets the bundle's state to
UNINSTALLED. To whatever extent possible, the Framework must remove any resources related to the bundle. This method must always uninstall the bundle from the persistent storage of the Framework.

Once this method returns, the state of the OSGi Service Platform must be the same as if the bundle had never been installed, unless:

- The uninstalled bundle has exported any packages (via its Export-Package manifest header)
- The uninstalled bundle was selected by the Framework as the exporter of these packages.

If none of the old exports are used, then the old exports must be removed. Otherwise, all old exports must remain available for existing bundles and future resolves until the refreshPackages method is called or the Framework is restarted.

4.4.11   ## Detecting Bundle Changes

The Bundle object provides a convenient way to detect changes in a bundle. The Framework must keep the time that a bundle is changed by any of the life cycle operations. The getLastModified() method will return the last time the bundle was installed, updated, or uninstalled. This last modified time must be stored persistently.

The method must return the number of milliseconds since midnight Jan. 1, 1970 UTC with the condition that a change must always result in a higher value than the previous last modified time of any bundle.

The getLastModified() is very useful when a bundle is caching resources from another bundle and needs to refresh the cache when the bundle changes. This life cycle change of the target bundle can happen while the caching bundle is not active. The last modified time is therefore a convenient way to track these target bundles.

4.4.12   **Retrieving Manifest Headers**

The Bundle interface defines two methods to return manifest header information: getHeaders() and getHeaders(String).

- getHeaders() – Returns a Dictionary object that contains the bundle's manifest headers and values as key/value pairs. The values returned are localized according to the default locale returned by java.util.Locale.getDefault.
- getHeaders(String) – Returns a Dictionary object that contains the bundle's manifest headers and values as key/value pairs. The returned values are localized using the specified locale. The locale may take the following values:
  - null – The default locale returned by java.util.Locale.getDefault is used. This makes this method identical to the getHeaders() method.
  - *Empty string* – The dictionary will contain the raw (unlocalized) manifest headers including any leading '%'.
  - *A Specific Locale* – The given locale is used to localize the manifest headers.

Localization is performed according to the description in *Localization* on page 58. If no translation is found for a specific key, the Dictionary returned by Bundle.getHeaders will return the raw values as specified in the manifest header values without the leading '%' character.

These methods require AdminPermission[<bundle>, METADATA] because some of the manifest header information may be sensitive, such as the packages listed in the Export-Package header. Bundles always have permission to read their own headers.

The getHeaders methods must continue to provide the manifest header information after the bundle enters the UNINSTALLED state. After the bundle has been uninstalled, this method will only return manifest headers that are raw or localized for the default locale at the time the bundle was uninstalled.

A framework implementation must use only the raw (unlocalized) manifest headers when processing manifest headers. Localizations must not influence the operations of the Framework.

4.4.13   **Loading Classes**

In certain cases, it is necessary to load classes as if they were loaded from inside the bundle. The loadClass(String) method gives access to the bundle class loader. This method can be used to:

- Load plugins from another bundle
- Start an application model activator
- Interact with legacy code

For example, an application model could use this feature to load the initial class from the bundle and start it according to the rules of the application model.

```
void appStart() {
   Class initializer =  bundle.loadClass(activator);
   if ( initializer != null ) {
      App app = (App) initializer.newInstance();
      app.activate();
   }
}
```

Loading a class from a bundle can cause it to be activated if the bundle uses a lazy activation policy.

4.4.14   **Access to Resources**

The resources from a bundle can come from different sources. They can come from the raw JAR file, Fragment bundles, imported packages, or the bundle class path. Different use cases require a different resource search strategy. The Bundle interface provides a number of methods that access resources but use different strategies. The following search strategies are supported:

- *Class Space* – The getResource(String) and getResources(String) provide access to resources that is consistent with the class space as described in *Overall Search Order* on page 49. Following the search order can make certain parts of the JAR files inaccessible. These methods require that the bundle is resolved. If the bundle is not resolved, the Framework must attempt to resolve it. The search order can hide certain directories of the JAR file. Split packages are taken into account; therefore, resources with the same package names can come from different JARs. If the bundle is unresolved (or cannot be resolved), the getResource and getResources methods must only load resources from the bundle class path. This search strategy should be used by code that wants to access its own resources. Calling either method can cause the creation of a class loader and force the bundle to become resolved.
- *JAR File* – The getEntry(String) and getEntryPaths(String) methods provide access to the resources in the bundle's JAR file. No searching is involved, only the raw JAR file is taken into account. The purpose of these methods is to provide low-level access without requiring that the bundle is resolved.
- *Bundle Space* – The findEntries(String,String,boolean) is an intermediate form. Useful when configuration or setup information is needed from another bundle. It considers Fragment bundles but it must never create a class loader. The method provides access to all directories in the associated JAR files.

For example, consider the following setup:

```
A: Require-Bundle: D
   Import-Package: q,t
   Export-Package: t
B: Export-Package: q,t
C: Fragment-Host: A
D: Export-Package: s
```

This setup is depicted in Figure 4.39.

Figure 4.39   *Setup for showing the difference between getResource and getEntry*

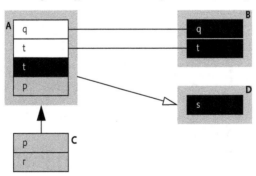

The following table shows the effect of getting a resource from this setup when bundle A is resolved.

Table 4.2 shows the same cases as the previous table but now for an unresolved bundle A.

Table 4.1   *Differences between getResource, getEntry, and findEntries for resolved bundle A*

Resource	getResource	getEntry	findEntries
q	B.q	null	null
p	A.p > C.p	A.p	A.p > C.p
r	C.r	null	C.r
s	D.s	null	null
t	B.t	A.t	A.t

Table 4.2   *Differences between getResource, getEntry, and findEntries for an unresolved bundle A*

Resource	getResource	getEntry	findEntries
q	null	null	null
p	A.p	A.p	A.p
r	null	null	null
s	null	null	null
t	A.t	A.t	A.t

4.4.15 Permissions of a Bundle

The Bundle interface defines a method for returning information pertaining to a bundle's permissions: hasPermission(Object). This method returns true if the bundle's Protection Domain has the specified permission, and false if it does not, or if the object specified by the argument is not an instance of java.security.Permission.

The parameter type is Object so that the Framework can be implemented on Java platforms that do not support Java 2 based security.

4.4.16 Access to a Bundle's Bundle Context

Bundles that have been started have a Bundle Context. This object is a *capability*; it is intended to be used only by the bundle. However, there are a number of cases where bundles must act on behalf of other bundles. For example, the Service Component Runtime registers services on behalf of other bundles. The framework therefore provides access to another bundle's context via the getBundleContext() method. If there is no Bundle Context for that Bundle because the bundle is a fragment bundle or the bundle state is not in { STARTING, ACTIVE, STOPPING }, then null must be returned.

This method is potentially harmful because it allows any bundle to act as any other bundle. In a secure system, the method is protected by requiring AdminPermission[*,CONTEXT].

4.5 The Bundle Context

The relationship between the Framework and its installed bundles is realized by the use of BundleContext objects. A BundleContext object represents the execution context of a single bundle within the OSGi Service Platform, and acts as a proxy to the underlying Framework.

A BundleContext object is created by the Framework when a bundle is started. The bundle can use this private BundleContext object for the following purposes:

- Installing new bundles into the OSGi environment. See *Installing Bundles* on page 84.
- Interrogating other bundles installed in the OSGi environment. See *Getting Bundle Information* on page 94.
- Obtaining a persistent storage area. See *Persistent Storage* on page 94.
- Retrieving service objects of registered services. See *Service References* on page 107.
- Registering services in the Framework service. See *Registering Services* on page 107.

- Subscribing or unsubscribing to events broadcast by the Framework. See *Listeners* on page 99.

When a bundle is started, the Framework creates a BundleContext object and provides this object as an argument to the start(BundleContext) method of the bundle's Bundle Activator. Each bundle is provided with its own BundleContext object; these objects should not be passed between bundles, since the BundleContext object is related to the security and resource allocation aspects of a bundle.

After the stop(BundleContext) method has returned, the BundleContext object must no longer be used. Framework implementations must throw an exception if the BundleContext object is used after a bundle is stopped.

4.5.1   Getting Bundle Information

The BundleContext interface defines methods to retrieve information about bundles installed in the OSGi Service Platform:

- getBundle() – Returns the single Bundle object associated with the BundleContext object.
- getBundles() – Returns an array of the bundles currently installed in the Framework.
- getBundle(long) – Returns the Bundle object specified by the unique identifier, or null if no matching bundle is found.

Bundle access is not restricted; any bundle can enumerate the set of installed bundles. Information that can identify a bundle, however (such as its location, or its header information), is only provided to callers that have AdminPermission[<bundle>,METADATA].

4.5.2   Persistent Storage

The Framework should provide a private persistent storage area for each installed bundle on platforms with some form of file system support.

The BundleContext interface defines access to this storage in terms of the File class, which supports platform-independent definitions of file and directory names.

The BundleContext interface defines a method to access the private persistent storage area: get-DataFile(String). This method takes a relative file name as an argument. It translates this file name into an absolute file name in the bundle's persistent storage area. It then returns a File object. This method returns null if there is no support for persistent storage.

The Framework must automatically provide the bundle with FilePermission[<storage area>, READ | WRITE | DELETE] to allow the bundle to read, write, and delete files in that storage area.

If EXECUTE permissions is required, then a relative path name can be used in the File Permission definition. For example, FilePermission[bin/*,EXECUTE] specifies that the sub-directory in the bundle's private data area may contain executables. This only provides execute permission within the Java environment and does not handle the potential underlying operating system issues related to executables.

This special treatment applies only to FilePermission objects assigned to a bundle. Default permissions must not receive this special treatment. A FilePermission for a relative path name assigned via the setDefaultPermission method must be ignored.

4.5.3   Environment Properties

The BundleContext interface defines a method for returning information pertaining to Framework properties: getProperty(String). This method can be used to return the following Framework properties. The alias column contains is names that have been reported to be returned by certain versions of the related operating systems. Frameworks should try to convert these aliases to the canonical OS or processor name. The bundle developer should use the canonical name in the Bundle-NativeCode manifest header.:

Table 4.3   *Property Names*

Property name	Description
org.osgi.framework.version	The specification version of the Framework, must be Version 1.5.
org.osgi.framework.vendor	The vendor of the Framework implementation.
org.osgi.framework.language	The language being used. See *ISO 639, International Standards Organization* See [45] *Codes for the Representation of Names of Languages* for valid values.
org.osgi.framework. « executionenvironment	A comma-separated list of provided execution environments (EE). All methods of each listed EE must be present on the Service Platform. For example, this property could contain: `CDC-1.1/Foundation-1.1,OSGi/Minimum-1.2` A Service Platform implementation must provide *all* the signatures that are defined in the mentioned EEs. Thus, the execution environment for a specific Service Platform Server must be the combined set of all signatures of all EEs in the org.osgi.framework.executionenvironment property.
org.osgi.framework.processor	Processor name. The following table defines a list of processor names. New processors are made available on the OSGi web site, see [50] *OSGi Reference Names*. Names should be matched case insensitive.

Name	Aliases	Description
68k		Motorola 68000
ARM		*Intel Strong ARM. Deprecated because it does not specify the endianness. See the following two rows.*
arm_le		Intel Strong ARM Little Endian mode
arm_be		Intel String ARM Big Endian mode
Alpha		Compaq (ex DEC)
ia64n		Hewlett Packard 64 bit
ia64w		Hewlett Packard 32 bit mode
Ignite	psc1k	PTSC
Mips		SGI
PArisc		Hewlett Packard
PowerPC	power ppc	Motorola/IBM Power PC
Sh4		Hitachi
Sparc		SUN
S390		IBM Mainframe 31 bit
S390x		IBM Mainframe 64-bit
V850E		NEC V850E
x86	pentium i386 i486 i586 i686	Intel& AMD 32 bit
x86-64	amd64 em64t x86_64	AMD/Intel 64 bit x86 architecture

Table 4.3   *Property Names*

Property name	Description
org.osgi.framework.os.version	The version of the operating system. If the version does not fit the standard x.y.z format (e.g. 2.4.32-kwt), then the Operator should define a System property with this name.
org.osgi.framework.os.name	The name of the operating system (OS) of the host computer. The following table defines a list of OS names. New OS names are made available on the OSGi web site, see [50] *OSGi Reference Names*. Names should be matched case insensitive.

Name	Aliases	Description
AIX		IBM
DigitalUnix		Compaq
Embos		Segger Embedded Software Solutions
Epoc32	SymbianOS	Symbian OS
FreeBSD		Free BSD
HPUX	hp-ux	Hewlett Packard
IRIX		Silicon Graphics
Linux		Open source
MacOS	"Mac OS"	Apple
MacOSX	"Mac OS X"	Apple
NetBSD		Open source
Netware		Novell
OpenBSD		Open source
OS2	OS/2	IBM
QNX	procnto	QNX
Solaris		Sun (almost an alias of SunOS)
SunOS		Sun Microsystems
VxWorks		WindRiver Systems
Windows95	Win95 "Windows 95" Win32	Microsoft Windows 95
Windows98	Win98 "Windows 98" Win32	Microsoft Windows 98
WindowsNT	WinNT "Windows NT" Win32	Microsoft Windows NT
WindowsCE	WinCE "Windows CE"	Microsoft Windows CE
Windows2000	Win2000 "Windows 2000" Win32	Microsoft Windows 2000
Windows2003	Win2003 "Windows 2003" Win32 "Windows Server 2003"	Microsoft Windows 2003

Table 4.3   *Property Names*

Property name	Description		
	WindowsXP	WinXP "Windows XP" Win32	Microsoft Windows XP
	WindowsVista	WinVista "Windows Vista" Win32	Microsoft Windows Vista
org.osgi.supports.« framework.extension	Support for framework extensions is mandatory, must therefore be set to true, see *Extension Bundles* on page 66.		
org.osgi.supports.« bootclasspath.extension	See *Requiring Bundles* on page 60.		
org.osgi.supports.« framework.fragment	Support for fragment bundles is mandatory, must therefore be set to true, see *Fragment Bundles* on page 63.		
org.osgi.supports.« framework.requirebundle	Support for Require Bundle is mandatory, must therefore be set to true, see *Requiring Bundles* on page 60.		
org.osgi.framework.« bootdelegation	See *Parent Delegation* on page 49		
org.osgi.framework.« system.packages	See *Parent Class Loader* on page 52		

All Framework properties may be defined by the Operator as System properties, or given as properties in the framework launching, see *Launching Properties* on page 76. If these properties are not defined as System properties or launching properties, then the Framework must construct required properties from relevant standard Java System properties.

Therefore, the search order for a property is:

- Framework constants (vendor, implementation, options, etc.).
- Launching properties
- System properties
- Framework default

4.6   **The System Bundle**

In addition to normal bundles, the Framework itself is represented as a bundle. The bundle representing the Framework is referred to as the *system bundle*. Through the system bundle, the Framework may register services that can be used by other bundles. Examples of such services are the Package Admin and Permission Admin services.

The system bundle resembles the framework object when a framework is launched, but implementations are not required to use the same object for the framework object and the system bundle. However, both objects must have bundle id 0, same location, and bundle symbolic name.

The system bundle is listed in the set of installed bundles returned by BundleContext.getBundles(), although it differs from other bundles in the following ways:

- The system bundle is always assigned a bundle identifier of zero (0).
- The system bundle getLocation method returns the string: "System Bundle", as defined in the Constants interface.

- The system bundle has a bundle symbolic name that is unique for a specific version. However, the name system.bundle must be recognized as an alias to this implementation-defined name.
- The system bundle's life cycle cannot be managed like normal bundles. Its life cycle methods must behave as follows:
  - *start* – Does nothing because the system bundle is already started.
  - *stop* – Returns immediately and shuts down the Framework on another thread.
  - *update* – Returns immediately, then stops and restarts the Framework on another thread.
  - *uninstall* – The Framework must throw a BundleException indicating that the system bundle cannot be uninstalled.
  - See *Frameworks* on page 74 for more information about the starting and stopping of the Framework.

4.6.1   System Bundle Headers

The system bundle's Bundle.getHeaders method returns a Dictionary object with implementation-specific manifest headers. The following headers of this OSGi specification can be returned in this dictionary. Headers not mentioned in this table should not be used.

Table 5   *Supported headers in the system bundle getHeaders method*

Header	Type	Description
Bundle-ContactAddress	optional	Recommended to provide the framework vendor's contact address.
Bundle-Copyright	optional	Recommended to provide the framework's copyright information.
Bundle-Description	optional	Recommended description of the framework.
Bundle-DocURL	optional	Recommended documentation URL pointing to further information about the framework.
Bundle-Icon	optional	Recommended pointer to a preferably PNG icon representing this framework.
Bundle-Localization	optional	Recommended localization information.
Bundle-License	optional	License information about this framework implementation.
Bundle-ManifestVersion	mandatory	The maximum version of the manifest version understood by this framework.
Bundle-Name	optional	Recommended human readable name of this framework.
Bundle-Required« ExecutionEnvironment	mandatory	Mandatory: the list of execution environments supported by this framework
Bundle-SymbolicName	mandatory	The implementation name for this framework.
Bundle-Vendor	optional	Recommended vendor information
Bundle-Version	mandatory	The version of this framework implementation.
Export-Package	mandatory	Contains packages that are exported by the Framework like org.osgi.framework but also the packages listed in the framework property org.osgi.framework.system.packages or org.osgi.framework.system.packages.extra

4.7 Events

The OSGi Framework Life Cycle layer supports the following types of events:

- BundleEvent – Reports changes in the life cycle of bundles.
- FrameworkEvent – Reports that the Framework is started, start level has changed, packages have been refreshed, or that an error has been encountered.

The actual event that is reported is available with the getType method. The integer that is returned from this method can be one of the constant names that are described in the class. However, events can, and will be, extended in the future. Unrecognized event types should be ignored.

4.7.1 Listeners

A listener interface is associated with each type of event. The following list describes these listeners.

- BundleListener and SynchronousBundleListener – Called with an event of type BundleEvent when a bundle's life cycle information has been changed.
  SynchronousBundleListener objects are called synchronously during the processing of the event and must be called before any BundleListener object is called. The following events are sent by the Framework after it has moved to a different state:
  - INSTALLED – Sent after a bundle is installed. The state is now Bundle INSTALLED state.
  - RESOLVED– Sent when the Framework has resolved a bundle. The state is now the Bundle RESOLVED state.
  - LAZY_ACTIVATION – The bundle has specified an activation policy; its activation is deferred to a later point in time. The state is set to the Bundle STARTING state. This is only sent to SynchronousBundleListener objects.
  - STARTING – Sent when the Framework is about to activate a bundle. This is only sent to SynchronousBundleListener objects. The state is now the Bundle STARTING state.
  - STARTED – Sent when the Framework has started a bundle. The state is now the Bundle ACTIVE state.
  - STOPPING – Sent when the Framework is about to stop a bundle or the start method of the Bundle Activator has thrown an exception and the bundle is stopped. This event indicates that the Bundle Context will be destroyed. This event is only sent to SynchronousBundleListener objects.
  - STOPPED– Sent when the Framework has stopped a bundle.
  - UNINSTALLED – Sent when the Framework has uninstalled a bundle
  - UNRESOLVED – Sent when the Framework detects that a bundle becomes unresolved; this could happen when the bundle is refreshed or updated. When a set of bundles are refreshed using the Package Admin API then each bundle in the set must have an UNRESOLVED BundleEvent published. The UNRESOLVED BundleEvent must be published after all the bundles in the set have been stopped and, in the case of a synchronous bundle listener, *before* any of the bundles in the set are re-started. RESOLVED and UNRESOLVED do not have to paired.
  - UPDATED – Sent after a bundle is updated.

- FrameworkListener – Called with an event of type FrameworkEvent. Framework events are of type:
  - ERROR – Important error that requires the immediate attention of an operator.
  - INFO – General information that is of interest in special situations.
  - PACKAGES_REFRESHED – The Framework has refreshed the packages.
  - STARTED – The Framework has performed all initialization and is running in normal mode.
  - STARTLEVEL_CHANGED – Is sent by the Framework after a new start level has been set and processed.

- STOPPED – Sent by the Framework because of a stop operation on the system bundle.
- STOPPED_BOOTCLASSPATH_MODIFIED –Sent by the Framework because of a stop operation on the system bundle and a boot class path extension bundle has been installed or updated.
- STOPPED_UPDATE – Sent by the Framework because of an update operation on the system bundle. The Framework will be restarted after this event is fired.
- WARNING – A warning to the operator that is not crucial but may indicate a potential error situation.
- WAIT_TIMEDOUT – Returned from the waitForStop method when the Framework did not stop before the given wait time-out expired.

BundleContext interface methods are defined which can be used to add and remove each type of listener.

Events can be asynchronously delivered, unless otherwise stated, meaning that they are not necessarily delivered by the same thread that generated the event. The thread used to call an event listener is not defined.

The Framework must publish a FrameworkEvent.ERROR if a callback to an event listener generates an unchecked exception - except when the callback happens while delivering a FrameworkEvent.ERROR (to prevent an infinite loop).

Synchronous events have the unfortunate effect that, in rare cases, events can be delivered out of order to a listener. For example, a Service Event UNREGISTERING can be delivered before its corresponding Service Event REGISTERED. One pathological case is when a service listener (for example a Service Tracker) unregisters a service that it receives in the REGISTERED event for. If there are listeners queued behind the pathological listener then they see the unregistering before they see the registration.

4.7.2   Delivering Events

If the Framework delivers an event asynchronously, it must:

- Collect a snapshot of the listener list at the time the event is published (rather than doing so in the future just prior to event delivery), but before the event is delivered, so that listeners do not enter the list after the event happened.
- Ensure, at the time the snapshot is taken, that listeners on the list still belong to active bundles at the time the event is delivered.
- It is possible to use more than one thread to deliver events. If this is the case then each handler must receive the events in the same order as the events were posted. This ensures that handlers see events in the expected order.

If the Framework did not capture the current listener list when the event was published, but instead waited until just prior to event delivery, then the following error could occur: a bundle could have started and registered a listener, and then the bundle could see its own BundleEvent.INSTALLED event.

The following three scenarios illustrate this concept.

1. Scenario one event sequence:
   - Event A is published.
   - Listener 1 is registered.
   - Asynchronous delivery of Event A is attempted.
   Expected Behavior: Listener 1 must not receive Event A, because it was not registered at the time the event was published.

2. Scenario two event sequence:
   - Listener 2 is registered.
   - Event B is published.

- Listener 2 is unregistered.
- Asynchronous delivery of Event B is attempted.

Expected Behavior: Listener 2 receives Event B, because Listener 2 was registered at the time Event B was published.

3. Scenario three event sequence:
   - Listener 3 is registered.
   - Event C is published.
   - The bundle that registered Listener 3 is stopped.
   - Asynchronous delivery of Event C is attempted.

Expected Behavior: Listener 3 must not receive Event C, because its Bundle Context object is invalid.

4.7.3 Synchronization Pitfalls

Generally, a bundle that calls a listener should not hold any Java monitors. This means that neither the Framework nor the originator of a synchronous event should be in a monitor when a callback is initiated.

The purpose of a Java monitor is to protect the update of data structures. This should be a small region of code that does not call any code the effect of which cannot be overseen. Calling the OSGi Framework from synchronized code can cause unexpected side effects. One of these side effects might be *deadlock*. A deadlock is the situation where two threads are blocked because they are waiting for each other.

Time-outs can be used to break deadlocks, but Java monitors do not have time-outs. Therefore, the code will hang forever until the system is reset (Java has deprecated all methods that can stop a thread). This type of deadlock is prevented by not calling the Framework (or other code that might cause callbacks) in a synchronized block.

If locks are necessary when calling other code, use the Java monitor to create semaphores that can time-out and thus provide an opportunity to escape a deadlocked situation.

4.8 Security

4.8.1 Admin Permission

The Admin Permission is a permission used to grant the right to manage the Framework with the option to restrict this right to a subset of bundles, called *targets*. For example, an Operator can give a bundle the right to only manage bundles of a signer that has a subject name of ACME:

```
org.osgi.framework.AdminPermission(
    "(signer=\*, o=ACME, c=us)", ... )
```

The actions of the Admin Permission are fine-grained. They allow the deployer to assign only the permissions that are necessary for a bundle. For example, an HTTP implementation could be granted access to all resources of all bundles.

```
org.osgi.framework.AdminPermission("*",
    "resource" )
```

Code that needs to check Admin Permission must always use the constructor that takes a bundle as parameter: AdminPermission(Bundle,String) with a single action.

For example, the implementation of the loadClass method must check that the caller has access to the class space:

```
public class BundleImpl implements Bundle {
```

```
      Class loadClass(String name) {
        securityManager.checkPermission(
          new AdminPermission(this,"class") );
            ...
      }
    }
```

The Admin Permission takes a filter as its name. Filter based permissions are described in *Filter Based Permissions* on page 19.

4.8.1.1   **Actions**

The action parameter of Admin Permission will specify the subset of privileged administrative operations that are allowed by the Framework. The actions that are architected are listed in table Table 4.1. Future versions of the specification, as well as additional system services, can add additional actions. The given set should therefore not be assumed to be a closed set.

Table 4.1   *Admin Permission actions*

Action	Used in
METADATA	Bundle.getHeaders
	Bundle.getLocation
RESOURCE	Bundle.getResource
	Bundle.getResources
	Bundle.getEntry
	Bundle.getEntryPaths
	Bundle.findEntries
	Bundle resource/entry URL creation
CLASS	Bundle.loadClass
LIFECYCLE	BundleContext.installBundle
	Bundle.update
	Bundle.uninstall
EXECUTE	Bundle.start
	Bundle.stop
	StartLevel.setBundleStartLevel
LISTENER	BundleContext.addBundleListener for SynchronousBundleListener
	BundleContext.removeBundleListener for SynchronousBundleListener
EXTENSIONLIFECYLE	BundleContext.installBundle for extension bundles
	Bundle.update for extension bundles
	Bundle.uninstall for extension bundles
RESOLVE	PackageAdmin.refreshPackages
	PackageAdmin.resolveBundles
STARTLEVEL	StartLevel.setStartLevel
	StartLevel.setInitialBundleStartLevel
CONTEXT	Bundle.getBundleContext

The special action "*" will represent all actions.

Each bundle must be given AdminPermission(<bundle identifier>, "resource,metadata,class, context") so that it can access its own resources and context. This is an implicit permission that must be automatically given to all bundles by the Framework.

4.8.2   **Privileged Callbacks**

The following interfaces define bundle callbacks that are invoked by the Framework:

- BundleActivator
- ServiceFactory
- Bundle-, Service-, and FrameworkListener.

When any of these callbacks are invoked by the Framework, the bundle that caused the callback may still be on the stack. For example, when one bundle installs and then starts another bundle, the installer bundle may be on the stack when the BundleActivator.start method of the installed bundle is called. Likewise, when a bundle registers a service object, it may be on the stack when the Framework calls back the serviceChanged method of all qualifying ServiceListener objects.

Whenever any of these bundle callbacks try to access a protected resource or operation, the access control mechanism should consider not only the permissions of the bundle receiving the callback, but also those of the Framework and any other bundles on the stack. This means that in these callbacks, bundle programmers normally would use doPrivileged calls around any methods protected by a permission check (such as getting or registering service objects).

In order to reduce the number of doPrivileged calls by bundle programmers, the Framework must perform a doPrivileged call around any bundle callbacks. The Framework should have java.security.AllPermission. Therefore, a bundle programmer can assume that the bundle is not further restricted except for its own permissions.

Bundle programmers do not need to use doPrivileged calls in their implementations of any callbacks registered with and invoked by the Framework.

For any other callbacks that are registered with a service object and therefore get invoked by the service-providing bundle directly, doPrivileged calls must be used in the callback implementation if the bundle's own privileges are to be exercised. Otherwise, the callback must fail if the bundle that initiated the callback lacks the required permissions.

A framework must never load classes in a doPrivileged region, but must instead use the current stack. This means that static initializers and constructors must not assume that they are privileged. Any privileged code in a static initializer must be guarded with a doPrivileged region in the static initializer. Likewise, a framework must not instantiate a BundleActivator object in a doPrivileged region, but must instead use the current stack. This means that the BundleActivator constructor must not assume that it is privileged.

4.8.3 Lazy Activation

The activation policy, see *Activation Policies* on page 87, can indirectly cause the activation of a bundle. AdminPermission[*,CLASS] therefore implies the EXECUTE action during a loadClass method call.

Normal class loading caused by executing Java class code must not require AdminPermission[*, EXECUTE].

4.9 Changes

- Added demon thread section, see *Daemon Threads* on page 82.
- Made it more clear that when the BundleActivator.start() method throws an exception, the BundleActivator.stop() method is never called for that instance.
- Highlighted that an update operation must restore the same state based on the same option. See *Updating Bundles* on page 89.
- Bundle Exception has now an integer error type.
- Made the Export-Package header mandatory for the System Bundle.
- Added additional environment properties, see 4.5.3 *Environment Properties*
- Clarified what the system bundle should return for the getHeaders method, see 4.6.1 *System Bundle Headers*.
- Introduced framework launchers.

- Moved description of Admin Permission filter name to *Filter Based Permissions* on page 19.
- Removed advice to re-implement some of the OSGi classes and the suggested extension mechanism.

4.10   References

[38]   *The Standard for the Format of ARPA Internet Text Messages*
STD 11, RFC 822, UDEL, August 1982
http://www.ietf.org/rfc/rfc822.txt

[39]   *The Hypertext Transfer Protocol - HTTP/1.1*
RFC 2068 DEC, MIT/LCS, UC Irvine, January 1997
http://www.ietf.org/rfc/rfc2068.txt

[40]   *The Java 2 Platform API Specification*
Standard Edition, Sun Microsystems
http://java.sun.com/j2se

[41]   *The Java Language Specification*
Second Edition, Sun Microsystems, 2000
http://java.sun.com/docs/books/jls/index.html

[42]   *A String Representation of LDAP Search Filters*
RFC 1960, UMich, 1996
http://www.ietf.org/rfc/rfc1960.txt

[43]   *The Java Security Architecture for JDK 1.2*
Version 1.0, Sun Microsystems, October 1998

[44]   *The Java 2 Package Versioning Specification*
http://java.sun.com/j2se/1.4/docs/guide/versioning/index.html

[45]   *Codes for the Representation of Names of Languages*
ISO 639, International Standards Organization
http://lcweb.loc.gov/standards/iso639-2/langhome.html

[46]   *Manifest Format*
http://java.sun.com/j2se/1.4/docs/guide/jar/jar.html#JAR%20Manifest

[47]   *W3C EBNF*
http://www.w3c.org/TR/REC-xml#sec-notation

[48]   *Lexical Structure Java Language*
http://java.sun.com/docs/books/jls/second_edition/html/lexical.doc.html

[49]   *Interval Notation*
http://www.math.ohio-state.edu/courses/math104/interval.pdf

[50]   *OSGi Reference Names*
http://www.osgi.org/Specifications/Reference

[51]   *JKS Keystore Format (reverse engineered)*
http://metastatic.org/source/JKS.html

[52]   *Java Service Provider Configuration*
http://java.sun.com/javase/6/docs/technotes/guides/jar/jar.html#Service%20Provider

5   Service Layer

Version 1.5

5.1   Introduction

The OSGi Service Layer defines a dynamic collaborative model that is highly integrated with the Life Cycle Layer. The *service* model is a publish, find and bind model. A service is a normal Java object that is registered under one or more Java interfaces with the service registry. Bundles can register services, search for them, or receive notifications when their registration state changes.

5.1.1   Essentials

- *Collaborative* – The service layer must provide a mechanism for bundles to publish, find, and bind to each other's services without having a priori knowledge of those bundles.
- *Dynamic* – The service mechanism must be able to handle changes in the outside world and underlying structures directly.
- *Secure* – It must be possible to restrict access to services.
- *Reflective* – Provide full access to the Service Layer's internal state.
- *Versioning* – Provide mechanisms that make it possible to handle the fact that bundles and their services evolve over time.
- *Persistent Identifier* – Provide a means for bundles to track services across Framework restarts.

5.1.2   Entities

- *Service* – An object registered with the service registry under one or more interfaces together with properties. This object can be discovered and used by bundles.
- *Service Registry* – Holds the service registrations.
- *Service Reference* – A reference to a service. Provides access to the service's properties but not the actual service object. The service object must be acquired through a bundle's Bundle Context.
- *Service Registration* – The receipt provided when a service is registered. The service registration allows the update of the service properties and the unregistration of the service.
- *Service Permission* – The permission to use an interface name when registering or using a service.
- *Service Factory* – A facility to let the registering bundle customize the service object for each using bundle.
- *Service Listener* – A listener to Service Events.
- *Service Event* – An event holding information about the registration, modification, or unregistration of a service object.
- *Filter* – An object that implements a simple but powerful filter language. It can select on properties.
- *Invalid Syntax Exception* – The exception thrown when a filter expression contains an error.

Figure 5.40   *Class Diagram* org.osgi.framework *Service Layer*

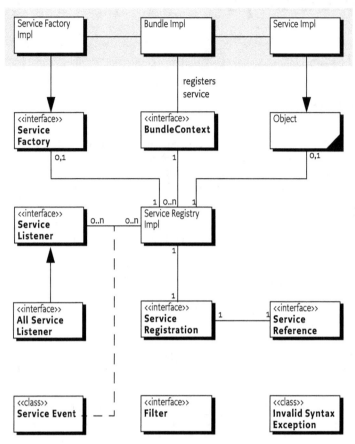

5.2   **Services**

In the OSGi Service Platform, bundles are built around a set of cooperating services available from a shared service registry. Such an OSGi service is defined semantically by its *service interface* and implemented as a *service object.*

The service interface should be specified with as few implementation details as possible. OSGi has specified many service interfaces for common needs and will specify more in the future.

The service object is owned by, and runs within, a bundle. This bundle must register the service object with the Framework service registry so that the service's functionality is available to other bundles under control of the Framework.

Dependencies between the bundle owning the service and the bundles using it are managed by the Framework. For example, when a bundle is stopped, all the services registered with the Framework by that bundle must be automatically unregistered.

The Framework maps services to their underlying service objects, and provides a simple but powerful query mechanism that enables a bundle to request the services it needs. The Framework also provides an event mechanism so that bundles can receive events of services that are registered, modified, or unregistered.

5.2.1 Service References

In general, registered services are referenced through ServiceReference objects. This avoids creating unnecessary dynamic service dependencies between bundles when a bundle needs to know about a service but does not require the service object itself.

A ServiceReference object can be stored and passed on to other bundles without the implications of dependencies. When a bundle wishes to use the service, it can be obtained by passing the ServiceReference object to BundleContext.getService(ServiceReference). See *Locating Services* on page 111.

A ServiceReference object encapsulates the properties and other meta-information about the service object it represents. This meta-information can be queried by a bundle to assist in the selection of a service that best suits its needs.

When a bundle queries the Framework service registry for services, the Framework must provide the requesting bundle with the ServiceReference objects of the requested services, rather than with the services themselves.

A ServiceReference object may also be obtained from a ServiceRegistration object.

A ServiceReference object is valid only as long as the service object is registered. However, its properties must remain available as long as the ServiceReference object exists.

5.2.2 Service Interfaces

A *service interface* is the specification of the service's public methods.

In practice, a bundle developer creates a service object by implementing its service interface and registers the service with the Framework service registry. Once a bundle has registered a service object under an interface name, the associated service can be acquired by bundles under that interface name, and its methods can be accessed by way of its service interface. The Framework also supports registering service objects under a class name, so references to service interface in this specification can be interpreted to be an interface or class.

When requesting a service object from the Framework, a bundle can specify the name of the service interface that the requested service object must implement. In the request, the bundle may also specify a filter string to narrow the search.

Many service interfaces are defined and specified by organizations such as the OSGi Alliance. A service interface that has been accepted as a standard can be implemented and used by any number of bundle developers.

5.2.3 Registering Services

A bundle publishes a service by registering a service object with the Framework service registry. A service object registered with the Framework is exposed to other bundles installed in the OSGi environment.

Every registered service object has a unique ServiceRegistration object, and has one or more ServiceReference objects that refer to it. These ServiceReference objects expose the registration properties of the service object, including the set of service interfaces they implement. The ServiceReference object can then be used to acquire a service object that implements the desired service interface.

The Framework permits bundles to register and unregister service objects dynamically. Therefore, a bundle is permitted to register service objects at any time during the STARTING, ACTIVE or STOPPING states.

A bundle registers a service object with the Framework by calling one of the BundleContext.registerService methods on its BundleContext object:

- registerService(String,Object,Dictionary) – For a service object registered under a single service interface.
- registerService(String[],Object,Dictionary) – For a service object registered under multiple service interfaces.

The names of the service interfaces under which a bundle wants to register its service are provided as arguments to the registerService methods. The Framework must ensure that the service object actually is an instance of each specified service interfaces, unless the object is a Service Factory. See *Service Factory* on page 114.

To perform this check, the Framework must load the Class object for each specified service interface from either the bundle or a shared package. For each Class object, Class.isInstance must be called and return true on the Class object with the service object as the argument.

The service object being registered may be further described by a Dictionary object, which contains the properties of the service as a collection of key/value pairs.

The service interface names under which a service object has been successfully registered are automatically added to the service object's properties under the key objectClass. This value must be set automatically by the Framework and any value provided by the bundle must be overridden.

If the service object is successfully registered, the Framework must return a ServiceRegistration object to the caller. A service object can be unregistered only by the holder of its ServiceRegistration object (see the unregister() method). Every successful service object registration must yield a unique ServiceRegistration object even if the same service object is registered multiple times.

Using the ServiceRegistration object is the only way to reliably change the service object's properties after it has been registered (see setProperties(Dictionary)). Modifying a service object's Dictionary object after the service object is registered may not have any effect on the service's properties.

The process of registering a service object is subject to a permission check. The registering bundle must have ServicePermission[<name>,REGISTER] to register the service object under all the service interfaces specified. Otherwise, the service object must not be registered, and a SecurityException must be thrown.

5.2.4   Early Need for ServiceRegistration Object

The registration of a service object will cause all registered ServiceListener objects to be notified. This is a synchronous notification. This means that such a listener can get access to the service and call its methods before the registerService method has returned the ServiceRegistration object. In certain cases, access to the ServiceRegistration object is necessary in such a callback. However, the registering bundle has not yet received the ServiceRegistration object. Figure 5.41 on page 109 shows such a sequence.

Figure 5.41   *Service Registration and registration*

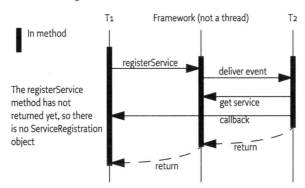

In a case as described previously, access to the registration object can be obtained via a ServiceFactory object. If a ServiceFactory object is registered, the Framework must call-back the registering bundle with the ServiceFactory method getService(Bundle,ServiceRegistration). The required ServiceRegistration object is passed as a parameter to this method.

5.2.5   Service Properties

Properties hold information as key/value pairs. The key must be a String object and the value should be a type recognized by Filter objects (see *Filters* on page 113 for a list). Multiple values for the same key are supported with arrays ([]) and Collection objects.

The values of properties should be limited to primitive or standard Java types to prevent unwanted inter bundle dependencies. The Framework cannot detect dependencies that are created by the exchange of objects between bundles via the service properties.

The key of a property is not case sensitive. ObjectClass, OBJECTCLASS and objectclass all are the same property key. A Framework must return the key in ServiceReference.getPropertyKeys in exactly the same case as it was last set. When a Dictionary object that contains keys that only differ in case is passed, the Framework must raise an exception.

The service properties are intended to provide information *about* the service object. The properties should not be used to participate in the actual function of the service. Modifying the properties for the service registration is a potentially expensive operation. For example, a Framework may pre-process the properties into an index during registration to speed up later look-ups.

The Filter interface supports complex filtering; it can be used to find matching service objects. Therefore, all properties share a single name space in the Framework service registry. As a result, it is important to use descriptive names or formal definitions of shorter names to prevent conflicts. Several OSGi specifications reserve parts of this name space. All properties starting with the prefix service. and the property objectClass are reserved for use by OSGi specifications.

Table 5.2 Standard Service Properties (+ indicates scalar, array of, or collection of) contains a list of pre-defined properties.

5.2.6   Persistent Identifier (PID)

The purpose of a Persistent Identifier (PID) is to identify a service across Framework restarts. Services that can reference the same underlying entity every time they are registered should therefore use a service property that contains a PID. The name of the service property for PID is defined as service.pid. The PID is a unique identifier for a service that persists over multiple invocations of the Framework. For a given service, the same PID should always be used. If the bundle is stopped and later started, the same PID must always be used.

The format of the PID should be:

Table 5.2   *Standard Service Properties (+ indicates scalar, array of, or collection of)*

Property Key	Type	Constants	Property Description
objectClass	String[]	OBJECTCLASS	The objectClass property contains the set of interface names under which a service object is registered with the Framework. The Framework must set this property automatically. The Framework must guarantee that when a service object is retrieved with BundleContext.getService(Service Reference), it can be cast to any of the interface names.
service.description	String	SERVICE_DESCRIPTION	The service.description property is intended to be used as documentation and is optional. Frameworks and bundles can use this property to provide a short description of a registered service object. The purpose is mainly for debugging because there is no support for localization.
service.id	Long	SERVICE_ID	Every registered service object is assigned a unique service.id by the Framework. This number is added to the service object's properties. The Framework assigns a unique value to every registered service object that is larger than values provided to all previously registered service objects.
service.pid	String+	SERVICE_PID	The service.pid property optionally identifies a persistent, unique identifier for the service object. See *Persistent Identifier (PID)* on page 109.
service.ranking	Integer	SERVICE_RANKING	When registering a service object, a bundle may optionally specify a service.ranking number as one of the service object's properties. If multiple qualifying service interfaces exist, a service with the highest SERVICE_RANKING number, or when equal to the lowest SERVICE_ID, determines which service object is returned by the Framework.
service.vendor	String	SERVICE_VENDOR	This optional property can be used by the bundle registering the service object to indicate the vendor.

```
        pid ::= symbolic-name              // See 1.3.2
```

5.2.7   Locating Services

In order to use a service object and call its methods, a bundle must first obtain a ServiceReference object. The BundleContext interface defines two methods a bundle can call to obtain ServiceReference objects from the Framework:

- getServiceReference(String) – This method returns a ServiceReference object to a service object that implements, and was registered under, the name of the service interface specified as String. If multiple such service objects exist, the service object with the highest SERVICE_RANKING is returned. If there is a tie in ranking, the service object with the lowest SERVICE_ID (the service object that was registered first) is returned.
- getServiceReferences(String,String) – This method returns an array of ServiceReference objects that:
  - Implement and were registered under the given service interface.
  - Satisfy the search filter specified. The filter syntax is further explained in *Filters* on page 113.

Both methods must return null if no matching service objects are returned. Otherwise, the caller receives one or more ServiceReference objects. These objects can be used to retrieve properties of the underlying service object, or they can be used to obtain the actual service object via the BundleContext object.

Both methods require that the caller has the required ServicePermission[ServiceReference, GET] to get the service object for the returned Service Reference. If the caller lacks the required permission, these methods must not include that Service Reference in the return.

5.2.8   Getting Service Properties

To allow for interrogation of service objects, the ServiceReference interface defines these two methods:

- getPropertyKeys() – Returns an array of the property keys that are available.
- getProperty(String) – Returns the value of a property.

Both of these methods must continue to provide information about the referenced service object, even after it has been unregistered from the Framework. This requirement can be useful when a ServiceReference object is stored with the Log Service.

5.2.9   Getting Service Objects

The BundleContext object is used to obtain the actual service object so that the Framework can manage dependencies. If a bundle retrieves a service object, that bundle becomes dependent upon the life cycle of that registered service object. This dependency is tracked by the BundleContext object used to obtain the service object, and is one reason that it is important to be careful when sharing BundleContext objects with other bundles.

The method BundleContext.getService(ServiceReference) returns an object that implements the interfaces as defined by the objectClass property.

This method has the following characteristics:

- Returns null if the underlying service object has been unregistered.
- Determines if the caller has ServicePermission[ServiceReference,GET], to get the service object associated with the Service Reference. This permission check is necessary so that ServiceReference objects can be passed around freely without compromising security.
- Increments the usage count of the service object by one for this BundleContext object.
- If the service object does not implement the ServiceFactory interface, it is returned. Otherwise, if the bundle context's usage count of the service object is one, the object is cast to a ServiceFactory object and the getService method is called to create a customized service object for the calling bundle which is then returned. Otherwise, a cached copy of this customized

object is returned. See *Service Factory* on page 114 for more information about ServiceFactory objects.

5.2.10 Information About Services

The Bundle interface defines these two methods for returning information pertaining to service usage of the bundles:

- getRegisteredServices() – Returns the ServiceReference objects that the bundle has registered with the Framework.
- getServicesInUse() – Returns the ServiceReference objects that the bundle is currently using.

5.2.11 Service Exceptions

The Service Exception is a Run Time exception that can be used by the Framework to report errors or user code that needs to signal a problem with a service. An exception type available from this exception provides the detailed information about the problem that caused the exception to be thrown.

Implementations of the framework or user code are allowed to throw sub classes of the ServiceException class. If a sub class is thrown for another reason than specified by one of the types, then the type should be set to SUBCLASS. Sub classes that provide additional information on existing types should keep the original type code.

5.2.12 Services and Concurrency

Services published on one thread and gotten on another thread must be safe to use. That is, the Framework must guarantee that there is a *happens-before* relationship between the time a service is registered and the time a service or Service Reference is gotten. That is both the registering and getting threads must be properly synchronized with each other.

5.3 Service Events

- ServiceEvent – Reports registration, unregistration, and property changes for service objects. All events of this kind must be delivered synchronously. The type of the event is given by the getType() method, which returns an int. Event types can be extended in the future; unknown event types should be ignored.

- ServiceListener – Called with a ServiceEvent when a service object has been registered or modified, or is in the process of unregistering. A security check must be performed for each registered listener when a ServiceEvent occurs. The listener must not be called unless the bundle which registered the listener has the required ServicePermission[ServiceReference,GET] for the corresponding Service Reference.

A bundle that uses a service object should register a ServiceListener object to track the availability of the service object, and take appropriate action when the service object is unregistering.

5.3.1 Service Event Types

The following service events are defined:

- REGISTERED – A service has been registered. This event is synchronously delivered after the service has been registered with the Framework.
- MODIFIED– The properties of a service have been modified. This event is synchronously delivered after the service properties have been modified.
- MODIFIED_ENDMATCH – Listeners registered with a filter can not see the MODIFIED event when a modification makes this filter no longer match. The lack of this notification complicates

tracking a service with a filter. The MODIFIED_ENDMATCH event is therefore delivered if the old service properties matched the given filter but the modified properties do not. This event is synchronously delivered after the service properties have been modified.

- UNREGISTERING – A service is in the process of being unregistered. This event is synchronously delivered before the service has completed unregistering. That is, the service object is still valid. The bundle receiving this event must release all references to this service before this method returns.

New service event types can be added in future specifications

5.4   **Stale References**

The Framework must manage the dependencies between bundles. This management is, however, restricted to Framework structures. Bundles must listen to events generated by the Framework to clean up and remove *stale references*.

A stale reference is a reference to a Java object that belongs to the class loader of a bundle that is stopped or is associated with a service object that is unregistered. Standard Java does not provide any generic means to clean up stale references, and bundle developers must analyze their code carefully to ensure that stale references are deleted.

Stale references are potentially harmful because they hinder the Java garbage collector from harvesting the classes, and possibly the instances, of stopped bundles. This may result in significantly increased memory usage and can cause updating native code libraries to fail. Bundles using services are strongly recommended to use either the Service Tracker or Declarative Services.

Service developers can minimize the consequences of (but not completely prevent) stale references by using the following mechanisms:

- Implement service objects using the ServiceFactory interface. The methods in the ServiceFactory interface simplify tracking bundles that use their service objects. See *Service Factory* on page 114.
- Use indirection in the service object implementations. Service objects handed out to other bundles should use a pointer to the actual service object implementation. When the service object becomes invalid, the pointer is set to null, effectively removing the reference to the actual service object.

The behavior of a service that becomes unregistered is undefined. Such services may continue to work properly or throw an exception at their discretion. This type of error should be logged.

5.5   **Filters**

The Framework provides a Filter interface, and uses a filter syntax in the getServiceReferences method that is defined in *Filter Syntax* on page 28. Filter objects can be created by calling BundleContext.createFilter(String) or FrameworkUtil.createFilter(String) with the chosen filter string. The filter supports the following match methods:

- match(ServiceReference) – Match the properties of the Service Reference performing key lookup in a case insensitive way.
- match(Dictionary) – Match the entries in the given Dictionary object performing key lookup in a case insensitive way.
- matchCase(Dictionary) – Match the entries in the given Dictionary object performing key lookup in a case sensitive way.

A Filter object can be used numerous times to determine if the match argument, a ServiceReference object or a Dictionary object, matches the filter string that was used to create the Filter object.

This matching requires comparing the value string in the filter to a target object from the service properties or dictionary. This comparison can be executed with the Comparable interface if the target object's class implements a constructor taking a single String object and the class implements the Comparable interface. That is, if the target object is of class Target, the class Target must implement:

* A constructor Target(String)
* Implement the java.lang.Comparable interface

If the target object does not implement java.lang.Comparable, the =, ~=, <= >= operators must return only true when the objects are equal (using the equals(Object) method). The Target class does not need to be a public class.

The following example shows how a class can verify the ordering of an enumeration with a filter.

```
public class B implements Comparable {
   String keys[] = {"bugs", "daffy", "elmer", "pepe"};
   int     index;

   public B(String s) {
      for ( index=0; index<keys.length; index++ )
        if ( keys[index].equals(s) )
           return;
   }

   public int compareTo( Object other ) {
      B vother = (B) other;
      return index - vother.index;
   }
}
```

The class could be used with the following filter:

```
(!(enum>=elmer))   -> matches bugs and daffy
```

The Filter.toString method must always return the filter string with unnecessary white space removed.

5.6   Service Factory

A Service Factory allows customization of the service object that is returned when a bundle calls BundleContext.getService(ServiceReference).

Often, the service object that is registered by a bundle is returned directly. If, however, the service object that is registered implements the ServiceFactory interface, the Framework must call methods on this object to create a unique service object for each distinct bundle that gets the service.

When the service object is no longer used by a bundle – for example, when that bundle is stopped – then the Framework must notify the ServiceFactory object.

ServiceFactory objects help manage bundle dependencies that are not explicitly managed by the Framework. By binding a returned service object to the requesting bundle, the service can be notified when that bundle ceases to use the service, such as when it is stopped, and release resources associated with providing the service to that bundle.

The ServiceFactory interface defines the following methods:

- getService(Bundle,ServiceRegistration) – This method is called by the Framework if a call is made to BundleContext.getService and the following are true:
  - The ServiceReference argument to BundleContext.getService refers to a service object that implements the ServiceFactory interface.
  - The bundle's usage count of that service object is zero; that is, the bundle currently does not have any dependencies on the service object.

  The call to BundleContext.getService must be routed by the Framework to this method, passing to it the Bundle object of the caller. The Framework must cache the mapping of the requesting bundle-to-service, and return the cached service object to the bundle on future calls to BundleContext.getService, as long as the requesting bundle's usage count of the service object is greater than zero.

  The Framework must check the service object returned by this method. If it is not an instance of all the classes named when the service factory was registered, null is returned to the caller that called getService. This check must be done as specified in *Registering Services* on page 107.
- ungetService(Bundle,ServiceRegistration,Object) – This method is called by the Framework if a call is made to BundleContext.ungetService and the following are true:
  - The ServiceReference argument to BundleContext.ungetService refers to a service object that implements the ServiceFactory interface.
  - The bundle's usage count for that service object must drop to zero after this call returns; that is, the bundle is about to release its last dependency on the service object.

  The call to BundleContext.ungetService must be routed by the Framework to this method so the ServiceFactory object can release the service object previously created.

  Additionally, the cached copy of the previously created service object must be unreferenced by the Framework so it may be garbage collected.

5.7 Releasing Services

In order for a bundle to release a service object, it must remove the dynamic dependency on the bundle that registered the service object. The Bundle
Context interface defines a method to release service objects: ungetService(ServiceReference). A ServiceReference object is passed as the argument of this method.

This method returns a boolean value:

- false if the bundle's usage count of the service object is already zero when the method was called, or the service object has already been unregistered.
- true if the bundle's usage count of the service object was more than zero before this method was called.

5.8 Unregistering Services

The ServiceRegistration interface defines the unregister() method to unregister the service object. This must remove the service object from the Framework service registry. The ServiceReference object for this ServiceRegistration object can no longer be used to access the service object.

The fact that this method is on the ServiceRegistration object ensures that only the bundle holding this object can unregister the associated service object. The bundle that unregisters a service object, however, might not be the same bundle that registered it. As an example, the registering bundle could have passed the ServiceRegistration object to another bundle, endowing that bundle with the responsibility of unregistering the service object. Passing ServiceRegistration objects should be done with caution.

After ServiceRegistration.unregister successfully completes, the service object must be:

- Completely removed from the Framework service registry. Therefore, ServiceReference objects obtained for that service object can no longer be used to access the service object. Calling BundleContext.getService method with the ServiceReference object must return null.
- Unregistered, even if other bundles had dependencies upon it. Bundles must be notified of the unregistration through the publishing of a ServiceEvent object of type ServiceEvent.UNREGISTERING. This event is sent synchronously in order to give bundles the opportunity to release the service object.
After receiving an event of type ServiceEvent.UNREGISTERING, a bundle should release the service object and release any references it has to this object, so that the service object can be garbage collected by the Java VM.
- Released by all using bundles. For each bundle whose usage count for the service object remains greater than zero after all invoked ServiceListener objects have returned, the Framework must set the usage count to zero and release the service object.

5.9 Multiple Version Export Considerations

Allowing multiple bundles to export a package with a given name causes some complications for Framework implementers and bundle programmers: The class name no longer uniquely identifies the exported class. This affects the service registry and permission checking.

5.9.1 Service Registry

Bundles must not be exposed to services for which there are conflicting class loaders. A bundle that gets a service should be able to expect that it can safely cast the service object to any of the associated interfaces or classes under which the service was registered and that it can access. No ClassCastExceptions should occur because those interfaces do not come from the same class loader. The service registry must therefore ensure that bundles can only see services that are *not incompatible* with them. A service is not incompatible with the bundle getting the service when that bundle is not wired to another source class loader for this interface package than the bundle registering the service. That is, it is either wired to the same source class loader or it has no wire for that package at all.

It is paramount that bundles are not accidentally confronted with incompatible services. Therefore, the following methods need to filter ServiceReference objects depending on the incompatibility of the interfaces with the calling bundle. The bundle is identified by the used Bundle Context:

- getServiceReference(String) – Only return a Service Reference that is not incompatible with the calling bundle for the specified interface.
- getServiceReferences(String,String) – Only return Service References that are not incompatible with the calling bundle for the specified interface.

The getAllServiceReferences(String,String) provides access to the service registry without any compatibility restrictions. Services acquired through this method can cause Class Cast Exceptions for the correct class names.

The ServiceReference isAssignableTo(Bundle,String) method is also available to test if the bundle that registered the service referenced by this ServiceReference and the specified bundle are both wired to same source for the specified interface.

5.9.2 Service Events

Service events must only be delivered to event listeners that are not incompatible with the Service Reference.

Some bundles need to listen to all service events regardless the compatibility issues. A new type of ServiceListener is therefore added: AllServiceListener. This is a marker interface; it extends ServiceListener. Listeners that use this marker interface indicate to the Framework that they want to see all services, including services that are incompatible with them.

5.10   Security

5.10.1   Service Permission

A ServicePermission has the following parameters.

- *Target* – Either the interface name or a filter expression for the GET action. The interface name may end with a wildcard to match multiple interface names. See java.security.BasicPermission for a discussion of wildcards. Filters are explained in *Filter Based Permissions* on page 19. The filter expression can additionally test for the service interface name with the objectClass key. Additionally, a service permission can also test for service properties that are part of the service registration. In general, all the service properties are usable in the filter expression. However, when there is a name conflict with the bundle identification properties, then the key can be prefixed with the commercial at sign ('@' 0u0040). For example, @id will refer to a service property with the name id.
- *Action* – Supported actions are:
  - REGISTER – Indicates that the permission holder may register the service object
  - GET – Indicates that the holder may get the service.

When an object is being registered as a service object using Bundle Context.registerService, the registering bundle must have the ServicePermission to register all the named classes. See *Registering Services* on page 107.

When a ServiceReference object is obtained from the service registry using BundleContext.getServiceReference or BundleContext.getServiceReferences, the calling bundle must have the required ServicePermission[ServiceReference, GET] to get the service object for each returned Service Reference. See *Service References* on page 107.

When a service object is obtained from a ServiceReference object using BundleContext.getService(ServiceReference), the calling code must have the required ServicePermission[ServiceReference, GET] to get the service object associated with the Service Reference.

ServicePermission must be used as a filter for the service events received by the Service Listener, as well as for the methods to enumerate services, including Bundle.getRegisteredServices and Bundle.getServicesInUse. The Framework must assure that a bundle must not be able to detect the presence of a service that it does not have permission to access.

5.11   Changes

- Added a section for concurrency and services.
- Added service event description, see *Service Event Types* on page 112.
- Introduced Service Exceptions, see *Service Exceptions* on page 112.
- Introduced new service properties and made SERVICE_PID potentially multi value. See *Service Properties* on page 109.
- Added filters to the Service Permission

6   Framework API

Version 1.5

6.1   org.osgi.framework

Framework Package Version 1.5.

Bundles wishing to use this package must list the package in the Import-Package header of the bundle's manifest. For example:

Import-Package: org.osgi.framework;version="[1.5,2.0)"

6.1.1   Summary

- AdminPermission - A bundle's authority to perform specific privileged administrative operations on or to get sensitive information about a bundle.
- AllServiceListener - A ServiceEvent listener that does not filter based upon package wiring.
- Bundle - An installed bundle in the Framework.
- BundleActivator - Customizes the starting and stopping of a bundle.
- BundleContext - A bundle's execution context within the Framework.
- BundleEvent - An event from the Framework describing a bundle lifecycle change.
- BundleException - A Framework exception used to indicate that a bundle lifecycle problem occurred.
- BundleListener - A BundleEvent listener.
- BundlePermission - A bundle's authority to require or provide a bundle or to receive or attach fragments.
- BundleReference - A reference to a Bundle.
- Configurable - Supports a configuration object.
- Constants - Defines standard names for the OSGi environment system properties, service properties, and Manifest header attribute keys.
- Filter - An RFC 1960-based Filter.
- FrameworkEvent - A general event from the Framework.
- FrameworkListener - A FrameworkEvent listener.
- FrameworkUtil - Framework Utility class.
- InvalidSyntaxException - A Framework exception used to indicate that a filter string has an invalid syntax.
- PackagePermission - A bundle's authority to import or export a package.
- ServiceEvent - An event from the Framework describing a service lifecycle change.
- ServiceException - A service exception used to indicate that a service problem occurred.
- ServiceFactory - Allows services to provide customized service objects in the OSGi environment.
- ServiceListener - A ServiceEvent listener.
- ServicePermission - A bundle's authority to register or get a service.
- ServiceReference - A reference to a service.
- ServiceRegistration - A registered service.
- SynchronousBundleListener - A synchronous BundleEvent listener.
- Version - Version identifier for bundles and packages.

6.1.2   **public final class AdminPermission**
              extends BasicPermission

A bundle's authority to perform specific privileged administrative operations on or to get sensitive information about a bundle. The actions for this permission are:

```
Action              Methods
class               Bundle.loadClass
execute             Bundle.start
                    Bundle.stop
                    StartLevel.setBundleStartLevel
extensionLifecycle  BundleContext.installBundle for extension bundles
                    Bundle.update for extension bundles
                    Bundle.uninstall for extension bundles
lifecycle           BundleContext.installBundle
                    Bundle.update
                    Bundle.uninstall
listener            BundleContext.addBundleListener for SynchronousBundleLis-
tener
                    BundleContext.removeBundleListener for SynchronousBundleL-
istener
metadata            Bundle.getHeaders
                    Bundle.getLocation
resolve             PackageAdmin.refreshPackages
                    PackageAdmin.resolveBundles
resource            Bundle.getResource
                    Bundle.getResources
                    Bundle.getEntry
                    Bundle.getEntryPaths
                    Bundle.findEntries
                    Bundle resource/entry URL creation
startlevel          StartLevel.setStartLevel
                    StartLevel.setInitialBundleStartLevel
context             Bundle.getBundleContext
```

The special action "*" will represent all actions. The resolve action is implied by the class, execute and resource actions.

The name of this permission is a filter expression. The filter gives access to the following attributes:

- signer - A Distinguished Name chain used to sign a bundle. Wildcards in a DN are not matched according to the filter string rules, but according to the rules defined for a DN chain.
- location - The location of a bundle.
- id - The bundle ID of the designated bundle.
- name - The symbolic name of a bundle.

Filter attribute names are processed in a case sensitive manner.

Concurrency Thread-safe

6.1.2.1   **public static final String CLASS = "class"**

The action string class. The class action implies the resolve action.

Since 1.3

6.1.2.2   **public static final String CONTEXT = "context"**

The action string context.

Since 1.4

6.1.2.3   **public static final String EXECUTE = "execute"**

The action string execute. The execute action implies the resolve action.

Since 1.3

6.1.2.4   **public static final String EXTENSIONLIFECYCLE = "extensionLifecycle"**

The action string extensionLifecycle.

Since 1.3

6.1.2.5   **public static final String LIFECYCLE = "lifecycle"**

The action string lifecycle.

Since 1.3

6.1.2.6   **public static final String LISTENER = "listener"**

The action string listener.

Since 1.3

6.1.2.7   **public static final String METADATA = "metadata"**

The action string metadata.

Since 1.3

6.1.2.8   **public static final String RESOLVE = "resolve"**

The action string resolve. The resolve action is implied by the class, execute and resource actions.

Since 1.3

6.1.2.9   **public static final String RESOURCE = "resource"**

The action string resource. The resource action implies the resolve action.

Since 1.3

6.1.2.10   **public static final String STARTLEVEL = "startlevel"**

The action string startlevel.

Since 1.3

6.1.2.11   **public AdminPermission( )**

☐ Creates a new AdminPermission object that matches all bundles and has all actions. Equivalent to AdminPermission("*","*");

6.1.2.12   **public AdminPermission(String filter, String actions)**

filter A filter expression that can use signer, location, id, and name keys. A value of "*" or null matches all bundle. Filter attribute names are processed in a case sensitive manner.

actions class, execute, extensionLifecycle, lifecycle, listener, metadata, resolve , resource, startlevel or context. A value of "*" or null indicates all actions.

☐ Create a new AdminPermission. This constructor must only be used to create a permission that is going to be checked.

Examples:

```
(signer=\*,o=ACME,c=US)
(&(signer=\*,o=ACME,c=US)(name=com.acme.*)(location=http://www.acme.com/bundles/
```

```
*))
  (id>=1)
```

When a signer key is used within the filter expression the signer value must escape the special filter chars ('*', '(', ')').

Null arguments are equivalent to "*".

Throws   IllegalArgumentException – If the filter has an invalid syntax.

6.1.2.13   **public AdminPermission(Bundle bundle, String actions)**

bundle   A bundle.

actions   class, execute, extensionLifecycle, lifecycle, listener, metadata, resolve , resource, startlevel, context.
A value of "*" or null indicates all actions.

□ Creates a new requested AdminPermission object to be used by the code that must perform check-
Permission. AdminPermission objects created with this constructor cannot be added to an Admin-
Permission permission collection.

Since   1.3

6.1.2.14   **public boolean equals(Object obj)**

obj   The object being compared for equality with this object.

□ Determines the equality of two AdminPermission objects.

Returns   true if obj is equivalent to this AdminPermission; false otherwise.

6.1.2.15   **public String getActions( )**

□ Returns the canonical string representation of the AdminPermission actions.

Always returns present AdminPermission actions in the following order: class, execute, extension-
Lifecycle, lifecycle, listener, metadata, resolve, resource, startlevel, context.

Returns   Canonical string representation of the AdminPermission actions.

6.1.2.16   **public int hashCode( )**

□ Returns the hash code value for this object.

Returns   Hash code value for this object.

6.1.2.17   **public boolean implies(Permission p)**

p   The requested permission.

□ Determines if the specified permission is implied by this object. This method throws an exception
if the specified permission was not constructed with a bundle.

This method returns true if the specified permission is an AdminPermission AND

• this object's filter matches the specified permission's bundle ID, bundle symbolic name, bundle
location and bundle signer distinguished name chain OR
• this object's filter is "*"

AND this object's actions include all of the specified permission's actions.

Special case: if the specified permission was constructed with "*" filter, then this method returns
true if this object's filter is "*" and this object's actions include all of the specified permission's
actions

Returns   true if the specified permission is implied by this object; false otherwise.

6.1.2.18   **public PermissionCollection newPermissionCollection( )**

□ Returns a new PermissionCollection object suitable for storing AdminPermissions.

Returns A new PermissionCollection object.

6.1.3 public interface AllServiceListener
extends ServiceListener

A ServiceEvent listener that does not filter based upon package wiring. AllServiceListener is a listener interface that may be implemented by a bundle developer. When a ServiceEvent is fired, it is synchronously delivered to an AllServiceListener. The Framework may deliver ServiceEvent objects to an AllServiceListener out of order and may concurrently call and/or reenter an AllServiceListener.

An AllServiceListener object is registered with the Framework using the BundleContext.addServiceListener method. AllServiceListener objects are called with a ServiceEvent object when a service is registered, modified, or is in the process of unregistering.

ServiceEvent object delivery to AllServiceListener objects is filtered by the filter specified when the listener was registered. If the Java Runtime Environment supports permissions, then additional filtering is done. ServiceEvent objects are only delivered to the listener if the bundle which defines the listener object's class has the appropriate ServicePermission to get the service using at least one of the named classes under which the service was registered.

Unlike normal ServiceListener objects, AllServiceListener objects receive all ServiceEvent objects regardless of whether the package source of the listening bundle is equal to the package source of the bundle that registered the service. This means that the listener may not be able to cast the service object to any of its corresponding service interfaces if the service object is retrieved.

See Also ServiceEvent, ServicePermission

Since 1.3

Concurrency Thread-safe

6.1.4 public interface Bundle

An installed bundle in the Framework.

A Bundle object is the access point to define the lifecycle of an installed bundle. Each bundle installed in the OSGi environment must have an associated Bundle object.

A bundle must have a unique identity, a long, chosen by the Framework. This identity must not change during the lifecycle of a bundle, even when the bundle is updated. Uninstalling and then reinstalling the bundle must create a new unique identity.

A bundle can be in one of six states:

- UNINSTALLED
- INSTALLED
- RESOLVED
- STARTING
- STOPPING
- ACTIVE

Values assigned to these states have no specified ordering; they represent bit values that may be ORed together to determine if a bundle is in one of the valid states.

A bundle should only execute code when its state is one of STARTING, ACTIVE, or STOPPING. An UNINSTALLED bundle can not be set to another state; it is a zombie and can only be reached because references are kept somewhere.

The Framework is the only entity that is allowed to create Bundle objects, and these objects are only valid within the Framework that created them.

Concurrency Thread-safe

6.1.4.1   **public static final int ACTIVE = 32**

The bundle is now running.

A bundle is in the ACTIVE state when it has been successfully started and activated.

The value of ACTIVE is 0x00000020.

6.1.4.2   **public static final int INSTALLED = 2**

The bundle is installed but not yet resolved.

A bundle is in the INSTALLED state when it has been installed in the Framework but is not or can-not be resolved.

This state is visible if the bundle's code dependencies are not resolved. The Framework may attempt to resolve an INSTALLED bundle's code dependencies and move the bundle to the RESOLVED state.

The value of INSTALLED is 0x00000002.

6.1.4.3   **public static final int RESOLVED = 4**

The bundle is resolved and is able to be started.

A bundle is in the RESOLVED state when the Framework has successfully resolved the bundle's code dependencies. These dependencies include:

- The bundle's class path from its Constants.BUNDLE_CLASSPATH Manifest header.
- The bundle's package dependencies from its Constants.EXPORT_PACKAGE and Con-stants.IMPORT_PACKAGE Manifest headers.
- The bundle's required bundle dependencies from its Constants.REQUIRE_BUNDLE Manifest header.
- A fragment bundle's host dependency from its Constants.FRAGMENT_HOST Manifest header.

Note that the bundle is not active yet. A bundle must be put in the RESOLVED state before it can be started. The Framework may attempt to resolve a bundle at any time.

The value of RESOLVED is 0x00000004.

6.1.4.4   **public static final int SIGNERS_ALL = 1**

Request that all certificates used to sign the bundle be returned.

See Also getSignerCertificates(int)

Since 1.5

6.1.4.5   **public static final int SIGNERS_TRUSTED = 2**

Request that only certificates used to sign the bundle that are trusted by the framework be returned.

See Also getSignerCertificates(int)

Since 1.5

6.1.4.6   **public static final int START_ACTIVATION_POLICY = 2**

The bundle start operation must activate the bundle according to the bundle's declared activation policy.

This bit may be set when calling start(int) to notify the framework that the bundle must be acti-vated using the bundle's declared activation policy.

See Also Constants.BUNDLE_ACTIVATIONPOLICY, start(int)

Since 1.4

6.1.4.7   **public static final int START_TRANSIENT = 1**

The bundle start operation is transient and the persistent autostart setting of the bundle is not modified.

This bit may be set when calling start(int) to notify the framework that the autostart setting of the bundle must not be modified. If this bit is not set, then the autostart setting of the bundle is modified.

See Also start(int)

Since 1.4

6.1.4.8   **public static final int STARTING = 8**

The bundle is in the process of starting.

A bundle is in the STARTING state when its start method is active. A bundle must be in this state when the bundle's BundleActivator.start is called. If the BundleActivator.start method completes without exception, then the bundle has successfully started and must move to the ACTIVE state.

If the bundle has a lazy activation policy, then the bundle may remain in this state for some time until the activation is triggered.

The value of STARTING is 0x00000008.

6.1.4.9   **public static final int STOP_TRANSIENT = 1**

The bundle stop is transient and the persistent autostart setting of the bundle is not modified.

This bit may be set when calling stop(int) to notify the framework that the autostart setting of the bundle must not be modified. If this bit is not set, then the autostart setting of the bundle is modified.

See Also stop(int)

Since 1.4

6.1.4.10   **public static final int STOPPING = 16**

The bundle is in the process of stopping.

A bundle is in the STOPPING state when its stop method is active. A bundle must be in this state when the bundle's BundleActivator.stop method is called. When the BundleActivator.stop method completes the bundle is stopped and must move to the RESOLVED state.

The value of STOPPING is 0x00000010.

6.1.4.11   **public static final int UNINSTALLED = 1**

The bundle is uninstalled and may not be used.

The UNINSTALLED state is only visible after a bundle is uninstalled; the bundle is in an unusable state but references to the Bundle object may still be available and used for introspection.

The value of UNINSTALLED is 0x00000001.

6.1.4.12   **public Enumeration findEntries(String path, String filePattern, boolean recurse)**

path The path name in which to look. The path is always relative to the root of this bundle and may begin with "/". A path value of "/" indicates the root of this bundle.

filePattern The file name pattern for selecting entries in the specified path. The pattern is only matched against the last element of the entry path. If the entry is a directory then the trailing "/" is not used for pattern matching. Substring matching is supported, as specified in the Filter specification, using the wild-card character ("*"). If null is specified, this is equivalent to "*" and matches all files.

recurse If true, recurse into subdirectories. Otherwise only return entries from the specified path.

☐ Returns entries in this bundle and its attached fragments. This bundle's class loader is not used to search for entries. Only the contents of this bundle and its attached fragments are searched for the specified entries. If this bundle's state is INSTALLED, this method must attempt to resolve this bundle before attempting to find entries.

This method is intended to be used to obtain configuration, setup, localization and other information from this bundle. This method takes into account that the "contents" of this bundle can be extended with fragments. This "bundle space" is not a namespace with unique members; the same entry name can be present multiple times. This method therefore returns an enumeration of URL objects. These URLs can come from different JARs but have the same path name. This method can either return only entries in the specified path or recurse into subdirectories returning entries in the directory tree beginning at the specified path. Fragments can be attached after this bundle is resolved, possibly changing the set of URLs returned by this method. If this bundle is not resolved, only the entries in the JAR file of this bundle are returned.

Examples:

```
// List all XML files in the OSGI-INF directory and below
Enumeration e = b.findEntries("OSGI-INF", "*.xml", true);

// Find a specific localization file
Enumeration e = b
.findEntries("OSGI-INF/l10n", "bundle_nl_DU.properties", false);
if (e.hasMoreElements())
return (URL) e.nextElement();
```

Note: Jar and zip files are not required to include directory entries. URLs to directory entries will not be returned if the bundle contents do not contain directory entries.

Returns An enumeration of URL objects for each matching entry, or null if an entry could not be found or if the caller does not have the appropriate AdminPermission[this,RESOURCE], and the Java Runtime Environment supports permissions. The URLs are sorted such that entries from this bundle are returned first followed by the entries from attached fragments in ascending bundle id order. If this bundle is a fragment, then only matching entries in this fragment are returned.

Throws IllegalStateException – If this bundle has been uninstalled.

Since 1.3

6.1.4.13   **public BundleContext getBundleContext( )**

☐ Returns this bundle's BundleContext. The returned BundleContext can be used by the caller to act on behalf of this bundle.

If this bundle is not in the STARTING, ACTIVE, or STOPPING states or this bundle is a fragment bundle, then this bundle has no valid BundleContext. This method will return null if this bundle has no valid BundleContext.

Returns A BundleContext for this bundle or null if this bundle has no valid BundleContext.

Throws SecurityException – If the caller does not have the appropriate AdminPermission[this,CON-TEXT], and the Java Runtime Environment supports permissions.

Since 1.4

6.1.4.14   **public long getBundleId( )**

☐ Returns this bundle's unique identifier. This bundle is assigned a unique identifier by the Framework when it was installed in the OSGi environment.

A bundle's unique identifier has the following attributes:

- Is unique and persistent.
- Is a long.
- Its value is not reused for another bundle, even after a bundle is uninstalled.
- Does not change while a bundle remains installed.
- Does not change when a bundle is updated.

This method must continue to return this bundle's unique identifier while this bundle is in the UNINSTALLED state.

Returns The unique identifier of this bundle.

6.1.4.15   **public URL getEntry(String path)**

path The path name of the entry.

☐ Returns a URL to the entry at the specified path in this bundle. This bundle's class loader is not used to search for the entry. Only the contents of this bundle are searched for the entry.

The specified path is always relative to the root of this bundle and may begin with "/". A path value of "/" indicates the root of this bundle.

Note: Jar and zip files are not required to include directory entries. URLs to directory entries will not be returned if the bundle contents do not contain directory entries.

Returns A URL to the entry, or null if no entry could be found or if the caller does not have the appropriate AdminPermission[this,RESOURCE] and the Java Runtime Environment supports permissions.

Throws IllegalStateException – If this bundle has been uninstalled.

Since 1.3

6.1.4.16   **public Enumeration getEntryPaths(String path)**

path The path name for which to return entry paths.

☐ Returns an Enumeration of all the paths (String objects) to entries within this bundle whose longest sub-path matches the specified path. This bundle's class loader is not used to search for entries. Only the contents of this bundle are searched.

The specified path is always relative to the root of this bundle and may begin with a "/". A path value of "/" indicates the root of this bundle.

Returned paths indicating subdirectory paths end with a "/". The returned paths are all relative to the root of this bundle and must not begin with "/".

Note: Jar and zip files are not required to include directory entries. Paths to directory entries will not be returned if the bundle contents do not contain directory entries.

Returns An Enumeration of the entry paths (String objects) or null if no entry could be found or if the caller does not have the appropriate AdminPermission[this,RESOURCE] and the Java Runtime Environment supports permissions.

Throws IllegalStateException – If this bundle has been uninstalled.

Since 1.3

6.1.4.17   **public Dictionary getHeaders( )**

☐ Returns this bundle's Manifest headers and values. This method returns all the Manifest headers and values from the main section of this bundle's Manifest file; that is, all lines prior to the first blank line.

Manifest header names are case-insensitive. The methods of the returned Dictionary object must operate on header names in a case-insensitive manner. If a Manifest header value starts with "%", it must be localized according to the default locale. If no localization is found for a header value, the header value without the leading "%" is returned.

For example, the following Manifest headers and values are included if they are present in the Manifest file:

```
Bundle-Name
Bundle-Vendor
Bundle-Version
Bundle-Description
Bundle-DocURL
Bundle-ContactAddress
```

This method must continue to return Manifest header information while this bundle is in the UNINSTALLED state.

Returns A Dictionary object containing this bundle's Manifest headers and values.

Throws SecurityException – If the caller does not have the appropriate AdminPermission[this,METADA-TA], and the Java Runtime Environment supports permissions.

See Also Constants.BUNDLE_LOCALIZATION

6.1.4.18   **public Dictionary getHeaders(String locale)**

locale The locale name into which the header values are to be localized. If the specified locale is null then the locale returned by java.util.Locale.getDefault is used. If the specified locale is the empty string, this method will return the raw (unlocalized) manifest headers including any leading "%".

☐ Returns this bundle's Manifest headers and values localized to the specified locale.

This method performs the same function as Bundle.getHeaders() except the manifest header values are localized to the specified locale.

If a Manifest header value starts with "%", it must be localized according to the specified locale. If a locale is specified and cannot be found, then the header values must be returned using the default locale. Localizations are searched for in the following order:

```
bn + "_" + Ls + "_" + Cs + "_" + Vs
bn + "_" + Ls + "_" + Cs
bn + "_" + Ls
bn + "_" + Ld + "_" + Cd + "_" + Vd
bn + "_" + Ld + "_" + Cd
bn + "_" + Ld
bn
```

Where bn is this bundle's localization basename, Ls, Cs and Vs are the specified locale (language, country, variant) and Ld, Cd and Vd are the default locale (language, country, variant). If null is specified as the locale string, the header values must be localized using the default locale. If the empty string ("") is specified as the locale string, the header values must not be localized and the raw (unlocalized) header values, including any leading "%", must be returned. If no localization is found for a header value, the header value without the leading "%" is returned.

This method must continue to return Manifest header information while this bundle is in the UNINSTALLED state, however the header values must only be available in the raw and default locale values.

Returns A Dictionary object containing this bundle's Manifest headers and values.

Throws SecurityException – If the caller does not have the appropriate AdminPermission[this,METADA-TA], and the Java Runtime Environment supports permissions.

See Also getHeaders(), Constants.BUNDLE_LOCALIZATION

Since 1.3

6.1.4.19   **public long getLastModified( )**

☐ Returns the time when this bundle was last modified. A bundle is considered to be modified when it is installed, updated or uninstalled.

The time value is the number of milliseconds since January 1, 1970, 00:00:00 GMT.

Returns The time when this bundle was last modified.

Since 1.3

6.1.4.20   **public String getLocation( )**

☐ Returns this bundle's location identifier.

The location identifier is the location passed to BundleContext.installBundle when a bundle is installed. The location identifier does not change while this bundle remains installed, even if this bundle is updated.

This method must continue to return this bundle's location identifier while this bundle is in the UNINSTALLED state.

Returns The string representation of this bundle's location identifier.

Throws SecurityException – If the caller does not have the appropriate AdminPermission[this,METADA-TA], and the Java Runtime Environment supports permissions.

6.1.4.21   **public ServiceReference[] getRegisteredServices( )**

☐ Returns this bundle's ServiceReference list for all services it has registered or null if this bundle has no registered services.

If the Java runtime supports permissions, a ServiceReference object to a service is included in the returned list only if the caller has the ServicePermission to get the service using at least one of the named classes the service was registered under.

The list is valid at the time of the call to this method, however, as the Framework is a very dynamic environment, services can be modified or unregistered at anytime.

Returns An array of ServiceReference objects or null.

Throws IllegalStateException – If this bundle has been uninstalled.

See Also ServiceRegistration, ServiceReference, ServicePermission

6.1.4.22   **public URL getResource(String name)**

name The name of the resource. See ClassLoader.getResource for a description of the format of a resource name.

     ❑ Find the specified resource from this bundle's class loader. This bundle's class loader is called to search for the specified resource. If this bundle's state is INSTALLED, this method must attempt to resolve this bundle before attempting to get the specified resource. If this bundle cannot be resolved, then only this bundle must be searched for the specified resource. Imported packages cannot be searched when this bundle has not been resolved. If this bundle is a fragment bundle then null is returned.

     Note: Jar and zip files are not required to include directory entries. URLs to directory entries will not be returned if the bundle contents do not contain directory entries.

Returns A URL to the named resource, or null if the resource could not be found or if this bundle is a fragment bundle or if the caller does not have the appropriate AdminPermission[this,RESOURCE], and the Java Runtime Environment supports permissions.

Throws IllegalStateException – If this bundle has been uninstalled.

See Also getEntry, findEntries

Since 1.1

6.1.4.23   **public Enumeration getResources(String name) throws IOException**

name The name of the resource. See ClassLoader.getResources for a description of the format of a resource name.

     ❑ Find the specified resources from this bundle's class loader. This bundle's class loader is called to search for the specified resources. If this bundle's state is INSTALLED, this method must attempt to resolve this bundle before attempting to get the specified resources. If this bundle cannot be resolved, then only this bundle must be searched for the specified resources. Imported packages cannot be searched when a bundle has not been resolved. If this bundle is a fragment bundle then null is returned.

     Note: Jar and zip files are not required to include directory entries. URLs to directory entries will not be returned if the bundle contents do not contain directory entries.

Returns An enumeration of URLs to the named resources, or null if the resource could not be found or if this bundle is a fragment bundle or if the caller does not have the appropriate AdminPermission[this,RE-SOURCE], and the Java Runtime Environment supports permissions.

Throws IllegalStateException – If this bundle has been uninstalled.

     IOException – If there is an I/O error.

Since 1.3

6.1.4.24   **public ServiceReference[] getServicesInUse( )**

     ❑ Returns this bundle's ServiceReference list for all services it is using or returns null if this bundle is not using any services. A bundle is considered to be using a service if its use count for that service is greater than zero.

     If the Java Runtime Environment supports permissions, a ServiceReference object to a service is included in the returned list only if the caller has the ServicePermission to get the service using at least one of the named classes the service was registered under.

     The list is valid at the time of the call to this method, however, as the Framework is a very dynamic environment, services can be modified or unregistered at anytime.

Returns An array of ServiceReference objects or null.

Throws IllegalStateException – If this bundle has been uninstalled.

See Also ServiceReference, ServicePermission

6.1.4.25   **public Map getSignerCertificates(int signersType)**

signersType If SIGNERS_ALL is specified, then information on all signers of this bundle is returned. If SIGNERS_TRUSTED is specified, then only information on the signers of this bundle trusted by the framework is returned.

☐ Return the certificates for the signers of this bundle and the certificate chains for those signers.

Returns The X509Certificates for the signers of this bundle and the X509Certificate chains for those signers. The keys of the Map are the X509Certificates of the signers of this bundle. The value for a key is a List containing the X509Certificate chain for the signer. The first item in the List is the signer's X509Certificate which is then followed by the rest of the X509Certificate chain. The returned Map will be empty if there are no signers. The returned Map is the property of the caller who is free to modify it.

Throws IllegalArgumentException – If the specified signersType is not SIGNERS_ALL or SIGNERS_TRUSTED.

Since 1.5

6.1.4.26   **public int getState( )**

☐ Returns this bundle's current state.

A bundle can be in only one state at any time.

Returns An element of UNINSTALLED,INSTALLED, RESOLVED,STARTING, STOPPING,ACTIVE.

6.1.4.27   **public String getSymbolicName( )**

☐ Returns the symbolic name of this bundle as specified by its Bundle-SymbolicName manifest header. The bundle symbolic name together with a version must identify a unique bundle. The bundle symbolic name should be based on the reverse domain name naming convention like that used for java packages.

This method must continue to return this bundle's symbolic name while this bundle is in the UNINSTALLED state.

Returns The symbolic name of this bundle or null if this bundle does not have a symbolic name.

Since 1.3

6.1.4.28   **public Version getVersion( )**

☐ Returns the version of this bundle as specified by its Bundle-Version manifest header. If this bundle does not have a specified version then Version.emptyVersion is returned.

This method must continue to return this bundle's version while this bundle is in the UNIN-STALLED state.

Returns The version of this bundle.

Since 1.5

6.1.4.29   **public boolean hasPermission(Object permission)**

permission The permission to verify.

☐ Determines if this bundle has the specified permissions.

If the Java Runtime Environment does not support permissions, this method always returns true.

permission is of type Object to avoid referencing the java.security.Permission class directly. This is to allow the Framework to be implemented in Java environments which do not support permissions.

If the Java Runtime Environment does support permissions, this bundle and all its resources including embedded JAR files, belong to the same java.security.ProtectionDomain; that is, they must share the same set of permissions.

Returns true if this bundle has the specified permission or the permissions possessed by this bundle imply the specified permission; false if this bundle does not have the specified permission or permission is not an instanceofjava.security.Permission.

Throws IllegalStateException – If this bundle has been uninstalled.

6.1.4.30 **public Class loadClass(String name) throws ClassNotFoundException**

name The name of the class to load.

☐ Loads the specified class using this bundle's class loader.

If this bundle is a fragment bundle then this method must throw a ClassNotFoundException.

If this bundle's state is INSTALLED, this method must attempt to resolve this bundle before attempting to load the class.

If this bundle cannot be resolved, a Framework event of type FrameworkEvent.ERROR is fired containing a BundleException with details of the reason this bundle could not be resolved. This method must then throw a ClassNotFoundException.

If this bundle's state is UNINSTALLED, then an IllegalStateException is thrown.

Returns The Class object for the requested class.

Throws ClassNotFoundException – If no such class can be found or if this bundle is a fragment bundle or if the caller does not have the appropriate AdminPermission[this,CLASS], and the Java Runtime Environment supports permissions.

IllegalStateException – If this bundle has been uninstalled.

Since 1.3

6.1.4.31 **public void start(int options) throws BundleException**

options The options for starting this bundle. See START_TRANSIENT and START_ACTIVATION_POLICY. The Framework must ignore unrecognized options.

☐ Starts this bundle.

If this bundle's state is UNINSTALLED then an IllegalStateException is thrown.

If the Framework implements the optional Start Level service and the current start level is less than this bundle's start level:

- If the START_TRANSIENT option is set, then a BundleException is thrown indicating this bundle cannot be started due to the Framework's current start level.
- Otherwise, the Framework must set this bundle's persistent autostart setting to Started with declared activation if the START_ACTIVATION_POLICY option is set or Started with eager activation if not set.

When the Framework's current start level becomes equal to or more than this bundle's start level, this bundle will be started.

Otherwise, the following steps are required to start this bundle:

1 If this bundle is in the process of being activated or deactivated then this method must wait for activation or deactivation to complete before continuing. If this does not occur in a reasonable time, a BundleException is thrown to indicate this bundle was unable to be started.
2 If this bundle's state is ACTIVE then this method returns immediately.
3 If the START_TRANSIENT option is not set then set this bundle's autostart setting to Started with declared activation if the START_ACTIVATION_POLICY option is set or Started with eager acti-

vation if not set. When the Framework is restarted and this bundle's autostart setting is not Stopped, this bundle must be automatically started.

4 If this bundle's state is not RESOLVED, an attempt is made to resolve this bundle. If the Framework cannot resolve this bundle, a BundleException is thrown.

5 If the START_ACTIVATION_POLICY option is set and this bundle's declared activation policy is lazy then:

If this bundle's state is STARTING then this method returns immediately.

This bundle's state is set to STARTING.

A bundle event of type BundleEvent.LAZY_ACTIVATION is fired.

This method returns immediately and the remaining steps will be followed when this bundle's activation is later triggered.

6 This bundle's state is set to STARTING.

7 A bundle event of type BundleEvent.STARTING is fired.

8 The BundleActivator.start method of this bundle's BundleActivator, if one is specified, is called. If the BundleActivator is invalid or throws an exception then:

This bundle's state is set to STOPPING.

A bundle event of type BundleEvent.STOPPING is fired.

Any services registered by this bundle must be unregistered.

Any services used by this bundle must be released.

Any listeners registered by this bundle must be removed.

This bundle's state is set to RESOLVED.

A bundle event of type BundleEvent.STOPPED is fired.

A BundleException is then thrown.

9 If this bundle's state is UNINSTALLED, because this bundle was uninstalled while the Bundle-Activator.start method was running, a BundleException is thrown.

10 This bundle's state is set to ACTIVE.

11 A bundle event of type BundleEvent.STARTED is fired.

Preconditions

- getState() in { INSTALLED, RESOLVED } or { INSTALLED, RESOLVED, STARTING } if this bundle has a lazy activation policy.

Postconditions, no exceptions thrown

- Bundle autostart setting is modified unless the START_TRANSIENT option was set.
- getState() in { ACTIVE } unless the lazy activation policy was used.
- BundleActivator.start() has been called and did not throw an exception unless the lazy activation policy was used.

Postconditions, when an exception is thrown

- Depending on when the exception occurred, bundle autostart setting is modified unless the START_TRANSIENT option was set.
- getState() not in { STARTING, ACTIVE }.

Throws BundleException – If this bundle could not be started. This could be because a code dependency could not be resolved or the specified BundleActivator could not be loaded or threw an exception or this bundle is a fragment.

IllegalStateException – If this bundle has been uninstalled or this bundle tries to change its own state.

SecurityException – If the caller does not have the appropriate AdminPermission[this,EXECUTE], and the Java Runtime Environment supports permissions.

Since 1.4

6.1.4.32   **public void start( ) throws BundleException**

☐ Starts this bundle with no options.

This method performs the same function as calling start(0).

Throws   BundleException – If this bundle could not be started. This could be because a code dependency could not be resolved or the specified BundleActivator could not be loaded or threw an exception or this bundle is a fragment.

IllegalStateException – If this bundle has been uninstalled or this bundle tries to change its own state.

SecurityException – If the caller does not have the appropriate AdminPermission[this,EXECUTE], and the Java Runtime Environment supports permissions.

See Also   start(int)

6.1.4.33   **public void stop(int options) throws BundleException**

options   The options for stoping this bundle. See STOP_TRANSIENT. The Framework must ignore unrecognized options.

☐ Stops this bundle.

The following steps are required to stop a bundle:

1   If this bundle's state is UNINSTALLED then an IllegalStateException is thrown.
2   If this bundle is in the process of being activated or deactivated then this method must wait for activation or deactivation to complete before continuing. If this does not occur in a reasonable time, a BundleException is thrown to indicate this bundle was unable to be stopped.
3   If the STOP_TRANSIENT option is not set then then set this bundle's persistent autostart setting to to Stopped. When the Framework is restarted and this bundle's autostart setting is Stopped, this bundle must not be automatically started.
4   If this bundle's state is not STARTING or ACTIVE then this method returns immediately.
5   This bundle's state is set to STOPPING.
6   A bundle event of type BundleEvent.STOPPING is fired.
7   If this bundle's state was ACTIVE prior to setting the state to STOPPING, the BundleActivator.stop method of this bundle's BundleActivator, if one is specified, is called. If that method throws an exception, this method must continue to stop this bundle and a BundleException must be thrown after completion of the remaining steps.
8   Any services registered by this bundle must be unregistered.
9   Any services used by this bundle must be released.
10 Any listeners registered by this bundle must be removed.
11 If this bundle's state is UNINSTALLED, because this bundle was uninstalled while the BundleActivator.stop method was running, a BundleException must be thrown.
12 This bundle's state is set to RESOLVED.
13 A bundle event of type BundleEvent.STOPPED is fired.

Preconditions

• getState() in { ACTIVE }.

Postconditions, no exceptions thrown

• Bundle autostart setting is modified unless the STOP_TRANSIENT option was set.
• getState() not in { ACTIVE, STOPPING }.
• BundleActivator.stop has been called and did not throw an exception.

Postconditions, when an exception is thrown

• Bundle autostart setting is modified unless the STOP_TRANSIENT option was set.

Throws BundleException – If this bundle's BundleActivator threw an exception or this bundle is a fragment.

IllegalStateException – If this bundle has been uninstalled or this bundle tries to change its own state.

SecurityException – If the caller does not have the appropriate AdminPermission[this,EXECUTE], and the Java Runtime Environment supports permissions.

Since 1.4

6.1.4.34 **public void stop( ) throws BundleException**

❑ Stops this bundle with no options.

This method performs the same function as calling stop(0).

Throws BundleException – If this bundle's BundleActivator threw an exception or this bundle is a fragment.

IllegalStateException – If this bundle has been uninstalled or this bundle tries to change its own state.

SecurityException – If the caller does not have the appropriate AdminPermission[this,EXECUTE], and the Java Runtime Environment supports permissions.

See Also start(int)

6.1.4.35 **public void uninstall( ) throws BundleException**

❑ Uninstalls this bundle.

This method causes the Framework to notify other bundles that this bundle is being uninstalled, and then puts this bundle into the UNINSTALLED state. The Framework must remove any resources related to this bundle that it is able to remove.

If this bundle has exported any packages, the Framework must continue to make these packages available to their importing bundles until the PackageAdmin.refreshPackages method has been called or the Framework is relaunched.

The following steps are required to uninstall a bundle:

1 If this bundle's state is UNINSTALLED then an IllegalStateException is thrown.
2 If this bundle's state is ACTIVE, STARTING or STOPPING, this bundle is stopped as described in the Bundle.stop method. If Bundle.stop throws an exception, a Framework event of type FrameworkEvent.ERROR is fired containing the exception.
3 This bundle's state is set to UNINSTALLED.
4 A bundle event of type BundleEvent.UNINSTALLED is fired.
5 This bundle and any persistent storage area provided for this bundle by the Framework are removed.

Preconditions

• getState() not in { UNINSTALLED }.

Postconditions, no exceptions thrown

• getState() in { UNINSTALLED }.
• This bundle has been uninstalled.

Postconditions, when an exception is thrown

• getState() not in { UNINSTALLED }.
• This Bundle has not been uninstalled.

Throws BundleException – If the uninstall failed. This can occur if another thread is attempting to change this bundle's state and does not complete in a timely manner.

IllegalStateException – If this bundle has been uninstalled or this bundle tries to change its own state.

SecurityException – If the caller does not have the appropriate AdminPermission[this,LIFECY-CLE], and the Java Runtime Environment supports permissions.

See Also stop()

### 6.1.4.36	public void update(InputStream input) throws BundleException

input The InputStream from which to read the new bundle or null to indicate the Framework must create the input stream from this bundle's Bundle-UpdateLocation Manifest header, if present, or this bundle's original location. The input stream must always be closed when this method completes, even if an exception is thrown.

☐ Updates this bundle from an InputStream.

If the specified InputStream is null, the Framework must create the InputStream from which to read the updated bundle by interpreting, in an implementation dependent manner, this bundle's Bundle-UpdateLocation Manifest header, if present, or this bundle's original location.

If this bundle's state is ACTIVE, it must be stopped before the update and started after the update successfully completes.

If this bundle has exported any packages that are imported by another bundle, these packages must not be updated. Instead, the previous package version must remain exported until the PackageAdmin.refreshPackages method has been has been called or the Framework is relaunched.

The following steps are required to update a bundle:

1 If this bundle's state is UNINSTALLED then an IllegalStateException is thrown.
2 If this bundle's state is ACTIVE, STARTING or STOPPING, this bundle is stopped as described in the Bundle.stop method. If Bundle.stop throws an exception, the exception is rethrown terminating the update.
3 The updated version of this bundle is read from the input stream and installed. If the Framework is unable to install the updated version of this bundle, the original version of this bundle must be restored and a BundleException must be thrown after completion of the remaining steps.
4 This bundle's state is set to INSTALLED.
5 If the updated version of this bundle was successfully installed, a bundle event of type BundleEvent.UPDATED is fired.
6 If this bundle's state was originally ACTIVE, the updated bundle is started as described in the Bundle.start method. If Bundle.start throws an exception, a Framework event of type FrameworkEvent.ERROR is fired containing the exception.

Preconditions

· getState() not in { UNINSTALLED }.

Postconditions, no exceptions thrown

· getState() in { INSTALLED, RESOLVED, ACTIVE }.
· This bundle has been updated.

Postconditions, when an exception is thrown

· getState() in { INSTALLED, RESOLVED, ACTIVE }.
· Original bundle is still used; no update occurred.

Throws BundleException – If the input stream cannot be read or the update fails.

IllegalStateException – If this bundle has been uninstalled or this bundle tries to change its own state.

SecurityException – If the caller does not have the appropriate AdminPermission[this,LIFECY-CLE] for both the current bundle and the updated bundle, and the Java Runtime Environment supports permissions.

See Also stop(), start()

6.1.4.37   **public void update( ) throws BundleException**

□ Updates this bundle.

This method performs the same function as calling update(InputStream) with a null InputStream.

Throws BundleException – If the update fails.

IllegalStateException – If this bundle has been uninstalled or this bundle tries to change its own state.

SecurityException – If the caller does not have the appropriate AdminPermission[this,LIFECY-CLE] for both the current bundle and the updated bundle, and the Java Runtime Environment supports permissions.

See Also update(InputStream)

6.1.5   public interface BundleActivator

Customizes the starting and stopping of a bundle.

BundleActivator is an interface that may be implemented when a bundle is started or stopped. The Framework can create instances of a bundle's BundleActivator as required. If an instance's Bundle-Activator.start method executes successfully, it is guaranteed that the same instance's BundleActivator.stop method will be called when the bundle is to be stopped. The Framework must not concurrently call a BundleActivator object.

BundleActivator is specified through the Bundle-Activator Manifest header. A bundle can only specify a single BundleActivator in the Manifest file. Fragment bundles must not have a BundleActivator. The form of the Manifest header is:

Bundle-Activator: *class-name*

where *class-name*

is a fully qualified Java classname.

The specified BundleActivator class must have a public constructor that takes no parameters so that a BundleActivator object can be created by Class.newInstance().

Concurrency Not Thread-safe

6.1.5.1   **public void start(BundleContext context) throws Exception**

context The execution context of the bundle being started.

□ Called when this bundle is started so the Framework can perform the bundle-specific activities necessary to start this bundle. This method can be used to register services or to allocate any resources that this bundle needs.

This method must complete and return to its caller in a timely manner.

Throws Exception – If this method throws an exception, this bundle is marked as stopped and the Framework will remove this bundle's listeners, unregister all services registered by this bundle, and release all services used by this bundle.

6.1.5.2   **public void stop(BundleContext context) throws Exception**

context The execution context of the bundle being stopped.

☐ Called when this bundle is stopped so the Framework can perform the bundle-specific activities necessary to stop the bundle. In general, this method should undo the work that the BundleActivator.start method started. There should be no active threads that were started by this bundle when this bundle returns. A stopped bundle must not call any Framework objects.

This method must complete and return to its caller in a timely manner.

Throws Exception – If this method throws an exception, the bundle is still marked as stopped, and the Framework will remove the bundle's listeners, unregister all services registered by the bundle, and release all services used by the bundle.

6.1.6   public interface BundleContext

A bundle's execution context within the Framework. The context is used to grant access to other methods so that this bundle can interact with the Framework.

BundleContext methods allow a bundle to:

- Subscribe to events published by the Framework.
- Register service objects with the Framework service registry.
- Retrieve ServiceReferences from the Framework service registry.
- Get and release service objects for a referenced service.
- Install new bundles in the Framework.
- Get the list of bundles installed in the Framework.
- Get the Bundle object for a bundle.
- Create File objects for files in a persistent storage area provided for the bundle by the Framework.

A BundleContext object will be created and provided to the bundle associated with this context when it is started using the BundleActivator.start method. The same BundleContext object will be passed to the bundle associated with this context when it is stopped using the BundleActivator.stop method. A BundleContext object is generally for the private use of its associated bundle and is not meant to be shared with other bundles in the OSGi environment.

The Bundle object associated with a BundleContext object is called the context bundle.

The BundleContext object is only valid during the execution of its context bundle; that is, during the period from when the context bundle is in the STARTING, STOPPING, and ACTIVE bundle states. If the BundleContext object is used subsequently, an IllegalStateException must be thrown. The BundleContext object must never be reused after its context bundle is stopped.

The Framework is the only entity that can create BundleContext objects and they are only valid within the Framework that created them.

Concurrency Thread-safe

6.1.6.1   **public void addBundleListener(BundleListener listener)**

listener The BundleListener to be added.

☐ Adds the specified BundleListener object to the context bundle's list of listeners if not already present. BundleListener objects are notified when a bundle has a lifecycle state change.

If the context bundle's list of listeners already contains a listener l such that (l==listener), this method does nothing.

Throws IllegalStateException – If this BundleContext is no longer valid.

SecurityException – If listener is a SynchronousBundleListener and the caller does not have the appropriate AdminPermission[context bundle,LISTENER], and the Java Runtime Environment supports permissions.

See Also BundleEvent, BundleListener

6.1.6.2   **public void addFrameworkListener(FrameworkListener listener)**

listener The FrameworkListener object to be added.

☐ Adds the specified FrameworkListener object to the context bundle's list of listeners if not already present. FrameworkListeners are notified of general Framework events.

If the context bundle's list of listeners already contains a listener l such that (l==listener), this method does nothing.

Throws IllegalStateException – If this BundleContext is no longer valid.

See Also FrameworkEvent, FrameworkListener

6.1.6.3   **public void addServiceListener(ServiceListener listener, String filter) throws InvalidSyntaxException**

listener The ServiceListener object to be added.

filter The filter criteria.

☐ Adds the specified ServiceListener object with the specified filter to the context bundle's list of listeners. See Filter for a description of the filter syntax. ServiceListener objects are notified when a service has a lifecycle state change.

If the context bundle's list of listeners already contains a listener l such that (l==listener), then this method replaces that listener's filter (which may be null) with the specified one (which may be null).

The listener is called if the filter criteria is met. To filter based upon the class of the service, the filter should reference the Constants.OBJECTCLASS property. If filter is null, all services are considered to match the filter.

When using a filter, it is possible that the ServiceEvents for the complete lifecycle of a service will not be delivered to the listener. For example, if the filter only matches when the property x has the value 1, the listener will not be called if the service is registered with the property x not set to the value 1. Subsequently, when the service is modified setting property x to the value 1, the filter will match and the listener will be called with a ServiceEvent of type MODIFIED. Thus, the listener will not be called with a ServiceEvent of type REGISTERED.

If the Java Runtime Environment supports permissions, the ServiceListener object will be notified of a service event only if the bundle that is registering it has the ServicePermission to get the service using at least one of the named classes the service was registered under.

Throws InvalidSyntaxException – If filter contains an invalid filter string that cannot be parsed.

IllegalStateException – If this BundleContext is no longer valid.

See Also ServiceEvent, ServiceListener, ServicePermission

6.1.6.4   **public void addServiceListener(ServiceListener listener)**

listener The ServiceListener object to be added.

☐ Adds the specified ServiceListener object to the context bundle's list of listeners.

This method is the same as calling BundleContext.addServiceListener(ServiceListener listener, String filter) with filter set to null.

Throws IllegalStateException – If this BundleContext is no longer valid.

See Also   addServiceListener(ServiceListener, String)

6.1.6.5   **public Filter createFilter(String filter) throws InvalidSyntaxException**

filter   The filter string.

□   Creates a Filter object. This Filter object may be used to match a ServiceReference object or a Dictionary object.

If the filter cannot be parsed, an InvalidSyntaxException will be thrown with a human readable message where the filter became unparsable.

Returns   A Filter object encapsulating the filter string.

Throws   InvalidSyntaxException – If filter contains an invalid filter string that cannot be parsed.

NullPointerException – If filter is null.

IllegalStateException – If this BundleContext is no longer valid.

See Also   Framework specification for a description of the filter string syntax., FrameworkUtil.createFilter(String)

Since   1.1

6.1.6.6   **public ServiceReference[] getAllServiceReferences(String clazz, String filter) throws InvalidSyntaxException**

clazz   The class name with which the service was registered or null for all services.

filter   The filter expression or null for all services.

□   Returns an array of ServiceReference objects. The returned array of ServiceReference objects contains services that were registered under the specified class and match the specified filter expression.

The list is valid at the time of the call to this method. However since the Framework is a very dynamic environment, services can be modified or unregistered at any time.

The specified filter expression is used to select the registered services whose service properties contain keys and values which satisfy the filter expression. See Filter for a description of the filter syntax. If the specified filter is null, all registered services are considered to match the filter. If the specified filter expression cannot be parsed, an InvalidSyntaxException will be thrown with a human readable message where the filter became unparsable.

The result is an array of ServiceReference objects for all services that meet all of the following conditions:

- If the specified class name, clazz, is not null, the service must have been registered with the specified class name. The complete list of class names with which a service was registered is available from the service's objectClass property.
- If the specified filter is not null, the filter expression must match the service.
- If the Java Runtime Environment supports permissions, the caller must have ServicePermission with the GET action for at least one of the class names under which the service was registered.

Returns   An array of ServiceReference objects or null if no services are registered which satisfy the search.

Throws   InvalidSyntaxException – If the specified filter contains an invalid filter expression that cannot be parsed.

IllegalStateException – If this BundleContext is no longer valid.

Since   1.3

6.1.6.7   **public Bundle getBundle( )**

□   Returns the Bundle object associated with this BundleContext. This bundle is called the context bundle.

Returns   The Bundle object associated with this BundleContext.

Throws   IllegalStateException – If this BundleContext is no longer valid.

6.1.6.8   **public Bundle getBundle(long id)**

id   The identifier of the bundle to retrieve.

□   Returns the bundle with the specified identifier.

Returns   A Bundle object or null if the identifier does not match any installed bundle.

6.1.6.9   **public Bundle[] getBundles( )**

□   Returns a list of all installed bundles.

This method returns a list of all bundles installed in the OSGi environment at the time of the call to this method. However, since the Framework is a very dynamic environment, bundles can be installed or uninstalled at anytime.

Returns   An array of Bundle objects, one object per installed bundle.

6.1.6.10   **public File getDataFile(String filename)**

filename   A relative name to the file to be accessed.

□   Creates a File object for a file in the persistent storage area provided for the bundle by the Framework. This method will return null if the platform does not have file system support.

A File object for the base directory of the persistent storage area provided for the context bundle by the Framework can be obtained by calling this method with an empty string as filename.

If the Java Runtime Environment supports permissions, the Framework will ensure that the bundle has the java.io.FilePermission with actions read,write,delete for all files (recursively) in the persistent storage area provided for the context bundle.

Returns   A File object that represents the requested file or null if the platform does not have file system support.

Throws   IllegalStateException – If this BundleContext is no longer valid.

6.1.6.11   **public String getProperty(String key)**

key   The name of the requested property.

□   Returns the value of the specified property. If the key is not found in the Framework properties, the system properties are then searched. The method returns null if the property is not found.

All bundles must have permission to read properties whose names start with "org.osgi.".

Returns   The value of the requested property, or null if the property is undefined.

Throws   SecurityException – If the caller does not have the appropriate PropertyPermission to read the property, and the Java Runtime Environment supports permissions.

6.1.6.12   **public Object getService(ServiceReference reference)**

reference   A reference to the service.

□   Returns the service object referenced by the specified ServiceReference object.

A bundle's use of a service is tracked by the bundle's use count of that service. Each time a service's service object is returned by getService(ServiceReference) the context bundle's use count for that service is incremented by one. Each time the service is released by ungetService(ServiceReference) the context bundle's use count for that service is decremented by one.

When a bundle's use count for a service drops to zero, the bundle should no longer use that service.

This method will always return null when the service associated with this reference has been unregistered.

The following steps are required to get the service object:

1 If the service has been unregistered, null is returned.
2 The context bundle's use count for this service is incremented by one.
3 If the context bundle's use count for the service is currently one and the service was registered with an object implementing the ServiceFactory interface, the ServiceFactory.get-Service(Bundle, ServiceRegistration) method is called to create a service object for the context bundle. This service object is cached by the Framework. While the context bundle's use count for the service is greater than zero, subsequent calls to get the services's service object for the context bundle will return the cached service object.
   If the service object returned by the ServiceFactory object is not an instanceof all the classes named when the service was registered or the ServiceFactory object throws an exception, null is returned and a Framework event of type FrameworkEvent.ERROR containing a ServiceException describing the error is fired.
4 The service object for the service is returned.

Returns A service object for the service associated with reference or null if the service is not registered, the service object returned by a ServiceFactory does not implement the classes under which it was registered or the ServiceFactory threw an exception.

Throws SecurityException – If the caller does not have the ServicePermission to get the service using at least one of the named classes the service was registered under and the Java Runtime Environment supports permissions.

IllegalStateException – If this BundleContext is no longer valid.

IllegalArgumentException – If the specified ServiceReference was not created by the same framework instance as this BundleContext.

See Also ungetService(ServiceReference), ServiceFactory

6.1.6.13   **public ServiceReference getServiceReference(String clazz)**

clazz The class name with which the service was registered.

☐ Returns a ServiceReference object for a service that implements and was registered under the specified class.

The returned ServiceReference object is valid at the time of the call to this method. However as the Framework is a very dynamic environment, services can be modified or unregistered at any time.

This method is the same as calling BundleContext.getServiceReferences(String, String) with a null filter expression. It is provided as a convenience for when the caller is interested in any service that implements the specified class.

If multiple such services exist, the service with the highest ranking (as specified in its Constants.SERVICE_RANKING property) is returned.

If there is a tie in ranking, the service with the lowest service ID (as specified in its Constants.SERVICE_ID property); that is, the service that was registered first is returned.

Returns A ServiceReference object, or null if no services are registered which implement the named class.

Throws IllegalStateException – If this BundleContext is no longer valid.

See Also getServiceReferences(String, String)

6.1.6.14   **public ServiceReference[] getServiceReferences(String clazz, String filter) throws InvalidSyntaxException**

clazz   The class name with which the service was registered or null for all services.

filter   The filter expression or null for all services.

☐   Returns an array of ServiceReference objects. The returned array of ServiceReference objects contains services that were registered under the specified class, match the specified filter expression, and the packages for the class names under which the services were registered match the context bundle's packages as defined in ServiceReference.isAssignableTo(Bundle, String).

The list is valid at the time of the call to this method. However since the Framework is a very dynamic environment, services can be modified or unregistered at any time.

The specified filter expression is used to select the registered services whose service properties contain keys and values which satisfy the filter expression. See Filter for a description of the filter syntax. If the specified filter is null, all registered services are considered to match the filter. If the specified filter expression cannot be parsed, an InvalidSyntaxException will be thrown with a human readable message where the filter became unparsable.

The result is an array of ServiceReference objects for all services that meet all of the following conditions:

- If the specified class name, clazz, is not null, the service must have been registered with the specified class name. The complete list of class names with which a service was registered is available from the service's objectClass property.
- If the specified filter is not null, the filter expression must match the service.
- If the Java Runtime Environment supports permissions, the caller must have ServicePermission with the GET action for at least one of the class names under which the service was registered.
- For each class name with which the service was registered, calling ServiceReference.isAssignableTo(Bundle, String) with the context bundle and the class name on the service's ServiceReference object must return true

Returns   An array of ServiceReference objects or null if no services are registered which satisfy the search.

Throws   InvalidSyntaxException – If the specified filter contains an invalid filter expression that cannot be parsed.

IllegalStateException – If this BundleContext is no longer valid.

6.1.6.15   **public Bundle installBundle(String location, InputStream input) throws BundleException**

location   The location identifier of the bundle to install.

input   The InputStream object from which this bundle will be read or null to indicate the Framework must create the input stream from the specified location identifier. The input stream must always be closed when this method completes, even if an exception is thrown.

☐   Installs a bundle from the specified InputStream object.

If the specified InputStream is null, the Framework must create the InputStream from which to read the bundle by interpreting, in an implementation dependent manner, the specified location.

The specified location identifier will be used as the identity of the bundle. Every installed bundle is uniquely identified by its location identifier which is typically in the form of a URL.

The following steps are required to install a bundle:

1   If a bundle containing the same location identifier is already installed, the Bundle object for that bundle is returned.
2   The bundle's content is read from the input stream. If this fails, a BundleException is thrown.

3   The bundle's associated resources are allocated. The associated resources minimally consist of a unique identifier and a persistent storage area if the platform has file system support. If this step fails, a BundleException is thrown.

4   The bundle's state is set to INSTALLED.

5   A bundle event of type BundleEvent.INSTALLED is fired.

6   The Bundle object for the newly or previously installed bundle is returned.

Postconditions, no exceptions thrown

- getState() in { INSTALLED, RESOLVED }.
- Bundle has a unique ID.

Postconditions, when an exception is thrown

- Bundle is not installed and no trace of the bundle exists.

Returns   The Bundle object of the installed bundle.

Throws   BundleException – If the input stream cannot be read or the installation failed.

SecurityException – If the caller does not have the appropriate AdminPermission[installed bundle,LIFECYCLE], and the Java Runtime Environment supports permissions.

IllegalStateException – If this BundleContext is no longer valid.

6.1.6.16   **public Bundle installBundle(String location) throws BundleException**

location   The location identifier of the bundle to install.

☐   Installs a bundle from the specified location identifier.

This method performs the same function as calling installBundle(String,InputStream) with the specified location identifier and a null InputStream.

Returns   The Bundle object of the installed bundle.

Throws   BundleException – If the installation failed.

SecurityException – If the caller does not have the appropriate AdminPermission[installed bundle,LIFECYCLE], and the Java Runtime Environment supports permissions.

IllegalStateException – If this BundleContext is no longer valid.

See Also   installBundle(String, InputStream)

6.1.6.17   **public ServiceRegistration registerService(String[] clazzes, Object service, Dictionary properties)**

clazzes   The class names under which the service can be located. The class names in this array will be stored in the service's properties under the key Constants.OBJECTCLASS.

service   The service object or a ServiceFactory object.

properties   The properties for this service. The keys in the properties object must all be String objects. See Constants for a list of standard service property keys. Changes should not be made to this object after calling this method. To update the service's properties the ServiceRegistration.setProperties method must be called. The set of properties may be null if the service has no properties.

☐   Registers the specified service object with the specified properties under the specified class names into the Framework. A ServiceRegistration object is returned. The ServiceRegistration object is for the private use of the bundle registering the service and should not be shared with other bundles. The registering bundle is defined to be the context bundle. Other bundles can locate the service by using either the getServiceReferences or getServiceReference method.

A bundle can register a service object that implements the ServiceFactory interface to have more flexibility in providing service objects to other bundles.

The following steps are required to register a service:

1 If service is not a ServiceFactory, an IllegalArgumentException is thrown if service is not an instanceof all the specified class names.
2 The Framework adds the following service properties to the service properties from the specified Dictionary (which may be null):
   A property named Constants.SERVICE_ID identifying the registration number of the service
   A property named Constants.OBJECTCLASS containing all the specified classes.
   Properties with these names in the specified Dictionary will be ignored.
3 The service is added to the Framework service registry and may now be used by other bundles.
4 A service event of type ServiceEvent.REGISTERED is fired.
5 A ServiceRegistration object for this registration is returned.

Returns A ServiceRegistration object for use by the bundle registering the service to update the service's properties or to unregister the service.

Throws IllegalArgumentException – If one of the following is true:
service is null.
service is not a ServiceFactory object and is not an instance of all the named classes in clazzes.
properties contains case variants of the same key name.

SecurityException – If the caller does not have the ServicePermission to register the service for all the named classes and the Java Runtime Environment supports permissions.

IllegalStateException – If this BundleContext is no longer valid.

See Also ServiceRegistration, ServiceFactory

6.1.6.18 **public ServiceRegistration registerService(String clazz, Object service, Dictionary properties)**

clazz The class name under which the service can be located.

service The service object or a ServiceFactory object.

properties The properties for this service.

☐ Registers the specified service object with the specified properties under the specified class name with the Framework.

This method is otherwise identical to registerService(String[], Object, Dictionary) and is provided as a convenience when service will only be registered under a single class name. Note that even in this case the value of the service's Constants.OBJECTCLASS property will be an array of string, rather than just a single string.

Returns A ServiceRegistration object for use by the bundle registering the service to update the service's properties or to unregister the service.

Throws IllegalStateException – If this BundleContext is no longer valid.

See Also registerService(String[], Object, Dictionary)

6.1.6.19 **public void removeBundleListener(BundleListener listener)**

listener The BundleListener object to be removed.

☐ Removes the specified BundleListener object from the context bundle's list of listeners.

If listener is not contained in the context bundle's list of listeners, this method does nothing.

Throws IllegalStateException – If this BundleContext is no longer valid.

SecurityException – If listener is a SynchronousBundleListener and the caller does not have the appropriate AdminPermission[context bundle,LISTENER], and the Java Runtime Environment supports permissions.

6.1.6.20   **public void removeFrameworkListener(FrameworkListener listener)**

listener The FrameworkListener object to be removed.

☐ Removes the specified FrameworkListener object from the context bundle's list of listeners.

If listener is not contained in the context bundle's list of listeners, this method does nothing.

Throws IllegalStateException – If this BundleContext is no longer valid.

6.1.6.21   **public void removeServiceListener(ServiceListener listener)**

listener The ServiceListener to be removed.

☐ Removes the specified ServiceListener object from the context bundle's list of listeners.

If listener is not contained in this context bundle's list of listeners, this method does nothing.

Throws IllegalStateException – If this BundleContext is no longer valid.

6.1.6.22   **public boolean ungetService(ServiceReference reference)**

reference A reference to the service to be released.

☐ Releases the service object referenced by the specified ServiceReference object. If the context bundle's use count for the service is zero, this method returns false. Otherwise, the context bundle's use count for the service is decremented by one.

The service's service object should no longer be used and all references to it should be destroyed when a bundle's use count for the service drops to zero.

The following steps are required to unget the service object:

1 If the context bundle's use count for the service is zero or the service has been unregistered, false is returned.
2 The context bundle's use count for this service is decremented by one.
3 If the context bundle's use count for the service is currently zero and the service was registered with a ServiceFactory object, the ServiceFactory.ungetService(Bundle, ServiceRegistration, Object) method is called to release the service object for the context bundle.
4 true is returned.

Returns false if the context bundle's use count for the service is zero or if the service has been unregistered; true otherwise.

Throws IllegalStateException – If this BundleContext is no longer valid.

IllegalArgumentException – If the specified ServiceReference was not created by the same framework instance as this BundleContext.

See Also getService, ServiceFactory

6.1.7   **public class BundleEvent**
                   extends EventObject

An event from the Framework describing a bundle lifecycle change.

BundleEvent objects are delivered to SynchronousBundleListeners and BundleListeners when a change occurs in a bundle's lifecycle. A type code is used to identify the event type for future extendability.

OSGi Alliance reserves the right to extend the set of types.

See Also BundleListener, SynchronousBundleListener

Concurrency Immutable

6.1.7.1   **public static final int INSTALLED = 1**

The bundle has been installed.

See Also BundleContext.installBundle(String)

6.1.7.2   **public static final int LAZY_ACTIVATION = 512**

The bundle will be lazily activated.

The bundle has a lazy activation policy and is waiting to be activated. It is now in the STARTING state and has a valid BundleContext. This event is only delivered to SynchronousBundleListeners. It is not delivered to BundleListeners.

Since 1.4

6.1.7.3   **public static final int RESOLVED = 32**

The bundle has been resolved.

See Also Bundle.RESOLVED

Since 1.3

6.1.7.4   **public static final int STARTED = 2**

The bundle has been started.

The bundle's BundleActivator start method has been executed if the bundle has a bundle activator class.

See Also Bundle.start()

6.1.7.5   **public static final int STARTING = 128**

The bundle is about to be activated.

The bundle's BundleActivator start method is about to be called if the bundle has a bundle activator class. This event is only delivered to SynchronousBundleListeners. It is not delivered to BundleListeners.

See Also Bundle.start()

Since 1.3

6.1.7.6   **public static final int STOPPED = 4**

The bundle has been stopped.

The bundle's BundleActivator stop method has been executed if the bundle has a bundle activator class.

See Also Bundle.stop()

6.1.7.7   **public static final int STOPPING = 256**

The bundle is about to deactivated.

The bundle's BundleActivator stop method is about to be called if the bundle has a bundle activator class. This event is only delivered to SynchronousBundleListeners. It is not delivered to BundleListeners.

See Also Bundle.stop()

Since 1.3

6.1.7.8   **public static final int UNINSTALLED = 16**

The bundle has been uninstalled.

See Also Bundle.uninstall

6.1.7.9   **public static final int UNRESOLVED = 64**

The bundle has been unresolved.

See Also   Bundle. INSTALLED

Since   1.3

6.1.7.10   **public static final int UPDATED = 8**

The bundle has been updated.

See Also   Bundle. update ()

6.1.7.11   **public BundleEvent(int type, Bundle bundle)**

type   The event type.

bundle   The bundle which had a lifecycle change.

❑   Creates a bundle event of the specified type.

6.1.7.12   **public Bundle getBundle( )**

❑   Returns the bundle which had a lifecycle change. This bundle is the source of the event.

Returns   The bundle that had a change occur in its lifecycle.

6.1.7.13   **public int getType( )**

❑   Returns the type of lifecyle event. The type values are:

- INSTALLED
- RESOLVED
- LAZY_ACTIVATION
- STARTING
- STARTED
- STOPPING
- STOPPED
- UPDATED
- UNRESOLVED
- UNINSTALLED

Returns   The type of lifecycle event.

6.1.8   public class BundleException
extends Exception

A Framework exception used to indicate that a bundle lifecycle problem occurred.

A BundleException object is created by the Framework to denote an exception condition in the life-cycle of a bundle. BundleExceptions should not be created by bundle developers. A type code is used to identify the exception type for future extendability.

OSGi Alliance reserves the right to extend the set of types.

This exception conforms to the general purpose exception chaining mechanism.

6.1.8.1   **public static final int ACTIVATOR_ERROR = 5**

The bundle activator was in error.

Since   1.5

6.1.8.2   **public static final int DUPLICATE_BUNDLE_ERROR = 9**

The install or update operation failed because another already installed bundle has the same symbolic name and version.

Since 1.5

6.1.8.3   **public static final int INVALID_OPERATION = 2**

The operation was invalid.

Since 1.5

6.1.8.4   **public static final int MANIFEST_ERROR = 3**

The bundle manifest was in error.

Since 1.5

6.1.8.5   **public static final int NATIVECODE_ERROR = 8**

The bundle could not be resolved due to an error with the Bundle-NativeCode header.

Since 1.5

6.1.8.6   **public static final int RESOLVE_ERROR = 4**

The bundle was not resolved.

Since 1.5

6.1.8.7   **public static final int SECURITY_ERROR = 6**

The operation failed due to insufficient permissions.

Since 1.5

6.1.8.8   **public static final int START_TRANSIENT_ERROR = 10**

The start transient operation failed because the start level of the bundle is greater than the current framework start level

Since 1.5

6.1.8.9   **public static final int STATECHANGE_ERROR = 7**

The operation failed to complete the requested lifecycle state change.

Since 1.5

6.1.8.10   **public static final int UNSPECIFIED = 0**

No exception type is unspecified.

Since 1.5

6.1.8.11   **public static final int UNSUPPORTED_OPERATION = 1**

The operation was unsupported.

Since 1.5

6.1.8.12   **public BundleException(String msg, Throwable cause)**

msg The associated message.

cause The cause of this exception.

□ Creates a BundleException with the specified message and exception cause.

6.1.8.13   **public BundleException(String msg)**

msg The message.

☐ Creates a BundleException with the specified message.

6.1.8.14   **public BundleException(String msg, int type, Throwable cause)**

msg The associated message.

type The type for this exception.

cause The cause of this exception.

☐ Creates a BundleException with the specified message, type and exception cause.

Since 1.5

6.1.8.15   **public BundleException(String msg, int type)**

msg The message.

type The type for this exception.

☐ Creates a BundleException with the specified message and type.

Since 1.5

6.1.8.16   **public Throwable getCause( )**

☐ Returns the cause of this exception or null if no cause was set.

Returns The cause of this exception or null if no cause was set.

Since 1.3

6.1.8.17   **public Throwable getNestedException( )**

☐ Returns the cause of this exception or null if no cause was specified when this exception was created.

This method predates the general purpose exception chaining mechanism. The getCause() method is now the preferred means of obtaining this information.

Returns The result of calling getCause().

6.1.8.18   **public int getType( )**

☐ Returns the type for this exception or UNSPECIFIED if the type was unspecified or unknown.

Returns The type of this exception.

Since 1.5

6.1.8.19   **public Throwable initCause(Throwable cause)**

cause The cause of this exception.

☐ Initializes the cause of this exception to the specified value.

Returns This exception.

Throws IllegalArgumentException – If the specified cause is this exception.

IllegalStateException – If the cause of this exception has already been set.

Since 1.3

6.1.9
public interface BundleListener
extends EventListener

A BundleEvent listener. BundleListener is a listener interface that may be implemented by a bundle developer. When a BundleEvent is fired, it is asynchronously delivered to a BundleListener. The Framework delivers BundleEvent objects to a BundleListener in order and must not concurrently call a BundleListener.

A BundleListener object is registered with the Framework using the BundleContext.addBundleListener method. BundleListeners are called with a BundleEvent object when a bundle has been installed, resolved, started, stopped, updated, unresolved, or uninstalled.

See Also BundleEvent

Concurrency Not Thread-safe

6.1.9.1
public void bundleChanged(BundleEvent event)

event The BundleEvent.

□ Receives notification that a bundle has had a lifecycle change.

6.1.10
public final class BundlePermission
extends BasicPermission

A bundle's authority to require or provide a bundle or to receive or attach fragments.

A bundle symbolic name defines a unique fully qualified name. Wildcards may be used.

```
name ::= <symbolic name> | <symbolic name ending in ".*"> | *
```

Examples:

```
org.osgi.example.bundle
org.osgi.example.*
*
```

BundlePermission has four actions: provide, require,host, and fragment. The provide action implies the require action.

Since 1.3

Concurrency Thread-safe

6.1.10.1
public static final String FRAGMENT = "fragment"

The action string fragment.

6.1.10.2
public static final String HOST = "host"

The action string host.

6.1.10.3
public static final String PROVIDE = "provide"

The action string provide. The provide action implies the require action.

6.1.10.4
public static final String REQUIRE = "require"

The action string require. The require action is implied by the provide action.

6.1.10.5
public BundlePermission(String symbolicName, String actions)

symbolicName The bundle symbolic name.

actions provide,require, host,fragment (canonical order).

□ Defines the authority to provide and/or require and or specify a host fragment symbolic name within the OSGi environment.

Bundle Permissions are granted over all possible versions of a bundle. A bundle that needs to provide a bundle must have the appropriate BundlePermission for the symbolic name; a bundle that requires a bundle must have the appropriate BundlePermssion for that symbolic name; a bundle that specifies a fragment host must have the appropriate BundlePermission for that symbolic name.

6.1.10.6   **public boolean equals(Object obj)**

obj The object to test for equality with this BundlePermission object.

□ Determines the equality of two BundlePermission objects. This method checks that specified bundle has the same bundle symbolic name and BundlePermission actions as this BundlePermission object.

Returns true if obj is a BundlePermission, and has the same bundle symbolic name and actions as this BundlePermission object; false otherwise.

6.1.10.7   **public String getActions( )**

□ Returns the canonical string representation of the BundlePermission actions.

Always returns present BundlePermission actions in the following order: provide, require, host, fragment.

Returns Canonical string representation of the BundlePermission actions.

6.1.10.8   **public int hashCode( )**

□ Returns the hash code value for this object.

Returns A hash code value for this object.

6.1.10.9   **public boolean implies(Permission p)**

p The requested permission.

□ Determines if the specified permission is implied by this object.

This method checks that the symbolic name of the target is implied by the symbolic name of this object. The list of BundlePermission actions must either match or allow for the list of the target object to imply the target BundlePermission action.

The permission to provide a bundle implies the permission to require the named symbolic name.

```
x.y.*,"provide" -> x.y.z,"provide" is true
*,"require" -> x.y, "require"     is true
*,"provide" -> x.y, "require"     is true
x.y,"provide" -> x.y.z, "provide" is false
```

Returns true if the specified BundlePermission action is implied by this object; false otherwise.

6.1.10.10   **public PermissionCollection newPermissionCollection( )**

□ Returns a new PermissionCollection object suitable for storing BundlePermission objects.

Returns A new PermissionCollection object.

6.1.11   public interface BundleReference

A reference to a Bundle.

Since 1.5

Concurrency Thread-safe

6.1.11.1   **public Bundle getBundle( )**

□ Returns the Bundle object associated with this BundleReference.

Returns The Bundle object associated with this BundleReference.

6.1.12   public interface Configurable

Supports a configuration object.

Configurable is an interface that should be used by a bundle developer in support of a configurable service. Bundles that need to configure a service may test to determine if the service object is an instanceof Configurable.

Deprecated As of 1.2. Please use Configuration Admin service.

6.1.12.1   **public Object getConfigurationObject( )**

□ Returns this service's configuration object.

Services implementing Configurable should take care when returning a service configuration object since this object is probably sensitive.

If the Java Runtime Environment supports permissions, it is recommended that the caller is checked for some appropriate permission before returning the configuration object.

Returns The configuration object for this service.

Throws SecurityException – If the caller does not have an appropriate permission and the Java Runtime Environment supports permissions.

Deprecated As of 1.2. Please use Configuration Admin service.

6.1.13   public interface Constants

Defines standard names for the OSGi environment system properties, service properties, and Manifest header attribute keys.

The values associated with these keys are of type String, unless otherwise indicated.

Since 1.1

6.1.13.1   **public static final String ACTIVATION_LAZY = "lazy"**

Bundle activation policy declaring the bundle must be activated when the first class load is made from the bundle.

A bundle with the lazy activation policy that is started with the START_ACTIVATION_POLICY option will wait in the STARTING state until the first class load from the bundle occurs. The bundle will then be activated before the class is returned to the requester.

The activation policy value is specified as in the Bundle-ActivationPolicy manifest header like:

        Bundle-ActivationPolicy: lazy

See Also BUNDLE_ACTIVATIONPOLICY, Bundle.start(int), Bundle.START_ACTIVATION_POLICY

Since 1.4

6.1.13.2   **public static final String BUNDLE_ACTIVATIONPOLICY = "Bundle-ActivationPolicy"**

Manifest header identifying the bundle's activation policy.

The attribute value may be retrieved from the Dictionary object returned by the Bundle.getHeaders method.

See Also ACTIVATION_LAZY, INCLUDE_DIRECTIVE, EXCLUDE_DIRECTIVE

Since 1.4

6.1.13.3   **public static final String BUNDLE_ACTIVATOR = "Bundle-Activator"**

Manifest header attribute identifying the bundle's activator class.

If present, this header specifies the name of the bundle resource class that implements the Bundle-Activator interface and whose start and stop methods are called by the Framework when the bundle is started and stopped, respectively.

The attribute value may be retrieved from the Dictionary object returned by the Bundle.getHeaders method.

6.1.13.4   **public static final String BUNDLE_CATEGORY = "Bundle-Category"**

Manifest header identifying the bundle's category.

The attribute value may be retrieved from the Dictionary object returned by the Bundle.getHeaders method.

6.1.13.5   **public static final String BUNDLE_CLASSPATH = "Bundle-ClassPath"**

Manifest header identifying a list of directories and embedded JAR files, which are bundle resources used to extend the bundle's classpath.

The attribute value may be retrieved from the Dictionary object returned by the Bundle.getHeaders method.

6.1.13.6   **public static final String BUNDLE_CONTACTADDRESS = "Bundle-ContactAddress"**

Manifest header identifying the contact address where problems with the bundle may be reported; for example, an email address.

The attribute value may be retrieved from the Dictionary object returned by the Bundle.getHeaders method.

6.1.13.7   **public static final String BUNDLE_COPYRIGHT = "Bundle-Copyright"**

Manifest header identifying the bundle's copyright information.

The attribute value may be retrieved from the Dictionary object returned by the Bundle.getHeaders method.

6.1.13.8   **public static final String BUNDLE_DESCRIPTION = "Bundle-Description"**

Manifest header containing a brief description of the bundle's functionality.

The attribute value may be retrieved from the Dictionary object returned by the Bundle.getHeaders method.

6.1.13.9   **public static final String BUNDLE_DOCURL = "Bundle-DocURL"**

Manifest header identifying the bundle's documentation URL, from which further information about the bundle may be obtained.

The attribute value may be retrieved from the Dictionary object returned by the Bundle.getHeaders method.

6.1.13.10   **public static final String BUNDLE_LOCALIZATION = "Bundle-Localization"**

Manifest header identifying the base name of the bundle's localization entries.

The attribute value may be retrieved from the Dictionary object returned by the Bundle.getHeaders method.

See Also BUNDLE_LOCALIZATION_DEFAULT_BASENAME

Since 1.3

6.1.13.11 **public static final String BUNDLE_LOCALIZATION_DEFAULT_BASENAME = "OSGI-INF/l10n/ bundle"**

Default value for the Bundle-Localization manifest header.

See Also BUNDLE_LOCALIZATION

Since 1.3

6.1.13.12 **public static final String BUNDLE_MANIFESTVERSION = "Bundle-ManifestVersion"**

Manifest header identifying the bundle manifest version. A bundle manifest may express the version of the syntax in which it is written by specifying a bundle manifest version. Bundles exploiting OSGi Release 4, or later, syntax must specify a bundle manifest version.

The bundle manifest version defined by OSGi Release 4 or, more specifically, by version 1.3 of the OSGi Core Specification is "2".

The attribute value may be retrieved from the Dictionary object returned by the Bundle.getHeaders method.

Since 1.3

6.1.13.13 **public static final String BUNDLE_NAME = "Bundle-Name"**

Manifest header identifying the bundle's name.

The attribute value may be retrieved from the Dictionary object returned by the Bundle.getHeaders method.

6.1.13.14 **public static final String BUNDLE_NATIVECODE = "Bundle-NativeCode"**

Manifest header identifying a number of hardware environments and the native language code libraries that the bundle is carrying for each of these environments.

The attribute value may be retrieved from the Dictionary object returned by the Bundle.getHeaders method.

6.1.13.15 **public static final String BUNDLE_NATIVECODE_LANGUAGE = "language"**

Manifest header attribute identifying the language in which the native bundle code is written specified in the Bundle-NativeCode manifest header. See ISO 639 for possible values.

The attribute value is encoded in the Bundle-NativeCode manifest header like:

        Bundle-NativeCode: http.so ; language=nl_be ...

See Also BUNDLE_NATIVECODE

6.1.13.16 **public static final String BUNDLE_NATIVECODE_OSNAME = "osname"**

Manifest header attribute identifying the operating system required to run native bundle code specified in the Bundle-NativeCode manifest header).

The attribute value is encoded in the Bundle-NativeCode manifest header like:

        Bundle-NativeCode: http.so ; osname=Linux ...

See Also BUNDLE_NATIVECODE

6.1.13.17 **public static final String BUNDLE_NATIVECODE_OSVERSION = "osversion"**

Manifest header attribute identifying the operating system version required to run native bundle code specified in the Bundle-NativeCode manifest header).

The attribute value is encoded in the Bundle-NativeCode manifest header like:

        Bundle-NativeCode: http.so ; osversion="2.34" ...

See Also BUNDLE_NATIVECODE

6.1.13.18   **public static final String BUNDLE_NATIVECODE_PROCESSOR = "processor"**

Manifest header attribute identifying the processor required to run native bundle code specified in the Bundle-NativeCode manifest header).

The attribute value is encoded in the Bundle-NativeCode manifest header like:

        Bundle-NativeCode: http.so ; processor=x86 ...

See Also BUNDLE_NATIVECODE

6.1.13.19   **public static final String BUNDLE_REQUIREDEXECUTIONENVIRONMENT = "Bundle-RequiredExecutionEnvironment"**

Manifest header identifying the required execution environment for the bundle. The service platform may run this bundle if any of the execution environments named in this header matches one of the execution environments it implements.

The attribute value may be retrieved from the Dictionary object returned by the Bundle.getHeaders method.

Since 1.2

6.1.13.20   **public static final String BUNDLE_SYMBOLICNAME = "Bundle-SymbolicName"**

Manifest header identifying the bundle's symbolic name.

The attribute value may be retrieved from the Dictionary object returned by the Bundle.getHeaders method.

Since 1.3

6.1.13.21   **public static final String BUNDLE_SYMBOLICNAME_ATTRIBUTE = "bundle-symbolic-name"**

Manifest header attribute identifying the symbolic name of a bundle that exports a package specified in the Import-Package manifest header.

The attribute value is encoded in the Import-Package manifest header like:

        Import-Package: org.osgi.framework; bundle-symbolic-name="com.acme.module.test"

See Also IMPORT_PACKAGE

Since 1.3

6.1.13.22   **public static final String BUNDLE_UPDATELOCATION = "Bundle-UpdateLocation"**

Manifest header identifying the location from which a new bundle version is obtained during a bundle update operation.

The attribute value may be retrieved from the Dictionary object returned by the Bundle.getHeaders method.

6.1.13.23   **public static final String BUNDLE_VENDOR = "Bundle-Vendor"**

Manifest header identifying the bundle's vendor.

The attribute value may be retrieved from the Dictionary object returned by the Bundle.getHeaders method.

6.1.13.24   **public static final String BUNDLE_VERSION = "Bundle-Version"**

Manifest header identifying the bundle's version.

The attribute value may be retrieved from the Dictionary object returned by the Bundle.getHeaders method.

6.1.13.25   **public static final String BUNDLE_VERSION_ATTRIBUTE = "bundle-version"**

Manifest header attribute identifying a range of versions for a bundle specified in the Require-Bundle or Fragment-Host manifest headers. The default value is 0.0.0.

The attribute value is encoded in the Require-Bundle manifest header like:

```
Require-Bundle: com.acme.module.test; bundle-version="1.1"
Require-Bundle: com.acme.module.test; bundle-version="[1.0,2.0)"
```

The bundle-version attribute value uses a mathematical interval notation to specify a range of bundle versions. A bundle-version attribute value specified as a single version means a version range that includes any bundle version greater than or equal to the specified version.

See Also REQUIRE_BUNDLE

Since 1.3

6.1.13.26   **public static final String DYNAMICIMPORT_PACKAGE = "DynamicImport-Package"**

Manifest header identifying the packages that the bundle may dynamically import during execution.

The attribute value may be retrieved from the Dictionary object returned by the Bundle.getHeaders method.

Since 1.2

6.1.13.27   **public static final String EXCLUDE_DIRECTIVE = "exclude"**

Manifest header directive identifying a list of classes to exclude in the exported package..

This directive is used by the Export-Package manifest header to identify a list of classes of the specified package which must not be allowed to be exported. The directive value is encoded in the Export-Package manifest header like:

```
Export-Package: org.osgi.framework; exclude:="*Impl"
```

This directive is also used by the Bundle-ActivationPolicy manifest header to identify the packages from which class loads will not trigger lazy activation. The directive value is encoded in the Bundle-ActivationPolicy manifest header like:

```
Bundle-ActivationPolicy: lazy; exclude:="org.osgi.framework"
```

See Also EXPORT_PACKAGE, BUNDLE_ACTIVATIONPOLICY

Since 1.3

6.1.13.28   **public static final String EXPORT_PACKAGE = "Export-Package"**

Manifest header identifying the packages that the bundle offers to the Framework for export.

The attribute value may be retrieved from the Dictionary object returned by the Bundle.getHeaders method.

6.1.13.29   **public static final String EXPORT_SERVICE = "Export-Service"**

Manifest header identifying the fully qualified class names of the services that the bundle may register (used for informational purposes only).

The attribute value may be retrieved from the Dictionary object returned by the Bundle.getHeaders method.

Deprecated   As of 1.2.

6.1.13.30   **public static final String EXTENSION_BOOTCLASSPATH = "bootclasspath"**

Manifest header directive value identifying the type of extension fragment. An extension fragment type of bootclasspath indicates that the extension fragment is to be loaded by the boot class loader.

The directive value is encoded in the Fragment-Host manifest header like:

```
Fragment-Host: system.bundle; extension:="bootclasspath"
```

See Also   EXTENSION_DIRECTIVE

Since   1.3

6.1.13.31   **public static final String EXTENSION_DIRECTIVE = "extension"**

Manifest header directive identifying the type of the extension fragment.

The directive value is encoded in the Fragment-Host manifest header like:

```
Fragment-Host: system.bundle; extension:="framework"
```

See Also   FRAGMENT_HOST, EXTENSION_FRAMEWORK, EXTENSION_BOOTCLASSPATH

Since   1.3

6.1.13.32   **public static final String EXTENSION_FRAMEWORK = "framework"**

Manifest header directive value identifying the type of extension fragment. An extension fragment type of framework indicates that the extension fragment is to be loaded by the framework's class loader.

The directive value is encoded in the Fragment-Host manifest header like:

```
Fragment-Host: system.bundle; extension:="framework"
```

See Also   EXTENSION_DIRECTIVE

Since   1.3

6.1.13.33   **public static final String FRAGMENT_ATTACHMENT_ALWAYS = "always"**

Manifest header directive value identifying a fragment attachment type of always. A fragment attachment type of always indicates that fragments are allowed to attach to the host bundle at any time (while the host is resolved or during the process of resolving the host bundle).

The directive value is encoded in the Bundle-SymbolicName manifest header like:

```
Bundle-SymbolicName: com.acme.module.test; fragment-attachment:="always"
```

See Also   FRAGMENT_ATTACHMENT_DIRECTIVE

Since   1.3

6.1.13.34   **public static final String FRAGMENT_ATTACHMENT_DIRECTIVE = "fragment-attachment"**

Manifest header directive identifying if and when a fragment may attach to a host bundle. The default value is always.

The directive value is encoded in the Bundle-SymbolicName manifest header like:

```
Bundle-SymbolicName: com.acme.module.test; fragment-attachment:="never"
```

See Also   BUNDLE_SYMBOLICNAME, FRAGMENT_ATTACHMENT_ALWAYS, FRAGMENT_ATTACHMENT_RESOLVETIME, FRAGMENT_ATTACHMENT_NEVER

Since   1.3

6.1.13.35   **public static final String FRAGMENT_ATTACHMENT_NEVER = "never"**

Manifest header directive value identifying a fragment attachment type of never. A fragment attachment type of never indicates that no fragments are allowed to attach to the host bundle at any time.

The directive value is encoded in the Bundle-SymbolicName manifest header like:

```
Bundle-SymbolicName: com.acme.module.test; fragment-attachment:="never"
```

See Also   FRAGMENT_ATTACHMENT_DIRECTIVE

Since   1.3

6.1.13.36   **public static final String FRAGMENT_ATTACHMENT_RESOLVETIME = "resolve-time"**

Manifest header directive value identifying a fragment attachment type of resolve-time. A fragment attachment type of resolve-time indicates that fragments are allowed to attach to the host bundle only during the process of resolving the host bundle.

The directive value is encoded in the Bundle-SymbolicName manifest header like:

```
Bundle-SymbolicName: com.acme.module.test; fragment-attachment:="resolve-
time"
```

See Also   FRAGMENT_ATTACHMENT_DIRECTIVE

Since   1.3

6.1.13.37   **public static final String FRAGMENT_HOST = "Fragment-Host"**

Manifest header identifying the symbolic name of another bundle for which that the bundle is a fragment.

The attribute value may be retrieved from the Dictionary object returned by the Bundle.getHeaders method.

Since   1.3

6.1.13.38   **public static final String FRAMEWORK_BEGINNING_STARTLEVEL = "org.osgi.framework.startlevel.beginning"**

Specifies the beginning start level of the framework.

See Also   Core Specification, section 8.2.3.

Since   1.5

6.1.13.39   **public static final String FRAMEWORK_BOOTDELEGATION = "org.osgi.framework.bootdelegation"**

Framework environment property identifying packages for which the Framework must delegate class loading to the parent class loader of the bundle.

The value of this property may be retrieved by calling the BundleContext.getProperty method.

See Also   FRAMEWORK_BUNDLE_PARENT

Since   1.3

6.1.13.40   **public static final String FRAMEWORK_BUNDLE_PARENT = "org.osgi.framework.bundle.parent"**

Specifies the parent class loader type for all bundle class loaders. Default value is boot.

See Also   FRAMEWORK_BUNDLE_PARENT_BOOT, FRAMEWORK_BUNDLE_PARENT_EXT, FRAMEWORK_BUNDLE_PARENT_APP, FRAMEWORK_BUNDLE_PARENT_FRAMEWORK

Since   1.5

6.1.13.41   **public static final String FRAMEWORK_BUNDLE_PARENT_APP = "app"**

Specifies to use the application class loader as the parent class loader for all bundle class loaders. Depending on how the framework is launched, this may refer to the same class loader as FRAMEWORK_BUNDLE_PARENT_FRAMEWORK.

See Also FRAMEWORK_BUNDLE_PARENT

Since 1.5

6.1.13.42   **public static final String FRAMEWORK_BUNDLE_PARENT_BOOT = "boot"**

Specifies to use of the boot class loader as the parent class loader for all bundle class loaders.

See Also FRAMEWORK_BUNDLE_PARENT

Since 1.5

6.1.13.43   **public static final String FRAMEWORK_BUNDLE_PARENT_EXT = "ext"**

Specifies to use the extension class loader as the parent class loader for all bundle class loaders.

See Also FRAMEWORK_BUNDLE_PARENT

Since 1.5

6.1.13.44   **public static final String FRAMEWORK_BUNDLE_PARENT_FRAMEWORK = "framework"**

Specifies to use the framework class loader as the parent class loader for all bundle class loaders. The framework class loader is the class loader used to load the framework implementation. Depending on how the framework is launched, this may refer to the same class loader as FRAMEWORK_BUNDLE_PARENT_APP.

See Also FRAMEWORK_BUNDLE_PARENT

Since 1.5

6.1.13.45   **public static final String FRAMEWORK_EXECPERMISSION = "org.osgi.framework.command.execpermission"**

Specifies an optional OS specific command to set file permissions on extracted native code. On some operating systems, it is required that native libraries be set to executable. This optional property allows you to specify the command. For example, on a UNIX style OS, this property could have the following value.

```
chmod +rx ${abspath}
```

The ${abspath} is used by the framework to substitute the actual absolute file path.

Since 1.5

6.1.13.46   **public static final String FRAMEWORK_EXECUTIONENVIRONMENT = "org.osgi.framework.executionenvironment"**

Framework environment property identifying execution environments provided by the Framework.

The value of this property may be retrieved by calling the BundleContext.getProperty method.

Since 1.2

6.1.13.47   **public static final String FRAMEWORK_LANGUAGE = "org.osgi.framework.language"**

Framework environment property identifying the Framework implementation language (see ISO 639 for possible values).

The value of this property may be retrieved by calling the BundleContext.getProperty method.

6.1.13.48   **public static final String FRAMEWORK_LIBRARY_EXTENSIONS =**

"org.osgi.framework.library.extensions"

Specifies a comma separated list of additional library file extensions that must be used when a bundle's class loader is searching for native libraries. If this property is not set, then only the library name returned by System.mapLibraryName(String) will be used to search. This is needed for certain operating systems which allow more than one extension for a library. For example, AIX allows library extensions of .a and .so, but System.mapLibraryName(String) will only return names with the .a extension.

Since 1.5

6.1.13.49 **public static final String FRAMEWORK_OS_NAME = "org.osgi.framework.os.name"**

Framework environment property identifying the Framework host-computer's operating system.

The value of this property may be retrieved by calling the BundleContext.getProperty method.

6.1.13.50 **public static final String FRAMEWORK_OS_VERSION = "org.osgi.framework.os.version"**

Framework environment property identifying the Framework host-computer's operating system version number.

The value of this property may be retrieved by calling the BundleContext.getProperty method.

6.1.13.51 **public static final String FRAMEWORK_PROCESSOR = "org.osgi.framework.processor"**

Framework environment property identifying the Framework host-computer's processor name.

The value of this property may be retrieved by calling the BundleContext.getProperty method.

6.1.13.52 **public static final String FRAMEWORK_SECURITY = "org.osgi.framework.security"**

Specifies the type of security manager the framework must use. If not specified then the framework will not set the VM security manager.

See Also FRAMEWORK_SECURITY_OSGI

Since 1.5

6.1.13.53 **public static final String FRAMEWORK_SECURITY_OSGI = "osgi"**

Specifies that a security manager that supports all security aspects of the OSGi core specification including postponed conditions must be installed.

If this value is specified and there is a security manager already installed, then a SecurityException must be thrown when the Framework is initialized.

See Also FRAMEWORK_SECURITY

Since 1.5

6.1.13.54 **public static final String FRAMEWORK_STORAGE = "org.osgi.framework.storage"**

Specified the persistent storage area used by the framework. The value of this property must be a valid file path in the file system to a directory. If the specified directory does not exist then the framework will create the directory. If the specified path exists but is not a directory or if the framework fails to create the storage directory, then framework initialization must fail. The framework is free to use this directory as it sees fit. This area can not be shared with anything else.

If this property is not set, the framework should use a reasonable platform default for the persistent storage area.

Since 1.5

6.1.13.55   **public static final String FRAMEWORK_STORAGE_CLEAN = "org.osgi.framework.storage.clean"**

Specifies if and when the persistent storage area for the framework should be cleaned. If this property is not set, then the framework storage area must not be cleaned.

See Also   FRAMEWORK_STORAGE_CLEAN_ONFIRSTINIT

Since   1.5

6.1.13.56   **public static final String FRAMEWORK_STORAGE_CLEAN_ONFIRSTINIT = "onFirstInit"**

Specifies that the framework storage area must be cleaned before the framework is initialized for the first time. Subsequent inits, starts or updates of the framework will not result in cleaning the framework storage area.

Since   1.5

6.1.13.57   **public static final String FRAMEWORK_SYSTEMPACKAGES = "org.osgi.framework.system.packages"**

Framework environment property identifying packages which the system bundle must export.

If this property is not specified then the framework must calculate a reasonable default value for the current execution environment.

The value of this property may be retrieved by calling the BundleContext.getProperty method.

Since   1.3

6.1.13.58   **public static final String FRAMEWORK_SYSTEMPACKAGES_EXTRA = "org.osgi.framework.system.packages.extra"**

Framework environment property identifying extra packages which the system bundle must export from the current execution environment.

This property is useful for configuring extra system packages in addition to the system packages calculated by the framework.

The value of this property may be retrieved by calling the BundleContext.getProperty method.

See Also   FRAMEWORK_SYSTEMPACKAGES

Since   1.5

6.1.13.59   **public static final String FRAMEWORK_TRUST_REPOSITORIES = "org.osgi.framework.trust.repositories"**

Specifies the trust repositories used by the framework. The value is a java.io.File.pathSeparator separated list of valid file paths to files that contain key stores of type JKS. The framework will use the key stores as trust repositories to authenticate certificates of trusted signers. The key stores are only used as read-only trust repositories to access public keys. No passwords are required to access the key stores' public keys.

Note that framework implementations are allowed to use other trust repositories in addition to the trust repositories specified by this property. How these other trust repositories are configured and populated is implementation specific.

Since   1.5

6.1.13.60   **public static final String FRAMEWORK_VENDOR = "org.osgi.framework.vendor"**

Framework environment property identifying the Framework implementation vendor.

The value of this property may be retrieved by calling the BundleContext.getProperty method.

6.1.13.61   **public static final String FRAMEWORK_VERSION = "org.osgi.framework.version"**

Framework environment property identifying the Framework version.

The value of this property may be retrieved by calling the BundleContext.getProperty method.

6.1.13.62   **public static final String FRAMEWORK_WINDOWSYSTEM = "org.osgi.framework.windowsystem"**

Specifies the current windowing system. The framework should provide a reasonable default if this is not set.

Since 1.5

6.1.13.63   **public static final String IMPORT_PACKAGE = "Import-Package"**

Manifest header identifying the packages on which the bundle depends.

The attribute value may be retrieved from the Dictionary object returned by the Bundle.getHeaders method.

6.1.13.64   **public static final String IMPORT_SERVICE = "Import-Service"**

Manifest header identifying the fully qualified class names of the services that the bundle requires (used for informational purposes only).

The attribute value may be retrieved from the Dictionary object returned by the Bundle.getHeaders method.

Deprecated As of 1.2.

6.1.13.65   **public static final String INCLUDE_DIRECTIVE = "include"**

Manifest header directive identifying a list of classes to include in the exported package.

This directive is used by the Export-Package manifest header to identify a list of classes of the specified package which must be allowed to be exported. The directive value is encoded in the Export-Package manifest header like:

```
Export-Package: org.osgi.framework; include:="MyClass*"
```

This directive is also used by the Bundle-ActivationPolicy manifest header to identify the packages from which class loads will trigger lazy activation. The directive value is encoded in the Bundle-ActivationPolicy manifest header like:

```
Bundle-ActivationPolicy: lazy; include:="org.osgi.framework"
```

See Also EXPORT_PACKAGE, BUNDLE_ACTIVATIONPOLICY

Since 1.3

6.1.13.66   **public static final String MANDATORY_DIRECTIVE = "mandatory"**

Manifest header directive identifying names of matching attributes which must be specified by matching Import-Package statements in the Export-Package manifest header.

The directive value is encoded in the Export-Package manifest header like:

```
Export-Package: org.osgi.framework; mandatory:="bundle-symbolic-name"
```

See Also EXPORT_PACKAGE

Since 1.3

6.1.13.67   **public static final String OBJECTCLASS = "objectClass"**

Service property identifying all of the class names under which a service was registered in the Framework. The value of this property must be of type String[].

This property is set by the Framework when a service is registered.

6.1.13.68   **public static final String PACKAGE_SPECIFICATION_VERSION = "specification-version"**

Manifest header attribute identifying the version of a package specified in the Export-Package or Import-Package manifest header.

Deprecated   As of 1.3. This has been replaced by VERSION_ATTRIBUTE.

6.1.13.69   **public static final String REQUIRE_BUNDLE = "Require-Bundle"**

Manifest header identifying the symbolic names of other bundles required by the bundle.

The attribute value may be retrieved from the Dictionary object returned by the Bundle.getHeaders method.

Since   1.3

6.1.13.70   **public static final String RESOLUTION_DIRECTIVE = "resolution"**

Manifest header directive identifying the resolution type in the Import-Package or Require-Bundle manifest header. The default value is mandatory.

The directive value is encoded in the Import-Package or Require-Bundle manifest header like:

```
Import-Package: org.osgi.framework; resolution:="optional"
Require-Bundle: com.acme.module.test; resolution:="optional"
```

See Also   IMPORT_PACKAGE, REQUIRE_BUNDLE, RESOLUTION_MANDATORY, RESOLUTION_OPTIONAL

Since   1.3

6.1.13.71   **public static final String RESOLUTION_MANDATORY = "mandatory"**

Manifest header directive value identifying a mandatory resolution type. A mandatory resolution type indicates that the import package or require bundle must be resolved when the bundle is resolved. If such an import or require bundle cannot be resolved, the module fails to resolve.

The directive value is encoded in the Import-Package or Require-Bundle manifest header like:

```
Import-Package: org.osgi.framework; resolution:="manditory"
Require-Bundle: com.acme.module.test; resolution:="manditory"
```

See Also   RESOLUTION_DIRECTIVE

Since   1.3

6.1.13.72   **public static final String RESOLUTION_OPTIONAL = "optional"**

Manifest header directive value identifying an optional resolution type. An optional resolution type indicates that the import or require bundle is optional and the bundle may be resolved without the import or require bundle being resolved. If the import or require bundle is not resolved when the bundle is resolved, the import or require bundle may not be resolved before the bundle is refreshed.

The directive value is encoded in the Import-Package or Require-Bundle manifest header like:

```
Import-Package: org.osgi.framework; resolution:="optional"
Require-Bundle: com.acme.module.test; resolution:="optional"
```

See Also   RESOLUTION_DIRECTIVE

Since   1.3

6.1.13.73   **public static final String SELECTION_FILTER_ATTRIBUTE = "selection-filter"**

Manifest header attribute is used for selection by filtering based upon system properties.

The attribute value is encoded in manifest headers like:

```
Bundle-NativeCode: libgtk.so; selection-filter="(ws=gtk)"; ...
```

See Also BUNDLE_NATIVECODE

Since 1.3

6.1.13.74   **public static final String SERVICE_DESCRIPTION = "service.description"**

Service property identifying a service's description.

This property may be supplied in the properties Dictionary object passed to the BundleContext.registerService method.

6.1.13.75   **public static final String SERVICE_ID = "service.id"**

Service property identifying a service's registration number. The value of this property must be of type Long.

The value of this property is assigned by the Framework when a service is registered. The Framework assigns a unique value that is larger than all previously assigned values since the Framework was started. These values are NOT persistent across restarts of the Framework.

6.1.13.76   **public static final String SERVICE_PID = "service.pid"**

Service property identifying a service's persistent identifier.

This property may be supplied in the propertiesDictionary object passed to the BundleContext.registerService method. The value of this property must be of type String, String[], or Collection of String.

A service's persistent identifier uniquely identifies the service and persists across multiple Framework invocations.

By convention, every bundle has its own unique namespace, starting with the bundle's identifier (see Bundle.getBundleId) and followed by a dot (.). A bundle may use this as the prefix of the persistent identifiers for the services it registers.

6.1.13.77   **public static final String SERVICE_RANKING = "service.ranking"**

Service property identifying a service's ranking number.

This property may be supplied in the properties Dictionary object passed to the BundleContext.registerService method. The value of this property must be of type Integer.

The service ranking is used by the Framework to determine the *natural order* of services, see ServiceReference.compareTo(Object), and the *default* service to be returned from a call to the BundleContext.getServiceReference method.

The default ranking is zero (0). A service with a ranking of Integer.MAX_VALUE is very likely to be returned as the default service, whereas a service with a ranking of Integer.MIN_VALUE is very unlikely to be returned.

If the supplied property value is not of type Integer, it is deemed to have a ranking value of zero.

6.1.13.78   **public static final String SERVICE_VENDOR = "service.vendor"**

Service property identifying a service's vendor.

This property may be supplied in the properties Dictionary object passed to the BundleContext.registerService method.

6.1.13.79   **public static final String SINGLETON_DIRECTIVE = "singleton"**

Manifest header directive identifying whether a bundle is a singleton. The default value is false.

The directive value is encoded in the Bundle-SymbolicName manifest header like:

```
Bundle-SymbolicName: com.acme.module.test; singleton:=true
```

The attribute value may be retrieved from the Dictionary object returned by the Bundle.getHeaders method.

See Also   BUNDLE_SYMBOLICNAME

Since   1.3

6.1.13.80   **public static final String SUPPORTS_BOOTCLASSPATH_EXTENSION = "org.osgi.supports.bootclasspath.extension"**

Framework environment property identifying whether the Framework supports bootclasspath extension bundles.

If the value of this property is true, then the Framework supports bootclasspath extension bundles. The default value is false.

The value of this property may be retrieved by calling the BundleContext.getProperty method.

Since   1.3

6.1.13.81   **public static final String SUPPORTS_FRAMEWORK_EXTENSION = "org.osgi.supports.framework.extension"**

Framework environment property identifying whether the Framework supports framework extension bundles.

As of version 1.4, the value of this property must be true. The Framework must support framework extension bundles.

The value of this property may be retrieved by calling the BundleContext.getProperty method.

Since   1.3

6.1.13.82   **public static final String SUPPORTS_FRAMEWORK_FRAGMENT = "org.osgi.supports.framework.fragment"**

Framework environment property identifying whether the Framework supports fragment bundles.

As of version 1.4, the value of this property must be true. The Framework must support fragment bundles.

The value of this property may be retrieved by calling the BundleContext.getProperty method.

Since   1.3

6.1.13.83   **public static final String SUPPORTS_FRAMEWORK_REQUIREBUNDLE = "org.osgi.supports.framework.requirebundle"**

Framework environment property identifying whether the Framework supports the Require-Bundle manifest header.

As of version 1.4, the value of this property must be true. The Framework must support the Require-Bundle manifest header.

The value of this property may be retrieved by calling the BundleContext.getProperty method.

Since   1.3

6.1.13.84   **public static final String SYSTEM_BUNDLE_LOCATION = "System Bundle"**

Location identifier of the OSGi *system bundle*, which is defined to be "System Bundle".

6.1.13.85   **public static final String SYSTEM_BUNDLE_SYMBOLICNAME = "system.bundle"**

Alias for the symbolic name of the OSGi *system bundle*. It is defined to be "system.bundle".

Since 1.3

6.1.13.86   **public static final String USES_DIRECTIVE = "uses"**

Manifest header directive identifying a list of packages that an exported package uses.

The directive value is encoded in the Export-Package manifest header like:

```
Export-Package: org.osgi.util.tracker; uses:="org.osgi.framework"
```

See Also   EXPORT_PACKAGE

Since 1.3

6.1.13.87   **public static final String VERSION_ATTRIBUTE = "version"**

Manifest header attribute identifying the version of a package specified in the Export-Package or Import-Package manifest header.

The attribute value is encoded in the Export-Package or Import-Package manifest header like:

```
Import-Package: org.osgi.framework; version="1.1"
```

See Also   EXPORT_PACKAGE, IMPORT_PACKAGE

Since 1.3

6.1.13.88   **public static final String VISIBILITY_DIRECTIVE = "visibility"**

Manifest header directive identifying the visibility of a required bundle in the Require-Bundle manifest header. The default value is private.

The directive value is encoded in the Require-Bundle manifest header like:

```
Require-Bundle: com.acme.module.test; visibility:="reexport"
```

See Also   REQUIRE_BUNDLE, VISIBILITY_PRIVATE, VISIBILITY_REEXPORT

Since 1.3

6.1.13.89   **public static final String VISIBILITY_PRIVATE = "private"**

Manifest header directive value identifying a private visibility type. A private visibility type indicates that any packages that are exported by the required bundle are not made visible on the export signature of the requiring bundle.

The directive value is encoded in the Require-Bundle manifest header like:

```
Require-Bundle: com.acme.module.test; visibility:="private"
```

See Also   VISIBILITY_DIRECTIVE

Since 1.3

6.1.13.90   **public static final String VISIBILITY_REEXPORT = "reexport"**

Manifest header directive value identifying a reexport visibility type. A reexport visibility type indicates any packages that are exported by the required bundle are re-exported by the requiring bundle. Any arbitrary arbitrary matching attributes with which they were exported by the required bundle are deleted.

The directive value is encoded in the Require-Bundle manifest header like:

```
Require-Bundle: com.acme.module.test; visibility:="reexport"
```

See Also   VISIBILITY_DIRECTIVE

Since 1.3

6.1.14   public interface Filter

An RFC 1960-based Filter.

Filters can be created by calling BundleContext.createFilter or FrameworkUtil.createFilter with a filter string.

A Filter can be used numerous times to determine if the match argument matches the filter string that was used to create the Filter.

Some examples of LDAP filters are:

```
"(cn=Babs Jensen)"
"(!(cn=Tim Howes))"
"(&(" + Constants.OBJECTCLASS + "=Person)(|(sn=Jensen)(cn=Babs J*)))"
"(o=univ*of*mich*)"
```

See Also   Core Specification, section 5.5, for a description of the filter string syntax.

Since   1.1

Concurrency   Thread-safe

6.1.14.1   public boolean equals(Object obj)

obj   The object to compare against this Filter.

☐   Compares this Filter to another Filter.

This method returns the result of calling this.toString().equals(obj.toString()).

Returns   If the other object is a Filter object, then returns the result of calling this.toString().equals(obj.toString()); false otherwise.

6.1.14.2   public int hashCode( )

☐   Returns the hashCode for this Filter.

This method returns the result of calling this.toString().hashCode().

Returns   The hashCode of this Filter.

6.1.14.3   public boolean match(ServiceReference reference)

reference   The reference to the service whose properties are used in the match.

☐   Filter using a service's properties.

This Filter is executed using the keys and values of the referenced service's properties. The keys are case insensitively matched with this Filter.

Returns   true if the service's properties match this Filter; false otherwise.

6.1.14.4   public boolean match(Dictionary dictionary)

dictionary   The Dictionary whose keys are used in the match.

☐   Filter using a Dictionary. This Filter is executed using the specified Dictionary's keys and values. The keys are case insensitively matched with this Filter.

Returns   true if the Dictionary's keys and values match this filter; false otherwise.

Throws   IllegalArgumentException – If dictionary contains case variants of the same key name.

6.1.14.5   public boolean matchCase(Dictionary dictionary)

dictionary   The Dictionary whose keys are used in the match.

☐   Filter with case sensitivity using a Dictionary. This Filter is executed using the specified Dictionary's keys and values. The keys are case sensitively matched with this Filter.

Returns true if the Dictionary's keys and values match this filter; false otherwise.

Since 1.3

6.1.14.6   **public String toString( )**

☐ Returns this Filter's filter string.

The filter string is normalized by removing whitespace which does not affect the meaning of the filter.

Returns This Filter's filter string.

6.1.15   public class FrameworkEvent
extends EventObject

A general event from the Framework.

FrameworkEvent objects are delivered to FrameworkListeners when a general event occurs within the OSGi environment. A type code is used to identify the event type for future extendability.

OSGi Alliance reserves the right to extend the set of event types.

See Also FrameworkListener

Concurrency Immutable

6.1.15.1   **public static final int ERROR = 2**

An error has occurred.

There was an error associated with a bundle.

6.1.15.2   **public static final int INFO = 32**

An informational event has occurred.

There was an informational event associated with a bundle.

Since 1.3

6.1.15.3   **public static final int PACKAGES_REFRESHED = 4**

A PackageAdmin.refreshPackage operation has completed.

This event is fired when the Framework has completed the refresh packages operation initiated by a call to the PackageAdmin.refreshPackages method. The source of this event is the System Bundle.

See Also PackageAdmin. refreshPackages

Since 1.2

6.1.15.4   **public static final int STARTED = 1**

The Framework has started.

This event is fired when the Framework has started after all installed bundles that are marked to be started have been started and the Framework has reached the initial start level. The source of this event is the System Bundle.

See Also The Start Level Service

6.1.15.5   **public static final int STARTLEVEL_CHANGED = 8**

A StartLevel.setStartLevel operation has completed.

This event is fired when the Framework has completed changing the active start level initiated by a call to the StartLevel.setStartLevel method. The source of this event is the System Bundle.

See Also The Start Level Service

Since 1.2

6.1.15.6 **public static final int STOPPED = 64**

The Framework has stopped.

This event is fired when the Framework has been stopped because of a stop operation on the system bundle. The source of this event is the System Bundle.

Since 1.5

6.1.15.7 **public static final int STOPPED_BOOTCLASSPATH_MODIFIED = 256**

The Framework has stopped and the boot class path has changed.

This event is fired when the Framework has been stopped because of a stop operation on the system bundle and a bootclasspath extension bundle has been installed or updated. The source of this event is the System Bundle.

Since 1.5

6.1.15.8 **public static final int STOPPED_UPDATE = 128**

The Framework has stopped during update.

This event is fired when the Framework has been stopped because of an update operation on the system bundle. The Framework will be restarted after this event is fired. The source of this event is the System Bundle.

Since 1.5

6.1.15.9 **public static final int WAIT_TIMEDOUT = 512**

The Framework did not stop before the wait timeout expired.

This event is fired when the Framework did not stop before the wait timeout expired. The source of this event is the System Bundle.

Since 1.5

6.1.15.10 **public static final int WARNING = 16**

A warning has occurred.

There was a warning associated with a bundle.

Since 1.3

6.1.15.11 **public FrameworkEvent(int type, Object source)**

type The event type.

source The event source object. This may not be null.

☐ Creates a Framework event.

Deprecated As of 1.2. This constructor is deprecated in favor of using the other constructor with the System Bundle as the event source.

6.1.15.12 **public FrameworkEvent(int type, Bundle bundle, Throwable throwable)**

type The event type.

bundle The event source.

throwable The related exception. This argument may be null if there is no related exception.

☐ Creates a Framework event regarding the specified bundle.

6.1.15.13   **public Bundle getBundle( )**

☐ Returns the bundle associated with the event. This bundle is also the source of the event.

Returns The bundle associated with the event.

6.1.15.14   **public Throwable getThrowable( )**

☐ Returns the exception related to this event.

Returns The related exception or null if none.

6.1.15.15   **public int getType( )**

☐ Returns the type of framework event.

The type values are:

- STARTED
- ERROR
- WARNING
- INFO
- PACKAGES_REFRESHED
- STARTLEVEL_CHANGED
- STOPPED
- STOPPED_BOOTCLASSPATH_MODIFIED
- STOPPED_UPDATE
- WAIT_TIMEDOUT

Returns The type of state change.

6.1.16   public interface FrameworkListener extends EventListener

A FrameworkEvent listener. FrameworkListener is a listener interface that may be implemented by a bundle developer. When a FrameworkEvent is fired, it is asynchronously delivered to a FrameworkListener. The Framework delivers FrameworkEvent objects to a FrameworkListener in order and must not concurrently call a FrameworkListener.

A FrameworkListener object is registered with the Framework using the BundleContext.addFrameworkListener method. FrameworkListener objects are called with a FrameworkEvent objects when the Framework starts and when asynchronous errors occur.

See Also FrameworkEvent

Concurrency Not Thread-safe

6.1.16.1   **public void frameworkEvent(FrameworkEvent event)**

event The FrameworkEvent object.

☐ Receives notification of a general FrameworkEvent object.

6.1.17   public class FrameworkUtil

Framework Utility class.

This class contains utility methods which access Framework functions that may be useful to bundles.

Since 1.3

Concurrency Thread-safe

6.1.17.1   **public static Filter createFilter(String filter) throws InvalidSyntaxException**

filter   The filter string.

□   Creates a Filter object. This Filter object may be used to match a ServiceReference object or a Dictionary object.

If the filter cannot be parsed, an InvalidSyntaxException will be thrown with a human readable message where the filter became unparsable.

This method returns a Filter implementation which may not perform as well as the framework implementation-specific Filter implementation returned by BundleContext.createFilter(String).

Returns   A Filter object encapsulating the filter string.

Throws   InvalidSyntaxException – If filter contains an invalid filter string that cannot be parsed.

NullPointerException – If filter is null.

See Also   Filter

6.1.17.2   **public static Bundle getBundle(Class classFromBundle)**

classFromBundle   A class defined by a bundle class loader.

□   Return a Bundle for the specified bundle class. The returned Bundle is the bundle associated with the bundle class loader which defined the specified class.

Returns   A Bundle for the specified bundle class or null if the specified class was not defined by a bundle class loader.

Since   1.5

6.1.17.3   **public static boolean matchDistinguishedNameChain(String matchPattern, List dnChain)**

matchPattern   The pattern against which to match the DN chain.

dnChain   The DN chain to match against the specified pattern. Each element of the chain must be of type String and use the format defined in RFC 2253.

□   Match a Distinguished Name (DN) chain against a pattern. DNs can be matched using wildcards. A wildcard ('*' \u002A) replaces all possible values. Due to the structure of the DN, the comparison is more complicated than string-based wildcard matching.

A wildcard can stand for zero or more DNs in a chain, a number of relative distinguished names (RDNs) within a DN, or the value of a single RDN. The DNs in the chain and the matching pattern are canonicalized before processing. This means, among other things, that spaces must be ignored, except in values.

The format of a wildcard match pattern is:

```
matchPattern ::= dn-match ( ';' dn-match ) *
dn-match ::= ( '*' | rdn-match ) ( ',' rdn-match ) * | '-'
rdn-match ::= name '=' value-match
value-match ::= '*' | value-star
value-star ::= < value, requires escaped '*' and '-' >
```

The most simple case is a single wildcard; it must match any DN. A wildcard can also replace the first list of RDNs of a DN. The first RDNs are the least significant. Such lists of matched RDNs can be empty.

For example, a match pattern with a wildcard that matches all all DNs that end with RDNs of o=ACME and c=US would look like this:

```
*, o=ACME, c=US
```

This match pattern would match the following DNs:

```
cn = Bugs Bunny, o = ACME, c = US
ou = Carrots, cn=Daffy Duck, o=ACME, c=US
street = 9C\, Avenue St. Dré zé ry, o=ACME, c=US
dc=www, dc=acme, dc=com, o=ACME, c=US
o=ACME, c=US
```

The following DNs would not match:

```
street = 9C\, Avenue St. Dré zé ry, o=ACME, c=FR
dc=www, dc=acme, dc=com, c=US
```

If a wildcard is used for a value of an RDN, the value must be exactly ∗. The wildcard must match any value, and no substring matching must be done. For example:

```
cn=*,o=ACME,c=*
```

This match pattern with wildcard must match the following DNs:

```
cn=Bugs Bunny,o=ACME,c=US
cn = Daffy Duck , o = ACME , c = US
cn=Road Runner, o=ACME, c=NL
```

But not:

```
o=ACME, c=NL
dc=acme.com, cn=Bugs Bunny, o=ACME, c=US
```

A match pattern may contain a chain of DN match patterns. The semicolon(';' \u003B) must be used to separate DN match patterns in a chain. Wildcards can also be used to match against a complete DN within a chain.

The following example matches a certificate signed by Tweety Inc. in the US.

```
* ; ou=S & V, o=Tweety Inc., c=US
```

The wildcard ('∗') matches zero or one DN in the chain, however, sometimes it is necessary to match a longer chain. The minus sign ('-' \u002D) represents zero or more DNs, whereas the asterisk only represents a single DN. For example, to match a DN where the Tweety Inc. is in the DN chain, use the following expression:

```
- ; *, o=Tweety Inc., c=US
```

Returns true If the pattern matches the DN chain; otherwise false is returned.

Throws IllegalArgumentException – If the specified match pattern or DN chain is invalid.

Since 1.5

6.1.18   public class InvalidSyntaxException
extends Exception

A Framework exception used to indicate that a filter string has an invalid syntax.

An InvalidSyntaxException object indicates that a filter string parameter has an invalid syntax and cannot be parsed. See Filter for a description of the filter string syntax.

This exception conforms to the general purpose exception chaining mechanism.

6.1.18.1   public InvalidSyntaxException(String msg, String filter)

msg The message.

filter The invalid filter string.

      □ Creates an exception of type InvalidSyntaxException.

This method creates an InvalidSyntaxException object with the specified message and the filter string which generated the exception.

6.1.18.2   **public InvalidSyntaxException(String msg, String filter, Throwable cause)**

msg The message.

filter The invalid filter string.

cause The cause of this exception.

      □ Creates an exception of type InvalidSyntaxException.

This method creates an InvalidSyntaxException object with the specified message and the filter string which generated the exception.

Since 1.3

6.1.18.3   **public Throwable getCause( )**

      □ Returns the cause of this exception or null if no cause was set.

Returns The cause of this exception or null if no cause was set.

Since 1.3

6.1.18.4   **public String getFilter( )**

      □ Returns the filter string that generated the InvalidSyntaxException object.

Returns The invalid filter string.

See Also BundleContext.getServiceReferences,
BundleContext.addServiceListener(ServiceListener,String)

6.1.18.5   **public Throwable initCause(Throwable cause)**

cause The cause of this exception.

      □ Initializes the cause of this exception to the specified value.

Returns This exception.

Throws IllegalArgumentException – If the specified cause is this exception.

IllegalStateException – If the cause of this exception has already been set.

Since 1.3

6.1.19   **public final class PackagePermission**
              extends BasicPermission

A bundle's authority to import or export a package.

A package is a dot-separated string that defines a fully qualified Java package.

For example:

   org.osgi.service.http

PackagePermission has three actions: exportonly, import and export. The export action, which is deprecated, implies the import action.

Concurrency Thread-safe

6.1.19.1   **public static final String EXPORT = "export"**

The action string export. The export action implies the import action.

Deprecated Since 1.5. Use exportonly instead.

6.1.19.2   **public static final String EXPORTONLY = "exportonly"**

The action string exportonly. The exportonly action does not imply the import action.

Since 1.5

6.1.19.3   **public static final String IMPORT = "import"**

The action string import.

6.1.19.4   **public PackagePermission(String name, String actions)**

name Package name or filter expression. A filter expression can only be specified if the specified action is import.

actions exportonly,import (canonical order).

☐ Creates a new PackagePermission object.

The name is specified as a normal Java package name: a dot-separated string. Wildcards may be used.

```
name ::= <package name> | <package name ending in ".*"> | *
```

Examples:

```
org.osgi.service.http
javax.servlet.*
*
```

For the import action, the name can also be a filter expression. The filter gives access to the following attributes:

- signer - A Distinguished Name chain used to sign the exporting bundle. Wildcards in a DN are not matched according to the filter string rules, but according to the rules defined for a DN chain.
- location - The location of the exporting bundle.
- id - The bundle ID of the exporting bundle.
- name - The symbolic name of the exporting bundle.
- package.name - The name of the requested package.

Filter attribute names are processed in a case sensitive manner.

Package Permissions are granted over all possible versions of a package. A bundle that needs to export a package must have the appropriate PackagePermission for that package; similarly, a bundle that needs to import a package must have the appropriate PackagePermssion for that package.

Permission is granted for both classes and resources.

6.1.19.5   **public PackagePermission(String name, Bundle exportingBundle, String actions)**

name The name of the requested package to import.

exportingBundle The bundle exporting the requested package.

actions The action import.

☐ Creates a new requested PackagePermission object to be used by code that must perform checkPermission for the import action. PackagePermission objects created with this constructor cannot be added to a PackagePermission permission collection.

Since 1.5

6.1.19.6   **public boolean equals(Object obj)**

obj   The object to test for equality with this PackagePermission object.

☐   Determines the equality of two PackagePermission objects. This method checks that specified package has the same package name and PackagePermission actions as this PackagePermission object.

Returns   true if obj is a PackagePermission, and has the same package name and actions as this PackagePermission object; false otherwise.

6.1.19.7   **public String getActions( )**

☐   Returns the canonical string representation of the PackagePermission actions.

Always returns present PackagePermission actions in the following order: EXPORTONLY,IMPORT.

Returns   Canonical string representation of the PackagePermission actions.

6.1.19.8   **public int hashCode( )**

☐   Returns the hash code value for this object.

Returns   A hash code value for this object.

6.1.19.9   **public boolean implies(Permission p)**

p   The requested permission.

☐   Determines if the specified permission is implied by this object.

This method checks that the package name of the target is implied by the package name of this object. The list of PackagePermission actions must either match or allow for the list of the target object to imply the target PackagePermission action.

The permission to export a package implies the permission to import the named package.

```
x.y.*,"export" -> x.y.z,"export" is true
*,"import" -> x.y, "import"      is true
*,"export" -> x.y, "import"      is true
x.y,"export" -> x.y.z, "export"  is false
```

Returns   true if the specified permission is implied by this object; false otherwise.

6.1.19.10   **public PermissionCollection newPermissionCollection( )**

☐   Returns a new PermissionCollection object suitable for storing PackagePermission objects.

Returns   A new PermissionCollection object.

6.1.20   **public class ServiceEvent**
extends EventObject

An event from the Framework describing a service lifecycle change.

ServiceEvent objects are delivered to ServiceListeners and AllServiceListeners when a change occurs in this service's lifecycle. A type code is used to identify the event type for future extendability.

OSGi Alliance reserves the right to extend the set of types.

See Also   ServiceListener, AllServiceListener

Concurrency   Immutable

6.1.20.1   **public static final int MODIFIED = 2**

The properties of a registered service have been modified.

This event is synchronously delivered after the service properties have been modified.

See Also   ServiceRegistration.setProperties

6.1.20.2   **public static final int MODIFIED_ENDMATCH = 8**

The properties of a registered service have been modified and the new properties no longer match the listener's filter.

This event is synchronously delivered after the service properties have been modified. This event is only delivered to listeners which were added with a non-null filter where the filter matched the service properties prior to the modification but the filter does not match the modified service properties.

See Also   ServiceRegistration.setProperties

Since   1.5

6.1.20.3   **public static final int REGISTERED = 1**

This service has been registered.

This event is synchronously delivered after the service has been registered with the Framework.

See Also   BundleContext.registerService(String[],Object,Dictionary)

6.1.20.4   **public static final int UNREGISTERING = 4**

This service is in the process of being unregistered.

This event is synchronously delivered before the service has completed unregistering.

If a bundle is using a service that is UNREGISTERING, the bundle should release its use of the service when it receives this event. If the bundle does not release its use of the service when it receives this event, the Framework will automatically release the bundle's use of the service while completing the service unregistration operation.

See Also   ServiceRegistration.unregister, BundleContext.ungetService

6.1.20.5   **public ServiceEvent(int type, ServiceReference reference)**

type   The event type.

reference   A ServiceReference object to the service that had a lifecycle change.

    □ Creates a new service event object.

6.1.20.6   **public ServiceReference getServiceReference( )**

    □ Returns a reference to the service that had a change occur in its lifecycle.

This reference is the source of the event.

Returns   Reference to the service that had a lifecycle change.

6.1.20.7   **public int getType( )**

    □ Returns the type of event. The event type values are:

- REGISTERED
- MODIFIED
- MODIFIED_ENDMATCH
- UNREGISTERING

Returns   Type of service lifecycle change.

6.1.21	**public class ServiceException** **extends RuntimeException**

A service exception used to indicate that a service problem occurred.

A ServiceException object is created by the Framework or service implementation to denote an exception condition in the service. A type code is used to identify the exception type for future extendability. Service implementations may also create subclasses of ServiceException. When subclassing, the subclass should set the type to SUBCLASSED to indicate that ServiceException has been subclassed.

This exception conforms to the general purpose exception chaining mechanism.

Since 1.5

6.1.21.1   **public static final int FACTORY_ERROR = 2**

The service factory produced an invalid service object.

6.1.21.2   **public static final int FACTORY_EXCEPTION = 3**

The service factory threw an exception.

6.1.21.3   **public static final int REMOTE = 5**

An error occurred invoking a remote service.

6.1.21.4   **public static final int SUBCLASSED = 4**

The exception is a subclass of ServiceException. The subclass should be examined for the type of the exception.

6.1.21.5   **public static final int UNREGISTERED = 1**

The service has been unregistered.

6.1.21.6   **public static final int UNSPECIFIED = 0**

No exception type is unspecified.

6.1.21.7   **public ServiceException(String msg, Throwable cause)**

msg The associated message.

cause The cause of this exception.

☐ Creates a ServiceException with the specified message and exception cause.

6.1.21.8   **public ServiceException(String msg)**

msg The message.

☐ Creates a ServiceException with the specified message.

6.1.21.9   **public ServiceException(String msg, int type, Throwable cause)**

msg The associated message.

type The type for this exception.

cause The cause of this exception.

☐ Creates a ServiceException with the specified message, type and exception cause.

6.1.21.10   **public ServiceException(String msg, int type)**

msg   The message.

type   The type for this exception.

   ☐ Creates a ServiceException with the specified message and type.

6.1.21.11   **public int getType( )**

   ☐ Returns the type for this exception or UNSPECIFIED if the type was unspecified or unknown.

Returns   The type of this exception.

6.1.22   public interface ServiceFactory

Allows services to provide customized service objects in the OSGi environment.

When registering a service, a ServiceFactory object can be used instead of a service object, so that the bundle developer can gain control of the specific service object granted to a bundle that is using the service.

When this happens, the BundleContext.getService(ServiceReference) method calls the ServiceFactory.getService method to create a service object specifically for the requesting bundle. The service object returned by the ServiceFactory is cached by the Framework until the bundle releases its use of the service.

When the bundle's use count for the service equals zero (including the bundle stopping or the service being unregistered), the ServiceFactory.ungetService method is called.

ServiceFactory objects are only used by the Framework and are not made available to other bundles in the OSGi environment. The Framework may concurrently call a ServiceFactory.

See Also   BundleContext.getService

Concurrency   Thread-safe

6.1.22.1   **public Object getService(Bundle bundle, ServiceRegistration registration)**

bundle   The bundle using the service.

registration   The ServiceRegistration object for the service.

   ☐ Creates a new service object.

The Framework invokes this method the first time the specified bundle requests a service object using the BundleContext.getService(ServiceReference) method. The service factory can then return a specific service object for each bundle.

The Framework caches the value returned (unless it is null), and will return the same service object on any future call to BundleContext.getService for the same bundle. This means the Framework must not allow this method to be concurrently called for the same bundle.

The Framework will check if the returned service object is an instance of all the classes named when the service was registered. If not, then null is returned to the bundle.

Returns   A service object that must be an instance of all the classes named when the service was registered.

See Also   BundleContext.getService

6.1.22.2   **public void ungetService(Bundle bundle, ServiceRegistration registration, Object service)**

bundle   The bundle releasing the service.

registration   The ServiceRegistration object for the service.

service   The service object returned by a previous call to the ServiceFactory.getService method.

        ☐ Releases a service object.

The Framework invokes this method when a service has been released by a bundle. The service object may then be destroyed.

See Also   BundleContext.ungetService

6.1.23   public interface ServiceListener
extends EventListener

A ServiceEvent listener. ServiceListener is a listener interface that may be implemented by a bundle developer. When a ServiceEvent is fired, it is synchronously delivered to a ServiceListener. The Framework may deliver ServiceEvent objects to a ServiceListener out of order and may concurrently call and/or reenter a ServiceListener.

A ServiceListener object is registered with the Framework using the BundleContext.addServiceListener method. ServiceListener objects are called with a ServiceEvent object when a service is registered, modified, or is in the process of unregistering.

ServiceEvent object delivery to ServiceListener objects is filtered by the filter specified when the listener was registered. If the Java Runtime Environment supports permissions, then additional filtering is done. ServiceEvent objects are only delivered to the listener if the bundle which defines the listener object's class has the appropriate ServicePermission to get the service using at least one of the named classes under which the service was registered.

ServiceEvent object delivery to ServiceListener objects is further filtered according to package sources as defined in ServiceReference.isAssignableTo(Bundle, String).

See Also   ServiceEvent, ServicePermission

Concurrency   Thread-safe

6.1.23.1   public void serviceChanged(ServiceEvent event)

event   The ServiceEvent object.

        ☐ Receives notification that a service has had a lifecycle change.

6.1.24   public final class ServicePermission
extends BasicPermission

A bundle's authority to register or get a service.

- The register action allows a bundle to register a service on the specified names.
- The get action allows a bundle to detect a service and get it.

ServicePermission to get the specific service.

Concurrency   Thread-safe

6.1.24.1   public static final String GET = "get"

The action string get.

6.1.24.2   public static final String REGISTER = "register"

The action string register.

6.1.24.3   public ServicePermission(String name, String actions)

name   The service class name

actions   get,register (canonical order)

□ Create a new ServicePermission.

The name of the service is specified as a fully qualified class name. Wildcards may be used.

```
name ::= <class name> | <class name ending in ".*"> | *
```

Examples:

```
org.osgi.service.http.HttpService
org.osgi.service.http.*
*
```

For the get action, the name can also be a filter expression. The filter gives access to the service properties as well as the following attributes:

- signer - A Distinguished Name chain used to sign the bundle publishing the service. Wildcards in a DN are not matched according to the filter string rules, but according to the rules defined for a DN chain.
- location - The location of the bundle publishing the service.
- id - The bundle ID of the bundle publishing the service.
- name - The symbolic name of the bundle publishing the service.

Since the above attribute names may conflict with service property names used by a service, you can prefix an attribute name with '@' in the filter expression to match against the service property and not one of the above attributes. Filter attribute names are processed in a case sensitive manner unless the attribute references a service property. Service properties names are case insensitive.

There are two possible actions: get and register. The get permission allows the owner of this permission to obtain a service with this name. The register permission allows the bundle to register a service under that name.

6.1.24.4   **public ServicePermission(ServiceReference reference, String actions)**

reference The requested service.

actions The action get.

□ Creates a new requested ServicePermission object to be used by code that must perform checkPermission for the get action. ServicePermission objects created with this constructor cannot be added to a ServicePermission permission collection.

Since 1.5

6.1.24.5   **public boolean equals(Object obj)**

obj The object to test for equality.

□ Determines the equality of two ServicePermission objects. Checks that specified object has the same class name and action as this ServicePermission.

Returns true if obj is a ServicePermission, and has the same class name and actions as this ServicePermission object; false otherwise.

6.1.24.6   **public String getActions( )**

□ Returns the canonical string representation of the actions. Always returns present actions in the following order: get, register.

Returns The canonical string representation of the actions.

6.1.24.7   **public int hashCode( )**

□ Returns the hash code value for this object.

Returns Hash code value for this object.

6.1.24.8   **public boolean implies(Permission p)**

  p The target permission to check.

   □ Determines if a ServicePermission object "implies" the specified permission.

 Returns true if the specified permission is implied by this object; false otherwise.

6.1.24.9   **public PermissionCollection newPermissionCollection( )**

   □ Returns a new PermissionCollection object for storing ServicePermission objects.

 Returns A new PermissionCollection object suitable for storing ServicePermission objects.

6.1.25   public interface ServiceReference extends Comparable

A reference to a service.

The Framework returns ServiceReference objects from the BundleContext.getServiceReference and BundleContext.getServiceReferences methods.

A ServiceReference object may be shared between bundles and can be used to examine the properties of the service and to get the service object.

Every service registered in the Framework has a unique ServiceRegistration object and may have multiple, distinct ServiceReference objects referring to it. ServiceReference objects associated with a ServiceRegistration object have the same hashCode and are considered equal (more specifically, their equals() method will return true when compared).

If the same service object is registered multiple times, ServiceReference objects associated with different ServiceRegistration objects are not equal.

 See Also BundleContext. getServiceReference, BundleContext. getServiceReferences, BundleContext. getService

 Concurrency Thread-safe

6.1.25.1   **public int compareTo(Object reference)**

 reference The ServiceReference to be compared.

   □ Compares this ServiceReference with the specified ServiceReference for order.

    If this ServiceReference and the specified ServiceReference have the same service id they are equal. This ServiceReference is less than the specified ServiceReference if it has a lower service ranking and greater if it has a higher service ranking. Otherwise, if this ServiceReference and the specified ServiceReference have the same service ranking, this ServiceReference is less than the specified ServiceReference if it has a higher service id and greater if it has a lower service id.

 Returns Returns a negative integer, zero, or a positive integer if this ServiceReference is less than, equal to, or greater than the specified ServiceReference.

 Throws IllegalArgumentException – If the specified ServiceReference was not created by the same framework instance as this ServiceReference.

 Since 1.4

6.1.25.2   **public Bundle getBundle( )**

   □ Returns the bundle that registered the service referenced by this ServiceReference object.

    This method must return null when the service has been unregistered. This can be used to determine if the service has been unregistered.

 Returns The bundle that registered the service referenced by this ServiceReference object; null if that service has already been unregistered.

See Also BundleContext.registerService(String[],Object,Dictionary)

6.1.25.3   **public Object getProperty(String key)**

key The property key.

☐ Returns the property value to which the specified property key is mapped in the properties Dictionary object of the service referenced by this ServiceReference object.

Property keys are case-insensitive.

This method must continue to return property values after the service has been unregistered. This is so references to unregistered services (for example, ServiceReference objects stored in the log) can still be interrogated.

Returns The property value to which the key is mapped; null if there is no property named after the key.

6.1.25.4   **public String[] getPropertyKeys( )**

☐ Returns an array of the keys in the properties Dictionary object of the service referenced by this ServiceReference object.

This method will continue to return the keys after the service has been unregistered. This is so references to unregistered services (for example, ServiceReference objects stored in the log) can still be interrogated.

This method is *case-preserving*; this means that every key in the returned array must have the same case as the corresponding key in the properties Dictionary that was passed to the BundleContext.registerService(String[],Object,Dictionary) or ServiceRegistration.setProperties methods.

Returns An array of property keys.

6.1.25.5   **public Bundle[] getUsingBundles( )**

☐ Returns the bundles that are using the service referenced by this ServiceReference object. Specifically, this method returns the bundles whose usage count for that service is greater than zero.

Returns An array of bundles whose usage count for the service referenced by this ServiceReference object is greater than zero; null if no bundles are currently using that service.

Since 1.1

6.1.25.6   **public boolean isAssignableTo(Bundle bundle, String className)**

bundle The Bundle object to check.

className The class name to check.

☐ Tests if the bundle that registered the service referenced by this ServiceReference and the specified bundle use the same source for the package of the specified class name.

This method performs the following checks:

1 Get the package name from the specified class name.
2 For the bundle that registered the service referenced by this ServiceReference (registrant bundle); find the source for the package. If no source is found then return true if the registrant bundle is equal to the specified bundle; otherwise return false.
3 If the package source of the registrant bundle is equal to the package source of the specified bundle then return true; otherwise return false.

Returns true if the bundle which registered the service referenced by this ServiceReference and the specified bundle use the same source for the package of the specified class name. Otherwise false is returned.

Throws IllegalArgumentException – If the specified Bundle was not created by the same framework instance as this ServiceReference.

Since 1.3

6.1.26   public interface ServiceRegistration

A registered service.

The Framework returns a ServiceRegistration object when a BundleContext.registerService method invocation is successful. The ServiceRegistration object is for the private use of the registering bundle and should not be shared with other bundles.

The ServiceRegistration object may be used to update the properties of the service or to unregister the service.

See Also   BundleContext.registerService(String[],Object,Dictionary)

Concurrency   Thread-safe

6.1.26.1   public ServiceReference getReference( )

□   Returns a ServiceReference object for a service being registered.

The ServiceReference object may be shared with other bundles.

Returns   ServiceReference object.

Throws   IllegalStateException – If this ServiceRegistration object has already been unregistered.

6.1.26.2   public void setProperties(Dictionary properties)

properties   The properties for this service. See Constants for a list of standard service property keys. Changes should not be made to this object after calling this method. To update the service's properties this method should be called again.

□   Updates the properties associated with a service.

The Constants.OBJECTCLASS and Constants.SERVICE_ID keys cannot be modified by this method. These values are set by the Framework when the service is registered in the OSGi environment.

The following steps are required to modify service properties:

1   The service's properties are replaced with the provided properties.
2   A service event of type ServiceEvent.MODIFIED is fired.

Throws   IllegalStateException – If this ServiceRegistration object has already been unregistered.

IllegalArgumentException – If properties contains case variants of the same key name.

6.1.26.3   public void unregister( )

□   Unregisters a service. Remove a ServiceRegistration object from the Framework service registry. All ServiceReference objects associated with this ServiceRegistration object can no longer be used to interact with the service once unregistration is complete.

The following steps are required to unregister a service:

1   The service is removed from the Framework service registry so that it can no longer be obtained.
2   A service event of type ServiceEvent.UNREGISTERING is fired so that bundles using this service can release their use of the service. Once delivery of the service event is complete, the ServiceReference objects for the service may no longer be used to get a service object for the service.
3   For each bundle whose use count for this service is greater than zero:
    The bundle's use count for this service is set to zero.
    If the service was registered with a ServiceFactory object, the ServiceFactory.ungetService method is called to release the service object for the bundle.

Throws   IllegalStateException – If this ServiceRegistration object has already been unregistered.

See Also   BundleContext.ungetService, ServiceFactory.ungetService

6.1.27   **public interface SynchronousBundleListener**
extends BundleListener

A synchronous BundleEvent listener. SynchronousBundleListener is a listener interface that may be implemented by a bundle developer. When a BundleEvent is fired, it is synchronously delivered to a SynchronousBundleListener. The Framework may deliver BundleEvent objects to a SynchronousBundleListener out of order and may concurrently call and/or reenter a SynchronousBundleListener.

A SynchronousBundleListener object is registered with the Framework using the BundleContext.addBundleListener method. SynchronousBundleListener objects are called with a BundleEvent object when a bundle has been installed, resolved, starting, started, stopping, stopped, updated, unresolved, or uninstalled.

Unlike normal BundleListener objects, SynchronousBundleListeners are synchronously called during bundle lifecycle processing. The bundle lifecycle processing will not proceed until all SynchronousBundleListeners have completed. SynchronousBundleListener objects will be called prior to BundleListener objects.

AdminPermission[bundle,LISTENER] is required to add or remove a SynchronousBundleListener object.

See Also BundleEvent

Since 1.1

Concurrency Thread-safe

6.1.28   **public class Version**
implements Comparable

Version identifier for bundles and packages.

Version identifiers have four components.

1 Major version. A non-negative integer.
2 Minor version. A non-negative integer.
3 Micro version. A non-negative integer.
4 Qualifier. A text string. See Version(String) for the format of the qualifier string.

Version objects are immutable.

Since 1.3

Concurrency Immutable

6.1.28.1   **public static final Version emptyVersion**

The empty version "0.0.0".

6.1.28.2   **public Version(int major, int minor, int micro)**

major Major component of the version identifier.

minor Minor component of the version identifier.

micro Micro component of the version identifier.

☐ Creates a version identifier from the specified numerical components.

The qualifier is set to the empty string.

Throws IllegalArgumentException – If the numerical components are negative.

6.1.28.3   **public Version(int major, int minor, int micro, String qualifier)**

major Major component of the version identifier.

minor Minor component of the version identifier.

micro Micro component of the version identifier.

qualifier Qualifier component of the version identifier. If null is specified, then the qualifier will be set to the empty string.

☐ Creates a version identifier from the specified components.

Throws IllegalArgumentException – If the numerical components are negative or the qualifier string is invalid.

6.1.28.4   **public Version(String version)**

version String representation of the version identifier.

☐ Created a version identifier from the specified string.

Here is the grammar for version strings.

```
version ::= major('.'minor('.'micro('.'qualifier)?)?)?
major ::= digit+
minor ::= digit+
micro ::= digit+
qualifier ::= (alpha|digit|'_'|'-')+
digit ::= [0..9]
alpha ::= [a..zA..Z]
```

There must be no whitespace in version.

Throws IllegalArgumentException – If version is improperly formatted.

6.1.28.5   **public int compareTo(Object object)**

object The Version object to be compared.

☐ Compares this Version object to another object.

A version is considered to be **less than** another version if its major component is less than the other version's major component, or the major components are equal and its minor component is less than the other version's minor component, or the major and minor components are equal and its micro component is less than the other version's micro component, or the major, minor and micro components are equal and it's qualifier component is less than the other version's qualifier component (using String.compareTo).

A version is considered to be **equal to** another version if the major, minor and micro components are equal and the qualifier component is equal (using String.compareTo).

Returns A negative integer, zero, or a positive integer if this object is less than, equal to, or greater than the specified Version object.

Throws ClassCastException – If the specified object is not a Version.

6.1.28.6   **public boolean equals(Object object)**

object The Version object to be compared.

☐ Compares this Version object to another object.

A version is considered to be **equal to** another version if the major, minor and micro components are equal and the qualifier component is equal (using String.equals).

Returns true if object is a Version and is equal to this object; false otherwise.

6.1.28.7   **public int getMajor( )**

☐ Returns the major component of this version identifier.

Returns The major component.

6.1.28.8   **public int getMicro( )**

☐ Returns the micro component of this version identifier.

Returns The micro component.

6.1.28.9   **public int getMinor( )**

☐ Returns the minor component of this version identifier.

Returns The minor component.

6.1.28.10   **public String getQualifier( )**

☐ Returns the qualifier component of this version identifier.

Returns The qualifier component.

6.1.28.11   **public int hashCode( )**

☐ Returns a hash code value for the object.

Returns An integer which is a hash code value for this object.

6.1.28.12   **public static Version parseVersion(String version)**

version String representation of the version identifier. Leading and trailing whitespace will be ignored.

☐ Parses a version identifier from the specified string.

See Version(String) for the format of the version string.

Returns A Version object representing the version identifier. If version is null or the empty string then emptyVersion will be returned.

Throws IllegalArgumentException – If version is improperly formatted.

6.1.28.13   **public String toString( )**

☐ Returns the string representation of this version identifier.

The format of the version string will be major.minor.micro if qualifier is the empty string or major.minor.micro.qualifier otherwise.

Returns The string representation of this version identifier.

6.2   org.osgi.framework.launch

Framework Launch Package Version 1.0.

Bundles wishing to use this package must list the package in the Import-Package header of the bundle's manifest. For example:

```
Import-Package: org.osgi.framework.launch;version="[1.0,2.0)"
```

6.2.1   Summary

- Framework - A Framework instance.
- FrameworkFactory - A factory for creating Framework instances.

6.2.2   **public interface Framework**
                   extends Bundle

A Framework instance. A Framework is also known as a System Bundle.

Framework instances are created using a `FrameworkFactory`. The methods of this interface can be used to manage and control the created framework instance.

Concurrency   Thread-safe

6.2.2.1   **public long getBundleId( )**

☐ Returns the Framework unique identifier. This Framework is assigned the unique identifier zero (0) since this Framework is also a System Bundle.

Returns   0.

See Also   `Bundle.getBundleId()`

6.2.2.2   **public String getLocation( )**

☐ Returns the Framework location identifier. This Framework is assigned the unique location "System Bundle" since this Framework is also a System Bundle.

Returns   The string "System Bundle".

Throws   `SecurityException` – If the caller does not have the appropriate AdminPermission[this,METADA-TA], and the Java Runtime Environment supports permissions.

See Also   `Bundle.getLocation()`, `Constants.SYSTEM_BUNDLE_LOCATION`

6.2.2.3   **public String getSymbolicName( )**

☐ Returns the symbolic name of this Framework. The symbolic name is unique for the implementation of the framework. However, the symbolic name "system.bundle" must be recognized as an alias to the implementation-defined symbolic name since this Framework is also a System Bundle.

Returns   The symbolic name of this Framework.

See Also   `Bundle.getSymbolicName()`, `Constants.SYSTEM_BUNDLE_SYMBOLICNAME`

6.2.2.4   **public void init( ) throws BundleException**

☐ Initialize this Framework. After calling this method, this Framework must:

- Be in the STARTING state.
- Have a valid Bundle Context.
- Be at start level 0.
- Have event handling enabled.
- Have reified Bundle objects for all installed bundles.
- Have registered any framework services. For example, PackageAdmin, ConditionalPermission-Admin, StartLevel.

This Framework will not actually be started until start is called.

This method does nothing if called when this Framework is in the STARTING, ACTIVE or STOPPING states.

Throws   `BundleException` – If this Framework could not be initialized.

`SecurityException` – If the Java Runtime Environment supports permissions and the caller does not have the appropriate AdminPermission[this,EXECUTE] or if there is a security manager already installed and the `Constants.FRAMEWORK_SECURITY` configuration property is set.

6.2.2.5   **public void start( ) throws BundleException**

☐ Start this Framework.

The following steps are taken to start this Framework:

1 If this Framework is not in the STARTING state, initialize this Framework.
2 All installed bundles must be started in accordance with each bundle's persistent *autostart setting*. This means some bundles will not be started, some will be started with *eager activation* and some will be started with their *declared activation* policy. If this Framework implements the optional *Start Level Service Specification*, then the start level of this Framework is moved to the start level specified by the beginning start level framework property, as described in the *Start Level Service Specification*. If this framework property is not specified, then the start level of this Framework is moved to start level one (1). Any exceptions that occur during bundle starting must be wrapped in a BundleException and then published as a framework event of type FrameworkEvent.ERROR
3 This Framework's state is set to ACTIVE.
4 A framework event of type FrameworkEvent.STARTED is fired

Throws BundleException – If this Framework could not be started.

SecurityException – If the caller does not have the appropriate AdminPermission[this,EXECUTE], and the Java Runtime Environment supports permissions.

See Also Start Level Service Specification

6.2.2.6 **public void start(int options) throws BundleException**

options Ignored. There are no start options for the Framework.

☐ Start this Framework.

Calling this method is the same as calling start(). There are no start options for the Framework.

Throws BundleException – If this Framework could not be started.

SecurityException – If the caller does not have the appropriate AdminPermission[this,EXECUTE], and the Java Runtime Environment supports permissions.

See Also start()

6.2.2.7 **public void stop( ) throws BundleException**

☐ Stop this Framework.

The method returns immediately to the caller after initiating the following steps to be taken on another thread.

1 This Framework's state is set to STOPPING.
2 All installed bundles must be stopped without changing each bundle's persistent *autostart setting*. If this Framework implements the optional *Start Level Service Specification*, then the start level of this Framework is moved to start level zero (0), as described in the *Start Level Service Specification*. Any exceptions that occur during bundle stopping must be wrapped in a BundleException and then published as a framework event of type FrameworkEvent.ERROR
3 Unregister all services registered by this Framework.
4 Event handling is disabled.
5 This Framework's state is set to RESOLVED.
6 All resources held by this Framework are released. This includes threads, bundle class loaders, open files, etc.
7 Notify all threads that are waiting at waitForStop that the stop operation has completed.

After being stopped, this Framework may be discarded, initialized or started.

Throws BundleException – If stopping this Framework could not be initiated.

SecurityException – If the caller does not have the appropriate AdminPermission[this,EXECUTE], and the Java Runtime Environment supports permissions.

See Also Start Level Service Specification

6.2.2.8   **public void stop(int options) throws BundleException**

options Ignored. There are no stop options for the Framework.

☐ Stop this Framework.

Calling this method is the same as calling stop(). There are no stop options for the Framework.

Throws BundleException – If stopping this Framework could not be initiated.

SecurityException – If the caller does not have the appropriate AdminPermission[this,EXECUTE], and the Java Runtime Environment supports permissions.

See Also stop()

6.2.2.9   **public void uninstall( ) throws BundleException**

☐ The Framework cannot be uninstalled.

This method always throws a BundleException.

Throws BundleException – This Framework cannot be uninstalled.

SecurityException – If the caller does not have the appropriate AdminPermission[this,LIFECY-CLE], and the Java Runtime Environment supports permissions.

6.2.2.10   **public void update( ) throws BundleException**

☐ Stop and restart this Framework.

The method returns immediately to the caller after initiating the following steps to be taken on another thread.

1   Perform the steps in the stop() method to stop this Framework.
2   Perform the steps in the start() method to start this Framework.

Throws BundleException – If stopping and restarting this Framework could not be initiated.

SecurityException – If the caller does not have the appropriate AdminPermission[this,LIFECY-CLE], and the Java Runtime Environment supports permissions.

6.2.2.11   **public void update(InputStream in) throws BundleException**

in Any provided InputStream is immediately closed before returning from this method and otherwise ignored.

☐ Stop and restart this Framework.

Calling this method is the same as calling update() except that any provided InputStream is immediately closed.

Throws BundleException – If stopping and restarting this Framework could not be initiated.

SecurityException – If the caller does not have the appropriate AdminPermission[this,LIFECY-CLE], and the Java Runtime Environment supports permissions.

6.2.2.12   **public FrameworkEvent waitForStop(long timeout) throws InterruptedException**

timeout Maximum number of milliseconds to wait until this Framework has completely stopped. A value of zero will wait indefinitely.

☐ Wait until this Framework has completely stopped. The stop and update methods on a Framework performs an asynchronous stop of the Framework. This method can be used to wait until the asynchronous stop of this Framework has completed. This method will only wait if called when this Framework is in the STARTING, ACTIVE, or STOPPING states. Otherwise it will return immediately.

A Framework Event is returned to indicate why this Framework has stopped.

Returns A Framework Event indicating the reason this method returned. The following FrameworkEvent types may be returned by this method.

STOPPED - This Framework has been stopped.

STOPPED_UPDATE - This Framework has been updated which has shutdown and will now restart.

STOPPED_BOOTCLASSPATH_MODIFIED - This Framework has been stopped and a bootclasspath extension bundle has been installed or updated. The VM must be restarted in order for the changed boot class path to take affect.

ERROR - The Framework encountered an error while shutting down or an error has occurred which forced the framework to shutdown.

WAIT_TIMEDOUT - This method has timed out and returned before this Framework has stopped.

Throws InterruptedException – If another thread interrupted the current thread before or while the current thread was waiting for this Framework to completely stop. The *interrupted status* of the current thread is cleared when this exception is thrown.

IllegalArgumentException – If the value of timeout is negative.

6.2.3 public interface FrameworkFactory

A factory for creating Framework instances.

A framework implementation jar must contain the following resource:

/META-INF/services/org.osgi.framework.launch.FrameworkFactory

This UTF-8 encoded resource must contain the name of the framework implementation's FrameworkFactory implementation class. Space and tab characters, including blank lines, in the resource must be ignored. The number sign ('#' \u0023) and all characters following it on each line are a comment and must be ignored.

Launchers can find the name of the FrameworkFactory implementation class in the resource and then load and construct a FrameworkFactory object for the framework implementation. The FrameworkFactory implementation class must have a public, no-argument constructor. Java™ SE 6 introduced the ServiceLoader class which can create a FrameworkFactory instance from the resource.

Concurrency Thread-safe

6.2.3.1 public Framework newFramework(Map configuration)

configuration The framework properties to configure the new framework instance. If framework properties are not provided by the configuration argument, the created framework instance must use some reasonable default configuration appropriate for the current VM. For example, the system packages for the current execution environment should be properly exported. The specified configuration argument may be null. The created framework instance must copy any information needed from the specified configuration argument since the configuration argument can be changed after the framework instance has been created.

□ Create a new Framework instance.

Returns A new, configured Framework instance. The framework instance must be in the Bundle.INSTALLED state.

Throws SecurityException – If the caller does not have AllPermission, and the Java Runtime Environment supports permissions.

7   Package Admin Service Specification

Version 1.2

7.1   Introduction

Bundles can export packages to other bundles. This exporting creates a dependency between the bundle exporting a package and the bundle using the package. When the exporting bundle is uninstalled or updated, a decision must be taken regarding any shared packages.

The Package Admin service provides an interface to let the Management Agent make this decision.

7.1.1   Essentials

- *Information* – The Package Admin service must provide the sharing status of all packages. This should include information about the importing bundles and exporting bundle.
- *Policy* – The Package Admin service must allow a management agent to provide a policy for package sharing when bundles are updated and uninstalled.
- *Minimal update* – Only bundles that depend on the package that needs to be resolved should have to be restarted when packages are forced to be refreshed.

7.1.2   Entities

- PackageAdmin – The interface that provides access to the internal Framework package sharing mechanism.
- ExportedPackage – The interface provides package information and its sharing status.
- RequiredBundle – The interfaces provides information about the bindings of required bundles.
- *Management Agent* – A bundle that is provided by the Operator to implement an Operator specific policy.

Figure 7.42   *Class Diagram org.osgi.service.packageadmin*

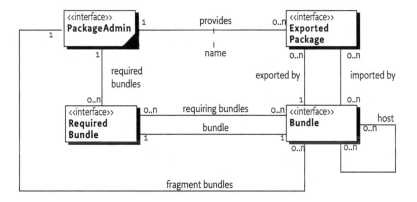

7.1.3   Operation

The Framework's system bundle should provide a Package Admin service for the Management Agent. The Package Admin service must be registered under the org.osgi.service.packageadmin.PackageAdmin interface by the system bundle. It provides access to the internal structures of the Framework related to package sharing, fragments and required bundles. This is an optional singleton service, so at most one Package Admin service must be registered at any moment in time.

The Framework must always leave the package sharing intact for packages exported by a bundle that is uninstalled or updated. A Management Agent can then choose to force the framework to refresh these packages using the Package Admin service. A policy of always using the most current packages exported by installed bundles can be implemented with a Management Agent that watches Framework events for bundles being uninstalled or updated, and then refreshes the packages of those bundles using the Package Admin service.

7.2   Package Admin

The Package Admin service is intended to allow a Management Agent to define the policy for managing package sharing. It provides methods for examining the status of the shared packages. It also allows the Management Agent to refresh the packages and stop and restart bundles as necessary.

7.2.1   Package Sharing

The PackageAdmin class provides the following methods:

- getExportedPackage(String) – Returns an ExportedPackage object that provides information about the requested package. This information can be used to make the decision to refresh the package.
- getExportedPackages(Bundle) – Returns a list of ExportedPackage objects for each package that the given bundle exports.
- refreshPackages(Bundle[]) – The management agent may call this method to refresh the exported packages of the specified bundles. The actual work must happen asynchronously. The Framework must send a Framework.PACKAGES_REFRESHED when all packages have been refreshed.
- resolveBundles(Bundle[]) – The Framework must attempt to resolve the given bundles.

7.2.2   Bundle Information

There is only the Bundle interface in the Framework API while bundles can perform different roles in the Framework. The Package Admin service provides access to this structural information.

- getBundle(Class) – Answer the bundle with the class loader that loaded the given class.
- getBundles(String,String)– Find a the set of bundles with the given bundle symbolic name and that fall within the given version. If the version is null, all bundles with the given bundle symbolic name are returned.
- getBundleType(Bundle) – Answer the type of the bundle. This is a bitmap of the different types. The following type is defined:
  - BUNDLE_TYPE_FRAGMENT– The bundle is a fragment.

7.2.3   Fragments and Required Bundles

The Package Admin service provides access to the network that is created by by requiring bundles and hosting fragments.

- getFragments(Bundle) – Return an array of bundles that currently act as fragment to the given bundle. If there are no fragments attached, null must be returned.

- getHosts(Bundle) – Return the bundles that acts as host to this fragment bundle. The given bundle should be an attached fragment bundle, otherwise null is returned.
- getRequiredBundles(String) – Return an array of RequiredBundle objects that match the given name (or all of the given name is null). The RequiredBundle object provides structural information about a required bundle.

7.2.4 Exported Package

Information about the shared packages is provided by the ExportedPackage objects. These objects provide detailed information about the bundles that import and export the package. This information can be used by a Management Agent to guide its decisions.

7.2.5 Refreshing Packages

Bundles may be stopped and later started again when the refreshPackages(Bundle[]) method is called. This starting must use the same option (e.g. START_TRANSIENT) that was used to start the bundle before the refreshPackages(Bundle[]) method was called.

If the Start Level Service is present, the stopping and starting of bundles must not violate the start level constraints. This implies that bundles with a higher start level must be stopped before bundles with a lower start level are stopped. Vice versa, bundles should not be started before all the bundles with a lower start level are started. See *Startup Sequence* on page 206.

The Bundle activation policies place additional rules on how a bundle should be restarted after a refresh, see *Restoring State After Refresh or Update* on page 89.

7.3 Security

The Package Admin service is a *system service* that can easily be abused because it provides access to the internal data structures of the Framework. Many bundles may have the ServicePermission[org.osgi.service.packageadmin.PackageAdmin, GET] because AdminPermission[System Bundle, RESOLVE] is required for calling any of the methods that modify the environment. No bundle must have ServicePermission[org.osgi.service.packageadmin.PackageAdmin, REGISTER], because only the Framework itself should register such a system service.

This service is intended for use by a Management Agent.

7.4 Changes

- Allow fragments to attach to multiple hosts.

7.5 org.osgi.service.packageadmin

Package Admin Package Version 1.2.

Bundles wishing to use this package must list the package in the Import-Package header of the bundle's manifest. For example:

```
Import-Package: org.osgi.service.packageadmin; version="[1.2,2.0)"
```

7.5.1 Summary

- ExportedPackage - An exported package.

- PackageAdmin - Framework service which allows bundle programmers to inspect the package wiring state of bundles in the Framework as well as other functions related to the class loader network among bundles.
- RequiredBundle - A required bundle.

7.5.2   public interface ExportedPackage

An exported package. Objects implementing this interface are created by the Package Admin service.

The term *exported package* refers to a package that has been exported from a resolved bundle. This package may or may not be currently wired to other bundles.

The information about an exported package provided by this object may change. An ExportedPackage object becomes stale if the package it references has been updated or removed as a result of calling PackageAdmin.refreshPackages(). If this object becomes stale, its getName() and getVersion() methods continue to return their original values, isRemovalPending() returns true, and getExportingBundle() and getImportingBundles() return null.

Concurrency Thread-safe

7.5.2.1   public Bundle getExportingBundle( )

□ Returns the bundle exporting the package associated with this exported package.

Returns The exporting bundle, or null if this ExportedPackage object has become stale.

7.5.2.2   public Bundle[] getImportingBundles( )

□ Returns the resolved bundles that are currently wired to this exported package.

Bundles which require the exporting bundle associated with this exported package are considered to be wired to this exported package are included in the returned array. See RequiredBundle.getRequiringBundles().

Returns The array of resolved bundles currently wired to this exported package, or null if this ExportedPackage object has become stale. The array will be empty if no bundles are wired to this exported package.

7.5.2.3   public String getName( )

□ Returns the name of the package associated with this exported package.

Returns The name of this exported package.

7.5.2.4   public String getSpecificationVersion( )

□ Returns the version of this exported package.

Returns The version of this exported package, or null if no version information is available.

Deprecated As of 1.2, replaced by getVersion.

7.5.2.5   public Version getVersion( )

□ Returns the version of this exported package.

Returns The version of this exported package, or Version.emptyVersion if no version information is available.

Since 1.2

7.5.2.6   public boolean isRemovalPending( )

□ Returns true if the package associated with this ExportedPackage object has been exported by a bundle that has been updated or uninstalled.

Returns true if the associated package is being exported by a bundle that has been updated or uninstalled, or if this ExportedPackage object has become stale; false otherwise.

7.5.3 public interface PackageAdmin

Framework service which allows bundle programmers to inspect the package wiring state of bundles in the Framework as well as other functions related to the class loader network among bundles.

If present, there will only be a single instance of this service registered with the Framework.

See Also org.osgi.service.packageadmin.ExportedPackage,
org.osgi.service.packageadmin.RequiredBundle

Concurrency Thread-safe

7.5.3.1 public static final int BUNDLE_TYPE_FRAGMENT = 1

Bundle type indicating the bundle is a fragment bundle.

The value of BUNDLE_TYPE_FRAGMENT is 0x00000001.

Since 1.2

7.5.3.2 public Bundle getBundle(Class clazz)

clazz The class object from which to locate the bundle.

☐ Returns the bundle from which the specified class is loaded. The class loader of the returned bundle must have been used to load the specified class. If the class was not loaded by a bundle class loader then null is returned.

Returns The bundle from which the specified class is loaded or null if the class was not loaded by a bundle class loader created by the same framework instance that registered this PackageAdmin service.

Since 1.2

7.5.3.3 public Bundle[] getBundles(String symbolicName, String versionRange)

symbolicName The symbolic name of the desired bundles.

versionRange The version range of the desired bundles, or null if all versions are desired.

☐ Returns the bundles with the specified symbolic name whose bundle version is within the specified version range. If no bundles are installed that have the specified symbolic name, then null is returned. If a version range is specified, then only the bundles that have the specified symbolic name and whose bundle versions belong to the specified version range are returned. The returned bundles are ordered by version in descending version order so that the first element of the array contains the bundle with the highest version.

Returns An array of bundles with the specified name belonging to the specified version range ordered in descending version order, or null if no bundles are found.

See Also org.osgi.framework.Constants.BUNDLE_VERSION_ATTRIBUTE

Since 1.2

7.5.3.4 public int getBundleType(Bundle bundle)

bundle The bundle for which to return the special type.

☐ Returns the special type of the specified bundle. The bundle type values are:

- BUNDLE_TYPE_FRAGMENT

If a bundle is not one or more of the defined types then 0x00000000 is returned.

Returns The special type of the bundle.

Throws IllegalArgumentException – If the specified Bundle was not created by the same framework instance that registered this PackageAdmin service.

Since 1.2

7.5.3.5　　　public ExportedPackage getExportedPackage(String name)

name The name of the exported package to be returned.

□ Gets the exported package for the specified package name.

If there are multiple exported packages with specified name, the exported package with the highest version will be returned.

Returns The exported package, or null if no exported package with the specified name exists.

See Also getExportedPackages(String)

7.5.3.6　　　public ExportedPackage[] getExportedPackages(Bundle bundle)

bundle The bundle whose exported packages are to be returned, or null if all exported packages are to be returned. If the specified bundle is the system bundle (that is, the bundle with id zero), this method returns all the packages known to be exported by the system bundle. This will include the package specified by the org.osgi.framework.system.packages system property as well as any other package exported by the framework implementation.

□ Gets the exported packages for the specified bundle.

Returns An array of exported packages, or null if the specified bundle has no exported packages.

Throws IllegalArgumentException – If the specified Bundle was not created by the same framework instance that registered this PackageAdmin service.

7.5.3.7　　　public ExportedPackage[] getExportedPackages(String name)

name The name of the exported packages to be returned.

□ Gets the exported packages for the specified package name.

Returns An array of the exported packages, or null if no exported packages with the specified name exists.

Since 1.2

7.5.3.8　　　public Bundle[] getFragments(Bundle bundle)

bundle The bundle whose attached fragment bundles are to be returned.

□ Returns an array of attached fragment bundles for the specified bundle. If the specified bundle is a fragment then null is returned. If no fragments are attached to the specified bundle then null is returned.

This method does not attempt to resolve the specified bundle. If the specified bundle is not resolved then null is returned.

Returns An array of fragment bundles or null if the bundle does not have any attached fragment bundles or the bundle is not resolved.

Throws IllegalArgumentException – If the specified Bundle was not created by the same framework instance that registered this PackageAdmin service.

Since 1.2

7.5.3.9　　　public Bundle[] getHosts(Bundle bundle)

bundle The fragment bundle whose host bundles are to be returned.

□ Returns the host bundles to which the specified fragment bundle is attached.

Returns   An array containing the host bundles to which the specified fragment is attached or null if the specified bundle is not a fragment or is not attached to any host bundles.

Throws   IllegalArgumentException – If the specified Bundle was not created by the same framework instance that registered this PackageAdmin service.

Since   1.2

7.5.3.10   **public RequiredBundle[] getRequiredBundles(String symbolicName)**

symbolicName   The bundle symbolic name or null for all required bundles.

☐   Returns an array of required bundles having the specified symbolic name.

If null is specified, then all required bundles will be returned.

Returns   An array of required bundles or null if no required bundles exist for the specified symbolic name.

Since   1.2

7.5.3.11   **public void refreshPackages(Bundle[] bundles)**

bundles   The bundles whose exported packages are to be updated or removed, or null for all bundles updated or uninstalled since the last call to this method.

☐   Forces the update (replacement) or removal of packages exported by the specified bundles.

If no bundles are specified, this method will update or remove any packages exported by any bundles that were previously updated or uninstalled since the last call to this method. The technique by which this is accomplished may vary among different Framework implementations. One permissible implementation is to stop and restart the Framework.

This method returns to the caller immediately and then performs the following steps on a separate thread:

1   Compute a graph of bundles starting with the specified bundles. If no bundles are specified, compute a graph of bundles starting with bundle updated or uninstalled since the last call to this method. Add to the graph any bundle that is wired to a package that is currently exported by a bundle in the graph. The graph is fully constructed when there is no bundle outside the graph that is wired to a bundle in the graph. The graph may contain UNINSTALLED bundles that are currently still exporting packages.
2   Each bundle in the graph that is in the ACTIVE state will be stopped as described in the Bundle.stop method.
3   Each bundle in the graph that is in the RESOLVED state is unresolved and thus moved to the INSTALLED state. The effect of this step is that bundles in the graph are no longer RESOLVED.
4   Each bundle in the graph that is in the UNINSTALLED state is removed from the graph and is now completely removed from the Framework.
5   Each bundle in the graph that was in the ACTIVE state prior to Step 2 is started as described in the Bundle.start method, causing all bundles required for the restart to be resolved. It is possible that, as a result of the previous steps, packages that were previously exported no longer are. Therefore, some bundles may be unresolvable until another bundle offering a compatible package for export has been installed in the Framework.
6   A framework event of type FrameworkEvent.PACKAGES_REFRESHED is fired.

For any exceptions that are thrown during any of these steps, a FrameworkEvent of type ERROR is fired containing the exception. The source bundle for these events should be the specific bundle to which the exception is related. If no specific bundle can be associated with the exception then the System Bundle must be used as the source bundle for the event.

Throws   SecurityException – If the caller does not have AdminPermission[System Bundle,RESOLVE] and the Java runtime environment supports permissions.

IllegalArgumentException – If the specified Bundles were not created by the same framework instance that registered this PackageAdmin service.

7.5.3.12   **public boolean resolveBundles(Bundle[] bundles)**

bundles   The bundles to resolve or null to resolve all unresolved bundles installed in the Framework.

□   Resolve the specified bundles. The Framework must attempt to resolve the specified bundles that are unresolved. Additional bundles that are not included in the specified bundles may be resolved as a result of calling this method. A permissible implementation of this method is to attempt to resolve all unresolved bundles installed in the framework.

If null is specified then the Framework will attempt to resolve all unresolved bundles. This method must not cause any bundle to be refreshed, stopped, or started. This method will not return until the operation has completed.

Returns   true if all specified bundles are resolved;

Throws   SecurityException – If the caller does not have AdminPermission[System Bundle,RESOLVE] and the Java runtime environment supports permissions.

IllegalArgumentException – If the specified Bundles were not created by the same framework instance that registered this PackageAdmin service.

Since   1.2

7.5.4   **public interface RequiredBundle**

A required bundle. Objects implementing this interface are created by the Package Admin service.

The term *required bundle* refers to a resolved bundle that has a bundle symbolic name and is not a fragment. That is, a bundle that may be required by other bundles. This bundle may or may not be currently required by other bundles.

The information about a required bundle provided by this object may change. A RequiredBundle object becomes stale if an exported package of the bundle it references has been updated or removed as a result of calling PackageAdmin.refreshPackages(). If this object becomes stale, its getSymbolicName() and getVersion() methods continue to return their original values, isRemoval-Pending() returns true, and getBundle() and getRequiringBundles() return null.

Since   1.2

Concurrency   Thread-safe

7.5.4.1   **public Bundle getBundle( )**

□   Returns the bundle associated with this required bundle.

Returns   The bundle, or null if this RequiredBundle object has become stale.

7.5.4.2   **public Bundle[] getRequiringBundles( )**

□   Returns the bundles that currently require this required bundle.

If this required bundle is required and then re-exported by another bundle then all the requiring bundles of the re-exporting bundle are included in the returned array.

Returns   An array of bundles currently requiring this required bundle, or null if this RequiredBundle object has become stale. The array will be empty if no bundles require this required package.

7.5.4.3   **public String getSymbolicName( )**

□   Returns the symbolic name of this required bundle.

Returns   The symbolic name of this required bundle.

7.5.4.4   **public Version getVersion( )**

☐ Returns the version of this required bundle.

Returns The version of this required bundle, or Version.emptyVersion if no version information is available.

7.5.4.5   **public boolean isRemovalPending( )**

☐ Returns true if the bundle associated with this RequiredBundle object has been updated or uninstalled.

Returns true if the required bundle has been updated or uninstalled, or if the RequiredBundle object has become stale; false otherwise.

8 Start Level Service Specification

Version 1.1

8.1 Introduction

This specification describes how to enable a Management Agent to control the relative starting and stopping order of bundles in an OSGi Service Platform.

The Start Level service assigns each bundle a *start level*. The Management Agent can modify the start levels for bundles and set the active start level of the Framework, which will start and stop the appropriate bundles. Only bundles that have a start level less or equal to this active start level must be active.

The purpose of the Start Level service is to allow the Management Agent to control, in detail, what bundles will be started and stopped and when this occurs.

8.1.1 Essentials

- *Ordering* – A management agent should be able to order the startup and shutdown sequences of bundles.
- *Levels* – The management agent should support a virtually unlimited number of levels.
- *Backward compatible* – The model for start levels should be compatible with the OSGi Service Platform Release 2 specifications.

8.1.2 Entities

- *Start Level Service* – The service that is used by a Management Agent to order the startup and shutdown sequences of bundles.
- *Management Agent* – See page 32.
- *Framework Event* – See page 99.
- *Framework Listener* – See page 99.

Figure 8.43   *Class Diagram org.osgi.service.startlevel package*

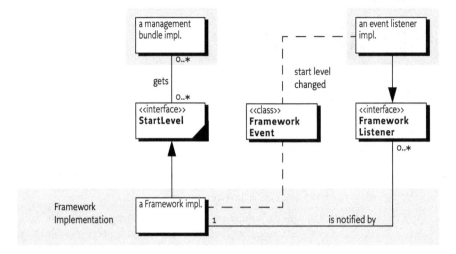

8.2   Start Level Service

The Start Level Service provides the following functions:

- Controls the beginning start level of the OSGi Framework.
- Is used to modify the active start level of the Framework.
- Can be used to assign a specific start level to a bundle.
- Can set the initial start level for newly installed bundles.

Defining the order in which bundles are started and stopped is useful for the following:

- *Safe mode* – The Management Agent can implement a *safe mode*. In this mode, only fully trusted bundles are started. Safe mode might be necessary when a bundle causes a failure at startup that disrupts normal operation and prevents correction of the problem.
- *Splash screen* – If the total startup time is long, it might be desirable to show a splash screen during initialization. This improves the user's perception of the boot time of the device. The startup ordering can ensure that the right bundle is started first.
- *Handling erratic bundles* – Problems can occur because bundles require services to be available when they are activated (this is a programming error). By controlling the start order, the Management Agent can prevent these problems.
- *High priority bundles* – Certain tasks such as metering need to run as quickly as possible and cannot have a long startup delay. These bundles can be started first.

8.2.1   The Concept of a Start Level

A *start level* is defined as a non-negative integer. A start level of 0 (zero) is the state in which the Framework has either not been launched or has completed shutdown (these two states are considered equivalent). In this state, no bundles are running. Progressively higher integral values represent progressively higher start levels. For example, 2 is a higher start level than 1. The Framework must support all positive int values (Integer.MAX_VALUE) for start levels.

The Framework has an *active start level* that is used to decide which bundles can be started. All bundles must be assigned a *bundle start level*. This is the minimum start level to start a bundle. The bundle start level can be set with the setBundleStartLevel(Bundle,int) method. When a bundle is installed, it is initially assigned the bundle start level returned by getInitialBundleStartLevel(). The initial bundle start level to be used when bundles are installed can be set with setInitialBundle-StartLevel(int).

In addition, a bundle can be persistently marked as *started* or *stopped* with the Bundle start and stop methods. A bundle cannot run unless it is marked started, regardless of the bundle's start level.

8.2.2   Changing the Active Start Level

A Management Agent can influence the active start level with the setStartLevel(int) method. The Framework must then increase or decrease the active start level by 1 until the requested start level is reached. The process of starting or stopping bundles, which is initiated by the setStartLevel(int) method, must take place asynchronously.

This means that the *active start level* (the one that is active at a certain moment in time) must be changed to a new start level, called the *requested start level*. The active and requested levels differ during a certain period when the Framework starts and stops the appropriate bundles. Moving from the active start level to the requested start level must take place in increments of one (1).

If the requested start level is higher than the active start level, the Framework must increase the start level by one and then start all bundles that meet the following criteria:

- Bundles that are persistently marked started, and
- Bundles that have a bundle start level equal to the new active start level.

The Framework continues increasing the active start level and starting the appropriate bundles until it has started all bundles with a bundle start level that equals the requested start level.

The Framework must not increase to the next active start level until all started bundles have returned from their BundleActivator.start method normally or with an exception. A FrameworkEvent.ERROR must be broadcast when the BundleActivator.start method throws an exception.

If the requested start level is lower than the active start level, the Framework must stop all bundles that have a bundle start level that is equal to the active start level. The Framework must then decrease the active start level by 1. If the active start level is still higher than the requested start level, it should continue stopping the appropriate bundles and decreasing the active start level until the requested start level is reached. A FrameworkEvent.ERROR must be broadcast when the BundleActivator.stop method throws an exception.

If the requested start level is the active start level, the Framework will not start or stop any bundles.

When the requested start level is reached and all bundles satisfy the condition that their bundle start level <= active start level in order to be started, then the FrameworkEvent.STARTLEVEL_CHANGED event must be sent to all registered FrameworkListener objects. If the requested start level and active start level are equal, then this event may arrive before the setStartLevel method has returned.

It must therefore always be true that:

- A bundle is started, or will be started soon, if the start level is less or equal to the active start level.
- A bundle is stopped, or will be stopped soon, when it has a start level more than the active start level.

These steps are depicted in the flow chart in Figure 8.44.

Figure 8.44   *Move to requested start level R, active level is A, B is a bundle's start level*

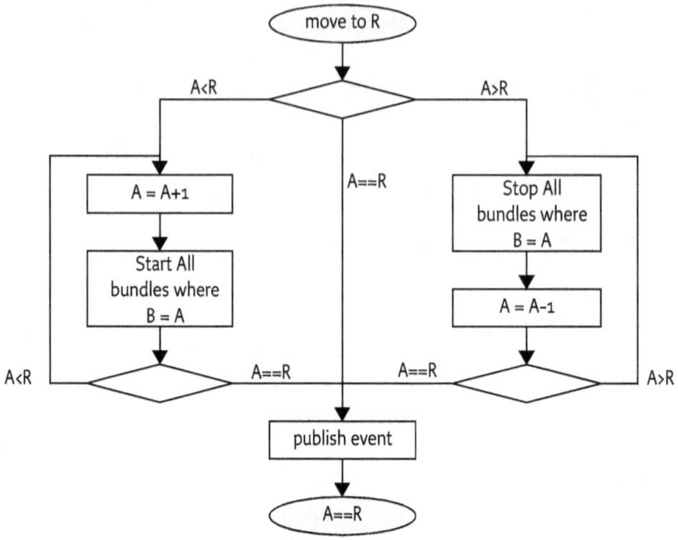

If the Framework is currently involved in changing the active start level, it must first reach the previously requested start level before it is allowed to continue with a newly requested start level. For example, assume the active start level is 5 and the Framework is requested to transition to start level 3. Before start level 3 is reached, another request is made to transition to start level 7. In this case, the OSGi Framework must first complete the transition to start level 3 before it transitions to start level 7.

8.2.3   Startup Sequence

At startup, the Framework must have an active start level of zero. It must then move the active start level to the *beginning start level*. The beginning start level is specified with an argument when starting the Framework or through some other means, which is left undefined here. If no beginning start level is given, the Framework must assume a beginning start level of one (1).

The Framework must launch and then set the requested start level to the beginning start level. It must then follow the procedure described in *Changing the Active Start Level* on page 205 to make the active start level equal the beginning start level, with the exception of the FrameworkEvent.START_LEVEL_CHANGED event broadcast. During launching, the Framework must broadcast a FrameworkEvent.STARTED event when the initial start level is reached.

8.2.4   Shutdown Sequence

When the Framework shuts down, the requested start level must be set to zero. The Framework must then follow the process described in *Changing the Active Start Level* on page 205 to make the active start level equal to zero.

8.2.5   Changing a Bundle's Start Level

Bundles are assigned an initial start level when they are installed. The default value for the initial start level is set to one, but can be changed with the setInitialBundleStartLevel(int) method. A bundle's start level will not change when the setInitialBundleStartLevel(int) method later modifies the default initial start level.

Once installed, the start level of a bundle can be changed with setBundleStartLevel(Bundle,int). When a bundle's start level is changed and the bundle is marked persistently to be started, then the OSGi Framework must compare the new bundle start level to the active start level. For example, assume that the active start level is 5 and a bundle with start level 5 is started. If the bundle's start level subsequently is changed to 6 then this bundle must be stopped by the OSGi Framework but it must still be marked persistently to be started.

8.2.6 Starting a Bundle

If a bundle is started by calling the Bundle.start method, then the OSGi Framework must mark the bundle as persistently started. The OSGi Framework must not actually start a bundle when the active start level is less than the bundle's start level. In that case, the state must not change.

8.2.7 Exceptions in the Bundle Activator

If the BundleActivator.start or stop method throws an Exception, then the handling of this Exception is different depending who invoked the start or stop method.

If the bundle is started/stopped due to a change in the active start level or the bundle's start level, then the Exception must be wrapped in a BundleException and broadcast as a FrameworkEvent.ERROR event. Otherwise, a new BundleException must be created containing the exception and this BundleException is then thrown to the caller.

8.2.8 System Bundle

The System Bundle is defined to have a start level of zero. The start level of the System Bundle cannot be changed. An IllegalArgumentException must be thrown if an attempt is made to change the start level of the System Bundle.

8.3 Compatibility Mode

Compatibility mode consists of a single start level for all bundles. All bundles are assigned a bundle start level of 1. In compatibility mode, the OSGi Framework is started and launched with an argument specifying a beginning start level of 1. The Framework then starts all bundles that are persistently marked to be started. When start level 1 is reached, all bundles have been started and the FrameworkEvent.STARTED event is published. This is considered compatible with prior OSGi Framework versions because all bundles are started and there is no control over the start order. Framework implementations must support compatibility mode.

8.4 Example Applications

The Start Level service allows a Management Agent to implement many different startup schemes. The following sections show some examples.

8.4.1 Safe Mode Startup Scheme

A Management Agent can implement a *safe mode* in which it runs trusted bundles at level 1 and runs itself on level 2. When the Management Agent gets control, it constructs a list of all applications to be started. This list can be constructed from BundleContext.getBundles(). The Management Agent checks each bundle to determine if it is not started but is marked to be started persistently by calling the isBundlePersistentlyStarted(Bundle) method of the Start Level service.

Before it starts each bundle, the Management Agent persistently records the bundle to be started and then starts the bundle. This continues until all bundles are started. When all bundles are successfully started, the Management Agent persistently records that all bundles started without problems.

If the Service Platform is restarted, the Management Agent should inspect the persistently recorded information. If the persistently recorded information indicates a bundle failure, the Management Agent should try to restart the system without that application bundle since that bundle failed. Alternatively, it could contact its Remote Manager and ask for assistance.

8.4.2 Splash Screen Startup Scheme

A splash screen is a popup containing startup information about an application. The popup provides feedback to the end user indicating that the system is still initializing. The Start Level service can be used by a bundle to pop-up a splash screen before any other bundle is started, and remove it once all bundles have been started. The splash-screen bundle would start at start level 1 and all other bundles would start at start level 2 or higher.

```
class SplashScreen implements
    BundleActivator, FrameworkListener {
    Screen    screen;
    public void start(BundleContext context) {
        context.addFrameworkListener( this );
        screen = createSplash();
        screen.open();
    }
    public void stop(BundleContext context) {
        screen.close();
    }
    public void frameworkEvent( FrameworkEvent event ) {
        if ( event.getType() == FrameworkEvent.STARTED )
            screen.close();
    }
    Screen createSplash() { ... }
}
```

8.5 Security

When the Start Level service is available, it is crucial to protect its usage from non-trusted bundles. A malicious bundle that can control start levels can control the whole service platform.

The Start Level service is for use by a Management Agent. This means that bundles that use this service must have AdminPermission[bundle,EXECUTE] to be able to modify a bundle's start level or AdminPermission[System Bundle,STARTLEVEL] to modify the Framework's active start level. Bundles that need only read access to this service should have ServicePermission[StartLevel, GET].

The Start Level service must be registered by the Framework so there is no reason for any bundle to have ServicePermission[StartLevel, REGISTER].

8.6 org.osgi.service.startlevel

Start Level Package Version 1.1.

Bundles wishing to use this package must list the package in the Import-Package header of the bundle's manifest. For example:

Import-Package: org.osgi.service.startlevel; version="[1.1,2.0)"

8.6.1   public interface StartLevel

The StartLevel service allows management agents to manage a start level assigned to each bundle and the active start level of the Framework. There is at most one StartLevel service present in the OSGi environment.

A start level is defined to be a state of execution in which the Framework exists. StartLevel values are defined as unsigned integers with 0 (zero) being the state where the Framework is not launched. Progressively higher integral values represent progressively higher start levels. e.g. 2 is a higher start level than 1.

Access to the StartLevel service is protected by corresponding ServicePermission. In addition AdminPermission is required to actually modify start level information.

Start Level support in the Framework includes the ability to control the beginning start level of the Framework, to modify the active start level of the Framework and to assign a specific start level to a bundle. How the beginning start level of a Framework is specified is implementation dependent. It may be a command line argument when invoking the Framework implementation.

When the Framework is first started it must be at start level zero. In this state, no bundles are running. This is the initial state of the Framework before it is launched. When the Framework is launched, the Framework will enter start level one and all bundles which are assigned to start level one and whose autostart setting indicates the bundle should be started are started as described in the Bundle.start method. The Framework will continue to increase the start level, starting bundles at each start level, until the Framework has reached a beginning start level. At this point the Framework has completed starting bundles and will then fire a Framework event of type FrameworkEvent.STARTED to announce it has completed its launch.

Within a start level, bundles may be started in an order defined by the Framework implementation. This may be something like ascending Bundle.getBundleId order or an order based upon dependencies between bundles. A similar but reversed order may be used when stopping bundles within a start level.

The StartLevel service can be used by management bundles to alter the active start level of the framework.

Concurrency Thread-safe

8.6.1.1   public int getBundleStartLevel(Bundle bundle)

bundle The target bundle.

□ Return the assigned start level value for the specified Bundle.

Returns The start level value of the specified Bundle.

Throws IllegalArgumentException – If the specified bundle has been uninstalled or if the specified bundle was not created by the same framework instance that registered this StartLevel service.

8.6.1.2   public int getInitialBundleStartLevel( )

□ Return the initial start level value that is assigned to a Bundle when it is first installed.

Returns The initial start level value for Bundles.

See Also setInitialBundleStartLevel

8.6.1.3   public int getStartLevel( )

□ Return the active start level value of the Framework. If the Framework is in the process of changing the start level this method must return the active start level if this differs from the requested start level.

Returns   The active start level value of the Framework.

8.6.1.4   **public boolean isBundleActivationPolicyUsed(Bundle bundle)**

bundle   The bundle whose autostart setting is to be examined.

□   Returns whether the specified bundle's autostart setting indicates that the activation policy declared in the bundle's manifest must be used.

The autostart setting of a bundle indicates whether the bundle's declared activation policy is to be used when the bundle is started.

Returns   true if the bundle's autostart setting indicates the activation policy declared in the manifest must be used. false if the bundle must be eagerly activated.

Throws   IllegalArgumentException – If the specified bundle has been uninstalled or if the specified bundle was not created by the same framework instance that registered this StartLevel service.

See Also   Bundle. START_ACTIVATION_POLICY

Since   1.1

8.6.1.5   **public boolean isBundlePersistentlyStarted(Bundle bundle)**

bundle   The bundle whose autostart setting is to be examined.

□   Returns whether the specified bundle's autostart setting indicates the bundle must be started.

The autostart setting of a bundle indicates whether the bundle is to be started when its start level is reached.

Returns   true if the autostart setting of the bundle indicates the bundle is to be started. false otherwise.

Throws   IllegalArgumentException – If the specified bundle has been uninstalled or if the specified bundle was not created by the same framework instance that registered this StartLevel service.

See Also   Bundle. START_TRANSIENT

8.6.1.6   **public void setBundleStartLevel(Bundle bundle, int startlevel)**

bundle   The target bundle.

startlevel   The new start level for the specified Bundle.

□   Assign a start level value to the specified Bundle.

The specified bundle will be assigned the specified start level. The start level value assigned to the bundle will be persistently recorded by the Framework.

If the new start level for the bundle is lower than or equal to the active start level of the Framework and the bundle's autostart setting indicates the bundle must be started, the Framework will start the specified bundle as described in the Bundle.start(int) method using the Bundle.START_TRANSIENT option. The Bundle.START_ACTIVATION_POLICY option must also be used if isBundleActivationPolicyUsed(Bundle) returns true for the bundle. The actual starting of this bundle must occur asynchronously.

If the new start level for the bundle is higher than the active start level of the Framework, the Framework will stop the specified bundle as described in the Bundle.stop(int) method using the Bundle.STOP_TRANSIENT option. The actual stopping of this bundle must occur asynchronously.

Throws   IllegalArgumentException – If the specified bundle has been uninstalled, or if the specified start level is less than or equal to zero, or if the specified bundle is the system bundle, or if the specified bundle was not created by the same framework instance that registered this StartLevel service.

SecurityException – If the caller does not have AdminPermission[bundle,EXECUTE] and the Java runtime environment supports permissions.

8.6.1.7   **public void setInitialBundleStartLevel(int startlevel)**

startlevel The initial start level for newly installed bundles.

☐   Set the initial start level value that is assigned to a Bundle when it is first installed.

The initial bundle start level will be set to the specified start level. The initial bundle start level value will be persistently recorded by the Framework.

When a Bundle is installed via BundleContext.installBundle, it is assigned the initial bundle start level value.

The default initial bundle start level value is 1 unless this method has been called to assign a different initial bundle start level value.

This method does not change the start level values of installed bundles.

Throws IllegalArgumentException – If the specified start level is less than or equal to zero.

SecurityException – If the caller does not have AdminPermission[System Bundle,STARTLEVEL] and the Java runtime environment supports permissions.

8.6.1.8   **public void setStartLevel(int startlevel)**

startlevel The requested start level for the Framework.

☐   Modify the active start level of the Framework.

The Framework will move to the requested start level. This method will return immediately to the caller and the start level change will occur asynchronously on another thread.

If the specified start level is higher than the active start level, the Framework will continue to increase the start level until the Framework has reached the specified start level. At each intermediate start level value on the way to and including the target start level, the Framework must:

1   Change the active start level to the intermediate start level value.
2   Start bundles at the intermediate start level whose autostart setting indicate they must be started. They are started as described in the Bundle.start(int) method using the Bundle.START_TRANSIENT option. The Bundle.START_ACTIVATION_POLICY option must also be used if isBundleActivationPolicyUsed(Bundle) returns true for the bundle.

FrameworkEvent.STARTLEVEL_CHANGED to announce it has moved to the specified start level.

If the specified start level is lower than the active start level, the Framework will continue to decrease the start level until the Framework has reached the specified start level. At each intermediate start level value on the way to and including the specified start level, the framework must:

1   Stop bundles at the intermediate start level as described in the Bundle.stop(int) method using the Bundle.STOP_TRANSIENT option.
2   Change the active start level to the intermediate start level value.

FrameworkEvent.STARTLEVEL_CHANGED to announce it has moved to the specified start level.

If the specified start level is equal to the active start level, then no bundles are started or stopped, however, the Framework must fire a Framework event of type FrameworkEvent.STARTLEVEL_CHANGED to announce it has finished moving to the specified start level. This event may arrive before this method return.

Throws IllegalArgumentException – If the specified start level is less than or equal to zero.

SecurityException – If the caller does not have AdminPermission[System Bundle,STARTLEVEL] and the Java runtime environment supports permissions.

9 Conditional Permission Admin Specification

Version 1.1

9.1 Introduction

The OSGi security model is based on the powerful and flexible Java 2 security architecture, specifically the permission model. This specification adds several new features to the Java 2 model to adapt it to the typical use cases of OSGi deployments.

Key aspects of this security management API is the use of policies. Policies contain a set of permissions that are applicable when the related conditions are met. A policy can both allow (the Java 2 model) as well as deny access when the permissions are implied. Deny permissions can significantly simplify security management. The real time management of Conditional Permission Admin enables management applications to control the permissions of other applications with immediate effect; no restart is required.

Policies are based on the very general concept of *conditions*. Conditions guard access to the policy's permissions. If they are not satisfied, then the permissions are not applicable. Conditions can be based on the bundle signer, the bundle location, as well as on user-defined conditions. The advantage of this model is that groups of permissions can be shared based on signers or locations. Conditions can also be used to enable or disable a group of permissions when an external condition is true, for example, an inserted SIM card, an online connection to the management system is established, a specific roaming area, or a user has approved a permission after prompting. This model allows an operator to create and enforce a dynamic security policies for its devices.

This specification defines a Conditional Permission Admin that supersedes the Permission Admin (albeit its relation to Permission Admin is well-defined in this specification).

9.1.1 Essentials

- *Policies* – Provide a security policy system where conditions control the actual permissions that bundles have at a certain moment in time to be allowed or denied access.
- *Java 2 Security* – Provide full compatibility with the existing Java 2 security model, existing applications must not require modifications.
- *Delegation* – Support a management delegation model where an Operator can delegate part of the management of a device to another party in a secure way.
- *Digital Signatures* – Support the use of digital signatures in a bundle's policy decisions.
- *Real Time* – Changes in the environment must be reflected immediately in the bundle's permissions.
- *Operator Specific Conditions* – It must be possible for operators, manufacturers, selected developers, and others to provide custom conditions.
- *User Confirmation* – The policy model must support end user prompting and confirmations.
- *Allow/Deny Policies* – It must be possible to both allow access as well as specifically deny access.
- *Ordering* – Policies must be ordered in a table and evaluated in the given order, which is from index 0 upwards.

- *Backward Compatibility* – The model must be backward compatible with the Permission Admin of earlier releases.

9.1.2   Entities

- *Conditional Permission Admin* – The administrative service that provides the functions to manipulate the *policy table*.
- *Policy* – Provides the information to allow or deny access to a resource. A policy contains a name, an access type, a set of conditions that must all be satisfied and a set of permissions of which at least one should be implied to specifically allow or deny access. A policy is encoded in a Conditional Permission Info.
- *Policy Table* – A conceptual table containing all the Conditional Permission Infos.
- *Conditional Permission Info* – The encoded form of a Policy.
- *Conditional Permission Update* – Holds a temporary copy of the Policy Table so that a number of changes can be committed as a whole.
- *Permission Info* – Holds a string based encoding of a Permission object.
- *Condition Info* – Holds a string based encoding of a Condition object.
- *Condition* – A Condition object is associated with a single Bundle Protection Domain. It abstracts an external condition that can be evaluated. A condition can be mutable or immutable as well as immediate or postponed.
- *Bundle Location Condition* – An immutable Condition object that is satisfied when the associated bundle has the given location.
- *Bundle Signer Condition* – An immutable Condition object that is satisfied when the associated bundle is signed by a certificate that matched the given DN.
- *Permission* – An object that defines a certain permission type. Same as the Java 2 Security model.
- *Bundle Protection Domain* – The class that implements the Protection Domain of a bundle, this specification does not define an interface for this class, but it plays an important role in this specification.

Figure 9.45   *org.osgi.service.condpermadmin package*

9.1.3 Synopsis

A Conditional Permission Admin service maintains a system wide ordered table of
ConditionalPermissionInfo objects. This table is called the *policy table*. The policy table holds an
encoded form of conditions, permissions, and their allow/deny access type. A manager can enumerate, delete, and add new policies to this table via a ConditionalPermissionsUpdate object.

When a bundle is created, it creates a Bundle Protection Domain. This protection domain calculates the system permissions for that bundle by instantiating the policy table, potentially pruning
any policies that can never apply to that bundle and optimizing entries that always apply.

A bundle can have local permissions defined in a Bundle Permission Resource. These are the actual
detailed permissions needed by this bundle to operate. A bundle's effective permissions are the
intersection of the local permissions and the system permissions. During the permission check of
the Java Security Manager, each Protection Domain is first checked for the local permissions, if this
fails, the complete check fails.

Otherwise, the Bundle Protection Domains of the calling bundles are consulted to see if they imply
the requested permission. To imply the requested permission, the Bundle Protection Domain must
find a policy in its policy table where all conditions are satisfied and where one of the policy's permissions imply the requested permission. If one of the permissions is implied, then the policy's
access type decides success or failure.

Certain conditions must postpone their evaluation so that their evaluation can be minimized and
grouped to prevent unwanted side effects. Postponed conditions can leverage a Dictionary object to
maintain state during a single permission check.

9.2   Permission Management Model

The Conditional Permission Admin provides a flexible security model for bundles. However, the price of this flexibility is additional complexity. The amount of configuration necessary to setup a working system can easily become overwhelming. It is therefore necessary to be very careful implementing a deployment security model. This section defines a series of possible deployment security models while simultaneously defining the terminology that is used in later sections.

9.2.1   Local Permissions

A good working principle is to minimize permissions as much as possible, as early as possible. This principle is embodied with the *local permissions* of a bundle. Local permissions are defined by a Bundle Permission Resource that is contained in the bundle; this resource defines a set of *permissions*. These permissions must be enforced by the Framework for the given bundle. That is, a bundle can get less permissions than the local permissions but it can never get more permissions. If no such permission resource is present then the local permissions must be All Permission. The Bundle Permission Resource is defined in *Bundle Permission Resource* on page 236.

For example, if the local permissions do not imply
ServicePermission[org.osgi.service.log.LogService,GET], then the bundle can never get the
LogService object, regardless of any other security setup in the device.

The fine-grained permissions allowed by the OSGi Service Platform are very effective with the local permissions because they can be defined by the developer instead of the deployer. The developer knows exactly what services are needed, what packages the bundle requires, and what network hosts are accessed. Tools can be used that analyze bundles and provide the appropriate local permissions to simplify the task of the developer. However, without detailed knowledge of the bundle's intrinsics, it is very difficult to create the local permissions due to their fine-grained granularity.

At first sight, it can seem odd that a bundle carries its own permissions. However, the local permissions define the *maximum* permissions that the bundle needs, providing more permissions to the bundle is irrelevant because the Framework must not allow the bundle to use them. The purpose of the local permissions is therefore *auditing* by the deployer. Analyzing a bundle's byte codes for its security requirements is cumbersome, if not impossible. Auditing a bundle's permission resource is (relatively) straightforward. For example, if the local permissions request permission to access the Internet, it is clear that the bundle has the potential to access the network. By inspecting the local permissions, the Operator can quickly see the security impact of the bundle. It can trust this audit because it must be enforced by the Framework when the bundle is executed.

An Operator that runs a fully closed system can use the local permissions to run third party applications that are not trusted to run unchecked, thereby mitigating risks. The Framework guarantees that a bundle is never granted a permission that is not implied by its local permissions. A simple audit of the application's local permissions will reveal any potential threats.

This scenario is depicted in Figure 9.46. A developer creates a bundle with local permissions, the operator verifies the local permissions, and if it matches the expectations, it is deployed to the device where the Framework verifies that the local permissions are never exceeded.

Figure 9.46   *Local permissions and Deployment*

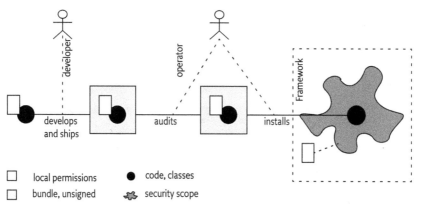

Summarizing, the benefits of local permissions are:

- *Fine-grained* – The developer has the knowledge to provide the fine-grained permissions that are necessary to minimize the sandbox of the bundle without constraining it.
- *Auditable* – The Operator has a relatively small and readable file that shows the required sandbox. It can therefore assesses the risk of running a bundle.
- *Sandboxed* – The Operator has the guarantee from the Framework that a bundle cannot escape its local permissions.

9.2.2   Open Deployment Channels

From a business perspective it is sometimes too restrictive to maintain a fully closed system. There are many use cases where users should be able to deploy bundles from a CD, via a PC, or from an Internet web sites. In those scenarios, relying on the local permissions is not sufficient because the Framework cannot verify that the local permissions have not been tampered with.

The de facto solution to tampering is to *digitally sign* the bundles. The rules for OSGi signing are defined in *Digitally Signed JAR Files* on page 10. A digital signing algorithm detects modifications of the JAR as well as provide the means for authenticating the signer. A Framework therefore must refuse to run a bundle when a signature does not match the contents or it does not recognize the signer. Signing makes it possible to use an untrusted deployment channel and still rely on the enforcement of the local permissions.

For example, an Operator can provision its applications via the Internet. When such an application is downloaded from an untrusted site, the Framework verifies the signature. It should install the application only when the signature is trusted or when it has default permissions for untrusted bundles.

Figure 9.47   *Local Scope and Deployment with signing*

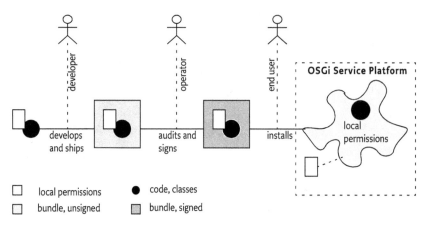

9.2.3   Delegation

A model where the local permissions are secured with a signature works for an Operator that fully controls a device. The operator must sign all bundles before they are provisioned. In this case, the Operator acts as a gatekeeper, no authority is delegated.

This can become expensive when there are third parties involved. For example, an Enterprise could provide applications to its employees on a mobile phone that is managed by an Operator. This model is depicted in Figure 9.48. If the Enterprise always has to contact the Operator before it can provision a new version, bottlenecks quickly arise.

Figure 9.48   *Delegation model*

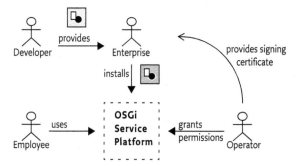

This bottleneck problem can also be solved with signing. Signing does not only provide tamper detection, it can also provide an authenticated *principal*. The principal can be authenticated with a certificate chain. The device contains a set of trusted certificates (depending on implementation) that are used to authenticate the certificate of the signer.

The operator can therefore safely associate a principal with a set of permissions. These permissions are called the *system permissions*. Bundles signed by that principal are then automatically granted those system permissions.

In this model, the Operator is still fully in control. At any moment in time, the Operator can change the system permissions associated with the principal and thereby immediately deny access to all bundles of that principal, while they are running. Alternatively, the Operator can add additional system permissions to the principal if a new service has become available to the signer's applications. For example, if the Operator installs a org.tourist.PointOfInterest service, it can grant the ServicePermission[org.tourist.PointOfInterest,GET] and PackagePermission[org.tourist, IMPORT] to all principals that are allowed to use this service. The Operator can inform the involved parties after the fact, if at all. This model therefore does not create a bottleneck.

Using digital signing to assign system permissions can therefore *delegate* the responsibility of provisioning to other parties. The Operator completely defines the limits of the permissions of the principal, but the signing and deployment can be done by the other parties.

For example, an Operator can define that the ACME company can provision bundles without any intervention of the Operator. The Operator has to provide ACME once with a signing certificate and the Operator must associate the ACME principal with the appropriate system permissions on the device.

The key advantage of this model is the reduced communication between ACME and the Operator: The Operator can modify the system permissions of ACME applications and be in control at any moment in time. The ACME company can develop new applications without the need to coordinate these efforts in any way with the Operator. This model is depicted in Figure 9.49, which also shows the possible sandboxes for Daffy Inc. and unsigned bundles.

Figure 9.49   *Typical Delegation model*

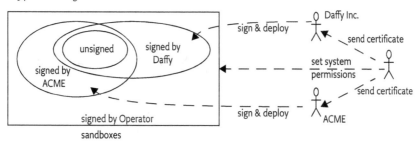

The local permissions can still play an important role in the delegation model because it provides the signer the possibility to mitigate its risk, just as it did for the Operator. Signers can verify the local permissions before they sign a bundle. Like the Operator in the earlier scenario, the signer can quickly verify the security requirements of a bundle. For example, if a game bundle requests AdminPermission[*,*], it is unlikely that the bundle will pass the security audit of the signer. However, in the unlikely case it did, it will not be granted this permission unless the Operator gave such a permission to the signer's principal on the device.

9.2.4   Grouping

The grouping model is traditionally used because it minimizes the administration of the security setup. For example, an operator can define the following security levels:

- *Untrusted* – Applications that are not trusted. These applications must run in a very limited security scope. They could be unsigned.
- *Trusted* – Applications that are trusted but that are not allowed to manage the device or provide system services.
- *System* – Applications that provide system services.
- *Manage* – Applications that manage the device.

The operator signs the bundle with an appropriate certificate before it is deployed, when the bundle is installed, it will be automatically be assigned to the appropriate security scope.

However, the behavior can also be obtained using the local permissions of a bundle.

9.2.5   Typical Example

This example provides a simple setup for a delegation model. The example is intended for readability, certain concepts will be explained later. The basic syntax for the policies is:

```
policy       ::= access '{' conditions permissions'}' name?
access       ::= 'ALLOW' | 'DENY'        // case insensitive
conditions   ::= ( '[' qname quoted-string* ']' )*
permissions  ::= ( '(' qname (quoted-string
                             quoted-string?)? ')' )+
name         ::= quoted-string
```

For readability, package prefixes that can be guessed are replaced with "..".

The following policy has a condition that limits the permissions to bundles that are signed by ACME. The permissions given are related to managing other bundles.

```
ALLOW {
    [ ..BundleSignerCondition "* ; o=ACME" ]

    ( ..AdminPermission "(signer=\* ; o=ACME)" "*" )
    ( ..ServicePermission "..ManagedService" "register" )
    ( ..ServicePermission "..ManagedServiceFactory"
                                    "register" )
} "1"
```

The next permission policy is for bundles signed by the operator. The operator bundles get full managing capabilities as well as permissions to provide any service.

```
ALLOW {
    [ ..BundleSignerCondition "*; o=Operator" ]
    ( ..AdminPermission "*" "*" )
    ( ..ServicePermission "*" "get,register" )
    ( ..PackagePermission "*" "import,exportonly" )
} "2"
```

The following block indicates that all bundles not signed by ACME will not have access to the com.acme.secret package, nor can they provide it. In this case, only bundles that are signed by ACME may use the com.acme.secret.* packages. Instead of explicitly specifying all allowed packages for bundles not signed by ACME, it is easier to deny them the protected packages. The "!" is a parameter for the Bundle Signer Condition to reverse its normal answer. This facility is also available in the Bundle Location Condition.

That is, the following policy specifies that bundles *not* signed by ACME will be denied permission to package com.acme.secret.*.

```
DENY {
    [ ..BundleSignerCondition "* ; o=ACME" "!" ]
    ( ..PackagePermission "com. acme. secret.*"
        "import,exportonly" )
} "3"
```

Basic permissions define the permissions that are available to all bundles. The basic permissions therefore have no conditions associated with them so all bundles will be able to use these permissions. All bundles may use the Log Service as well as use any package that was not yet denied earlier.

```
ALLOW {
    (..ServicePermission "..LogService" "get" )
    (..PackagePermission "*" "import" )
```

```
}  "4"
```

The resulting permissions are summarized in Table 9.3. The + indicates allow, the - means deny. The number is the deciding policy.

Table 9.3   Assigned Permissions. + indicates allow, - deny.

		Unsigned	ACME	Operator
..LogService	get	+4	+4	+2
..ManagedService*	register	–	+1	+2
..ManagedService*	get	–	–	+2
com.acme.FooService	get	–	–	+2
com.acme.secret	import	–3	+4	+2
com.acme.secret.bar	exportonly	–3	–	+2
com.acme.foo	import	+4	+4	+2
bundle signed by ACME	start	–	+1	+2
bundle signed by Operator	start	–	–	+2

9.3   Effective Permissions

Once a bundle is installed, it gets Java 2 *permissions* associated from the framework. Some of these permissions are *implied*. Implied permissions are given by the framework because they are required for normal operation, for example every bundle has the File Permission to read and write the bundle data area. See *Implied Permissions* on page 19.

A framework can also provide an administrative service to associate a set of permissions with a bundle. The set of permissions given by such an administrative agent to a bundle are called the *system permissions*. For example, the Permission Admin service and the Conditional Permission Admin service can be used by a managing application to define the *system permissions*. Additionally, a bundle can carry its own permissions; these are called the *local permissions*. All these permission sets interact in a non-trivial way to give the *effective permissions*.

The purpose of the local permissions is to mitigate the bundle signer's risk. The Framework guarantees that a bundle's effective permissions are always smaller or equal than the local permissions because the effective permissions are the intersection of the local permissions with the system permissions, except for the implied permissions that are always granted.

$$Effective = (Local \cap System) \cup Implied$$

The system permissions have two possible sources. The system permissions can be bound via the Permission Admin service to a location. This mechanism is provided for backward compatibility only. New management applications should use the Conditional Permission Admin service if possible.

If the Permission Admin location is not bound, all the *conditional permissions* from Conditional Permission Admin act as the system permissions. The relationship between the system permissions and local permissions is depicted in Figure 9.50.

Figure 9.50   *System, Local and Security permissions*

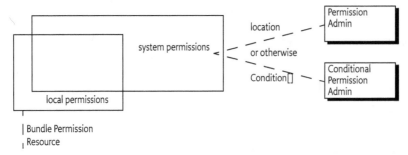

9.4   Conditional Permissions

The conditional permissions provide a very general model that is related to the Java 2 Security model. The Java 2 Security model assigns a set of permissions to a code base or signer. During the permission check, this set is consulted for permissions that imply the checked permissions. If the checked permission is implied, access is granted.

The Conditional Permission Admin service model assumes a more general approach. It conceptually has a system wide *policy table*, that is shared between all bundles.

A policy consists of:

- An access type (ALLOW or DENY)
- A set of conditions
- A set of permissions
- A name

During a permission check, the table is traversed in ascending index order and each policy is evaluated. The first policy that is *matching* controls the outcome of the permission check as given by its access type. A policy is only matching a permission P when:

- All of the policy's conditions are satisfied
- At least one of its permissions implies P, as defined by Java 2 security.

For example, assume the following setup for bundle A:

```
ALLOW {
    [ ...BundleSignerCondition "cn=*, o=ACME, c=US" ]
    [ com.acme.Online ]
      (...AdminPermission "*" "*")
}
```

In the example, both the BundleSignerCondition must be satisfied as well as the com.acme.Online condition before Admin Permission is granted.

Deny policies significantly simplify the security configuration setup because they handle the common case of an exception to a general rule. For example, a bundle that is allowed to use all package imports and exports *except* packages in the com.acme.secret.* name space. The set of all possible packages is impossible to enumerate because it is an infinite set. In this case, * cannot be used because the com.acme.secret.* should not be included. With a deny policy it is possible to first deny access to com.acme.secret.* for all bundles bar the exception, and then later allow * for everybody. The policies for this look like:

```
DENY {
    [...BundleSignerCondition "cn=*, o=ACME" "!" ]
     (...PackagePermission "com.acme.secret.*"
```

```
                    "import,exportonly" )
    }
    ALLOW {
        (...PackagePermission "*" "*" )
    }
```

9.4.1 Encoding versus Instantiation

The system wide policy table does not contain instances, it contains *encoded forms* of the permissions and conditions. The policy table acts as a *template* for each Bundle Protection Domain; the Bundle Protection Domain creates instances with the associated bundle as their context.

It is a dynamic template because a Bundle Protection Domain must track the changes to the framework's policy table immediately and update any instances from the new encoded forms. Once the atomic commit() method of the update object has successfully returned, all subsequent use of Bundle Protection Domains must be based on the new configuration. See *Permission Management* on page 231 for more information of how to manage this table.

The conditions and permissions of the policy table must be instantiated before the conditions can be checked. This instantiation can happen, when a Bundle Protection Domain is created, or the first time when the conditional permissions are needed because of a permission check. Figure 9.51 shows the central table and its instantiation for different Bundle Protection Domains.

Figure 9.51   *Instantiation of the policy table*

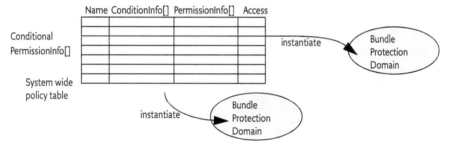

Condition objects must always belong to a single Bundle Protection Domain and must never be shared.

9.5 Conditions

The purpose of a Condition is to decide if a policy is applicable or not. That is, it acts as a guard for the permissions. The conditions must therefore be evaluated when a Permission object is checked against the effective permissions of a bundle.

The state of a Condition object can be obtained with its isSatisfied() method. A condition that returns true to this method is called to be *satisfied.* If the method throws an Exception, this should be logged and treated as if the condition is not satisfied.

Certain Condition objects could optimize their evaluations if they are activated multiple times in the same permission check. For example, a user prompt could appear several times in a permission check but the prompt should only be given once to the user. These conditions are called *postponed conditions*, conditions that can be verified immediately are called *immediate conditions*. The isPostponed() method can inform if the condition is immediate or postponed. A Condition must always return the same value for the isPostponed method so that the Conditional Permission Admin can cache this value. If this method returns false, the isSatisfied() method must be quick and can be called during the permission check, otherwise the decision must be postponed until the end of the permission check because it is potentially expensive to evaluate. Postponed conditions must always be postponed the first time they are evaluated.

For example, a condition could verify that a mobile phone is *roaming*. This information is readily available in memory and therefore the isPostponed() method could always return false. Alternatively, a Condition object that gets an authorization over the network should only be evaluated at most once during a permission check to minimize the delay caused by the network latency. Such a Condition object should return true for the isPostponed method so all the Condition objects are evaluated together at the end of the permission check.

Condition objects only need to be evaluated multiple times when the answer can change. A Condition object that can vary its satisfiability is called *mutable*, it can be checked with the isMutable() method. If the condition is *immutable*, the Condition object must always return the same result for the isSatisfied() method. The isMutable() method answers the mutability of the next isSatisfied() method. The answer of the next call to the isSatisfied method could still differ from the previous call, even if the isMutable method returns true.

A mutable Condition can become immutable over time but it cannot go from immutable to mutable. Optimizations can take advantage of the immutability by, for example, caching the result of the isSatisfied() method.

Except for immediate conditions, the isSatisfied method must only be called inside a permission check.

For example, the Bundle Protection Domain can prune any policy from its view of the policy table that contains a Condition object that is immutable and not satisfied. The Bundle Signer Condition and Bundle Location Condition are examples of immutable conditions that can easily be discarded when they do not match the context bundle when the policy table is instantiated. See *Optimizing Immutable Conditions* on page 237 for more information about optimizing immutable conditions.

9.6 The Permission Check

The Java 2 security model has both a Security Manager and an Access Controller to perform a permission check. The core functionality is located in the AccessController and the AccessControlContext classes that cooperate with ProtectionDomain objects to detect if a permission is allowed or denied. In the OSGi Framework, each bundle must have a single Bundle Protection Domain that holds the instantiated policy table.

The Access Controller provides the full functionality for checking a permission. However, all permission checks should be tunneled through the SecurityManager checkPermission methods. The Security Manager can be replaced by a custom implementation, unlike the Access Controller (it is a final class). This model is depicted in Figure 9.52.

The Framework must replace the Security Manager to implement the Conditional Permission Admin in a compliant implementation. If a Framework implementation is not able to take over the Security Manager because another party in the VM has already set it, then not all features of this specification can be implemented.

Figure 9.52   *Java 2 Permission checking in OSGi bundles*

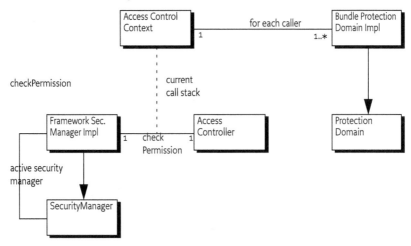

9.6.1   Security Manager checkPermission Method

A permission check starts when the Security Manager checkPermission method is called with permission P as argument. The current Security Manager must be implemented by the Framework and is therefore called the Framework Security Manager; it must be fully integrated with the Conditional Permission Admin service.

The Framework Security Manager must get the Access Control Context in effect. It must call the AccessController getContext() method to get the default context if it is not passed a specific context.

The AccessControlContext checkPermission method must then be called, which causes the call stack to be traversed. At each stack level the Bundle Protection Domain of the calling class is evaluated for the permission P using the ProtectionDomain implies method. The complete evaluation must take place on the same thread.

9.6.2   Bundle Protection Domain implies Method

Permission P must be implied by the local permissions of the Bundle Protection Domain. If this is not the case, the complete check must immediately end with a failure. Local permissions are described in *Local Permissions* on page 216 and *Bundle Permission Resource* on page 236.

The permission check now depends on the instantiated policy table, called Ts. During the Bundle Protection Domain implies method, the goal is to decide if the permission P is denied, or can progress because it is potentially allowed. Potentially, because the table can contain postponed conditions that need to be executed after all protection domains are checked.

The policy table must therefore be traversed in ascending index order until the first policy is matching that can give an immediate access type. If this access type is DENY, the implies method fails and aborts the check. If an ALLOW is found, the next domain must be checked. To ensure that there is at least one immediate matching policy in the table, a virtual DENY { (AllPermission) } is added at the end of the table. This virtual policy has the effect of making the default policy DENY when no matching entries are found.

During the traversal, an optimized policy list per bundle is constructed containing the postponed conditions and at the end a matching policy. This list is evaluated after all the protection domains are checked and none of them failed.

Therefore, the following definitions begin the Bundle Protection Domain implies method's algorithm:

```
Ts = instantiated policy table + DENY {(AllPermission)}
PL = {}
```

PL will be copied from Ts until the first policy that *matches*. A matching policy has all of its conditions immediately satisfied and one of the permissions implies permission P. If a policy can never be matched because it has an immediate condition that cannot be satisfied, then it is not copied to PL. At the end, PL contains zero or more postponed policies followed by exactly one matching policy.

In pseudo code:

```
policy:
for each policy T in Ts
        for each condition C in T conditions
                if C is immediate and C is not satisfied
                        continue policy

        found = false
        for permission X in T permissions
                found |= X implies P

        if not found
                continue policy

        add T to PL

        if T has no postponed conditions
                break
```

PL must now be optimized to remove superfluous policies. A postponed policy can be removed if it cannot change the outcome from the last (which is an immediate) policy. That is, if the immediate policy at the end has the same access type as the previous policy in PL, then it can be ignored. The following pseudo code removes these superfluous postponed conditions.

```
while PL length > 1
        if PL[PL length -2] access = PL[PL length -1] access
                remove PL[PL length -2]
        else
                break
```

After discarding these superfluous postponed conditions, the contents of PL has the structure outline in Figure 9.53, where Tp(x) is a postponed policy with a access type x, and Tm is a matching policy, ! is the not operator for the condition.

Figure 9.53   *Structure of Postponed List PL*

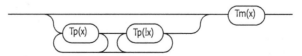

If PL contains only one policy and it is a DENY policy, then the Bundle Protection Domain can directly answer false from the implies method, which will abort the complete permission check evaluation. In all other cases, it must remember the postponed list PL for the given bundle, and return true.

```
if PL = {DENY{...}}
      return false
Bundle.pl = PL
return true
```

9.6.2.1   Example Bundle Protection Domain Check

This example demonstrated the per bundle evaluation aspect of the Bundle Protection Domain's implies method. Assume the following policies are active:

```
DENY {
   [ BundleSignerCondition "cn=ACME" "!" ]
   ( FilePermission "/tmp/acme/-" "READ,WRITE" )
} "0"
ALLOW {
   ( FilePermission "/tmp/-" "READ,WRITE" )
} "1"
ALLOW {
   [ PromptCondition "Allowed to Read?" ]
   ( FilePermission "*" "READ" )
} "2"
DENY {
    [ PromptCondition "Deny Writing?" ]
    ( FilePermission "*" "READ,WRITE" )
} "3"
```

This setup reserves unconditionally the /tmp/acme/- file system for bundles signed by ACME because the first line denies any bundle not signed by ACME access to this part of the file system. Reading and writing of the remainder of the /tmp file tree is allowed for all. For the rest of the file system, read access is prompted to allow, and write access is prompted to deny.

Assume that a bundle signed by ACME wants to read /etc/passwd. Policy 0, and 1 do not match because the File Permission in these policies are not applicable. Policy 2 has a permission that implies this file and its condition is postponed, so it will be postponed and policy 3 will also included. There is no matching policy, so a virtual matching DENY policy (D) will be included as the last entry. This makes PL: 2, 3, and D.

```
Tp(ALLOW)      # 2
Tp(DENY)       # 3
Tm(DENY)       # virtual (D)
```

In this case, there is a superfluous Tp(DENY) #3 because it can not change the final answer of the last matching DENY. It is therefore removed. The list is thus:

```
Tp(ALLOW)      # 2
Tm(DENY)       # virtual
```

This list must be saved for later evaluation when all the Bundle Protection Domains have finished successfully.

9.6.3   Postponed Evaluation

If all protection domains have been checked and none has denied the permission by returning false, then *each* checked Bundle Protection Domain has a postponed list.

This per bundle postponed list contains one or more policies that must now be evaluated in sequence. The first policy in the list that can satisfy all its postponed conditions decides the access. If this policy has an access type of ALLOW, the list of the next domain is evaluated otherwise the evaluation fails.

The evaluation always ends because the last entry in each of the postponed lists is guaranteed to be a matching policy. As a special case, a postponed list with one entry indicates success. this must be a matching ALLOW because an immediate DENY would have failed earlier.

For example, if bundle A postponed policy Tp1 and bundle B postponed policy Tp2, and bundle C was immediately satisfied for ALLOW, then the constellation would like Figure 9.54.

Figure 9.54   *Evaluation of postponed policies*

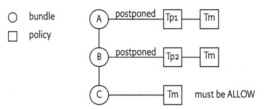

The Conditional Permission Admin provides a type specific Dictionary object to all evaluations of the same postponed Condition implementation class during a single permission check. It is the responsibility of the Condition implementer to use this Dictionary to maintain states between invocations. The condition is evaluated with a method that takes an array and a Dictionary object: isSatisfied(Condition[],Dictionary). The array always contains a single element that is the receiver. An array is used because an earlier version of this specification could verify multiple conditions simultaneously.

The Dictionary object has the following qualities:

• It is specific to a Condition implementation class, different implementation classes will not share this Dictionary object.
• It is created before the isSatisfied(Condition[],Dictionary) is called for the first time during this permission check.
• It is only valid during the invocation of a single checkPermission session. That is, it is not maintained between checkPermission invocations.
• It is shared between invocations of isSatisfied(Condition[], Dictionary) method for different Bundle Protection Domains.

The algorithm for the postponed processing can now be explained with the following pseudo code:

```
bundle:
for each bundle B
    policy:
    for each policy T in B.pl
        for C in T conditions
            if C is postponed and
                C is not satisfied with Dictionary
                continue policy

        if T access = DENY
            return false
        else
            continue bundle
assert false // can not reach
```

```
return true
```

9.6.4   Example

A permission P is checked while bundle A, B, and C are on the call stack. Their security setup is as follows:

- IC = a condition that is immediately evaluated,
- PC is a postponed condition,
- P, Q, and R are permissions.

The situation for C is as follows:

```
ALLOW {                    (Q)      }  "C1"
ALLOW { [IC0]              (P)      }  "C2"
ALLOW { [PC2]              (P)      }  "C3"
```

First, the Bundle Protection Domain of bundle C is asked if it implies permission P. Bundle C has three policies. Policy C1 has no conditions, only a permission that does not imply permission P, it is therefore ignored. The second policy has an immediate condition IC0, which is not satisfied. Therefore, the policy's permissions are not even considered. The last policy contains a mutable postponed condition PC2. The permission P is implied by the related permissions. However, it is not possible to make the decision at this moment in time, therefore the evaluation of policy C3 is postponed. The postponed list for bundle C is therefore:

```
ALLOW    {[PC2]}            "C3"
DENY     {(AllPermission)}
```

This list can not be optimized because the final access type differs from the earlier access types.

The setup for bundle B is as follows:

```
ALLOW { [IC1] [PC2] [PC1]  (P) (R) }   "B1"
ALLOW { [PC2]              (P) (R) }   "B2"
DENY  {                    (P)     }   "B3"
ALLOW {                    (Q)     }   "B4"
```

Bundle B is considered, its first policy has and immediate Condition object that is IC1. This condition turns out to be satisfied. This policy is a potential candidate because it has two postponed conditions left. It is a possibility because its permissions imply permission P. The policy is therefore placed on the postponed list.

Policy B2 is similar, it must also be placed on the postponed list because it implies permission P and it has a postponed condition PC2.

Policy B3 matches, it is therefore placed on the postponed list and the evaluation is stopped because there is an immediate decision, therefore it is not necessary to look at policy B4.

There are 2 policies postponed, the bundle is potentially permitted. Bundle's B postponed list therefore looks like:

```
ALLOW    {[PC2][PC1]}  "B1"
ALLOW    {[PC2]}       "B2"
DENY     { }
```

This list cannot be optimized because the final access type differs from the earlier postponed conditions.

Last and least, bundle A.

```
A: ALLOW {   [IC1] [PC1]    (P) (Q) }     "A1"
```

```
ALLOW {  [IC2]      (P) (R) }    "A2"
ALLOW {             (S)     }    "A3"
```

Bundle A's IC1 is evaluated first and it is satisfied. Permission P is implied by the policy A1's permissions, therefore this policy is postponed for evaluation.

Policy A2 is also satisfied and it directly implies permission P. This policy is therefore also placed on the postponed list and further evaluation is no longer necessary because it is the first matching policy. That is, policy A3 is ignored. The postponed list looks like:

```
ALLOW { [PC1] } "A1"
ALLOW { }       "A2"
```

This list is optimized to:

```
ALLOW {}        "A2"
```

After the checkPermission method of the Access Control Context method returns, the Framework Security Manager must evaluate the postponed lists of all the bundles. The list of postponed policies looks like Figure 9.54.

Figure 9.55　　　*Evaluation of postponed policies*

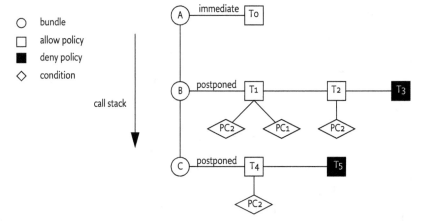

The Framework Security Manager must now evaluate the postponed lists for each bundle. In this example, postponed condition PC2 occurs 3 times. All these evaluations of PC2 get the same Dictionary object. If PC2 prompts the users with a specific question, then it should not ask the same question again when another PC2 is evaluated later. The Dictionary object can be used to maintain this state.

Both PC1 and PC2 prompt the user. PC1 will be rejected in this example, and PC2 will be affirmed.

First the postponed list of bundle A is evaluated. This is the trivial case of ALLOW {}, and the postponed list for bundle A succeeds with ALLOW.

For bundle B, policy T1 must prompt for PC2 and PC1. PC2 records the answer in the Dictionary that is specific for PC2. Because PC1 fails, T1 is not applicable and policy T2 must be evaluated. PC2 had recorded its answer so it does not prompt but returns true immediately. Policy T2 is an ALLOW policy and bundle B therefore ends positively.

Last, bundle C requires evaluation of policy T4. PC2 retrieves its answer from the given Dictionary object and succeeds. Policy T4 has an access type of ALLOW and this concludes the complete permission check positively.

9.6.5   Using the Access Control Context Directly

Bundle programmers should always use the Java Security Manager to do security checks. When the Access Controller is used directly (or the Access Control Context) to do the security check instead, then the evaluation cannot handle postponed conditions. Therefore, the postponed conditions must be treated as immediate conditions by the Bundle Protection Domain when the permissions check does not go through the Framework's security manager. The implication of this is that the result of checking a permission can depend on the way the check is initiated.

For example, a bundle on the stack has the needed permission P tied to a User Prompt Condition and another bundle on the stack does not have the Permission P. The check would fail if the Security Manager was called and the user would never be prompted because the failure was detected before the conditional permissions could be evaluated. However, if the Access Control Context was called directly, the user would be prompted and fail even if the user acknowledged the request.

9.7   Permission Management

The policy model provided by the Conditional Permission Admin service requires that the policies in the policy table are ordered. This requires a management interface that allows easy manipulation of the ordered table. The List interface fulfills this requirement, but an OSGi Framework is a dynamic environment and there can be other parties editing the same policy table. Therefore, the Conditional Permission Admin service uses an indirection. If a bundle wants to edit the table, it can get the table in a ConditonalPermissionUpdate object with the newConditionalPermissionUpdate() method from the Conditional Permission Admin service. This method creates a copy of the policy table in the returned *update* object. This update object provides access to a List object with ConditionalPermissionInfo objects, which are the encoded form of the policies.

New objects can be created with the newConditionalPermissionInfo(String,ConditionInfo[],PermissionInfo[],String) method on the Conditional Permission Admin service, and then added to this list. The method requires a name, an array of ConditionInfo objects, an array of PermissionInfo objects, and the access decision. The name parameter can be null. Each ConditionalPermissionInfo object has a name to distinguish it from others, as well as identifying it to a management server. If the name is null, the Conditional Permission Admin service will automatically create a unique name. Though it is possible to create policies with the same name, during the commit the names will be verified for uniqueness. If a duplicate name appears, an exception will be thrown.

Conditional Permission Infos can also be removed from this list. Modifications like remove, do not change or influence the running system, they only affect the update object.

All changes are effectuated when the commit method is called. If there had been a change in the underlying policy table since the update object was created, the commit method will abort and return false. Otherwise, the actual policy table is atomically updated and true is returned. There is no obligation to ever call commit; a canceled update can just be forgotten.

The data structures of the update model are depicted in Figure 9.56.

Figure 9.56   *Structure of the Info objects.*

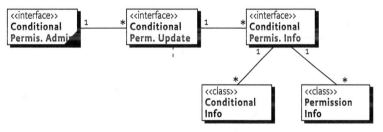

Both the ConditionalInfo and PermissionInfo objects can be constructed from encoded strings. The syntax for these strings are:

```
conditions    ::= ( '[' qname quoted-string* ']' )*
permissions   ::= ( '(' qname (quoted-string
                              quoted-string?)? ')' )+
```

The strings are converted by getting the class with the qname, and then creating an instance through a constructor that takes the given number of arguments. The exclamation mark is convention for a negated condition, it indicates that the condition should reverse its result. Deny policies often require the negation of the conditions. For example, often a bundle should *not* be signed by a specific signer to exclude it from a resource.

Both the PermissionInfo and ConditionInfo are concrete classes with appropriate methods to construct them from their encoded form. The encoded form given to a Condition implementation constructor must not contain the exclamation mark for negation.

A policy is specified with the following syntax:

```
policy        ::= access '{' conditions permissions'}' name?
access        ::= 'ALLOW' | 'DENY'         // case insensitive
name          ::= quoted-string
```

The Conditional Permission Admin provides a convenience method to create a ConditionalPermissionInfo object with the newConditionalPermissionInfo(String) method.

The following example is a code snippet the reads a stream with conditional permissions using the encoded form. The method parses the file line by line. Each line is scanned and split with regular expressions. The following example shows how a text string can be parsed and added to the update object.

```
static Pattern CP_MATCHER = Pattern.compiler(...);
public  void manage(ConditionalPermissionAdmin admin,
   String text) {
   ConditionalPermissionUpdate update = admin
      .newConditionalPermissionUpdate();
   List list = update.getConditionalPermissionInfos();
   list.clear();

   Matcher m = CP_MATCHER.matcher(text);
   int n = 1;
   while (m.find()) {
      String policy = m.group(1);
      ConditionalPermissionInfo info =
         admin.newConditionalPermissionInfo( policy );

      list.add(info);
   }
   if ( !update.commit() )
      throw new ConcurrentModificationException(
   "Conditional Permission Admin was updated concurrently");
}
```

9.7.1 Default Permissions

Conditional Permission Admin does not have a specific concept of default permissions. Default permissions are derived from the policies that do not have any Condition objects. These policies are applied to all bundles, effectively making them default permissions. This is a different from Permission Admin; in Permission Admin default permissions only apply when there are no specific permissions set.

9.8 Implementing Conditions

Condition objects are constructed from ConditionInfo objects when the policy table is instantiated for a Bundle Protection Domain. The ConditionInfo object supports a variable number of arguments.

The Conditional Permission Admin must use reflection to find a public static getCondition method on the Condition implementation class that takes a Bundle object and a ConditionInfo object as arguments. This method must return a object that implements the Condition interface.

However, this does not have to be a new object, the getCondition method can reuse objects if it so desires. For example, a Bundle Location Condition is immutable, it therefore maintains only 2 instances: One for bundles that match the given location and one for the others. In the getCondition method it can verify the bundle's location with argument and return either instance.

This is such a common pattern that the Condition interface provides two such immutable instances:

- TRUE – A condition object that will always evaluate to true and that is never postponed.
- FALSE – A condition object that will always evaluate to false and that is never postponed.

If no static getCondition method can be found, the Conditional Permission Admin service must try to find a public constructor that takes a Bundle object and a ConditionInfo object as arguments. For the com.acme.AcmeCondition, the Conditional Permission Admin must look for:

```
public static Condition com.acme.AcmeCondition.getCondition(
      Bundle, ConditionInfo )
public com.acme.AcmeCondition( Bundle, ConditionInfo )
```

If it is not possible to create a condition object, the given condition must be treated as a Condition.FALSE object and an error should be logged.

A Condition object will be unique to a Bundle Protection Domain as explained in *Encoding versus Instantiation* on page 223. Thus, any queries made on a Condition object will be with the given Bundle object as context.

The cheapest Condition objects are immutable; they have almost no overhead. If a Condition object is immutable directly after it is created, then the Framework Security Manager can immediately shortcut future evaluations. That is, if an immutable Condition object is not satisfied, its parent policy can be immediately be discarded; it is not even necessary to instantiate any further Condition or Permission objects for that policy.

Mutable Condition objects must be evaluated during a permission check. Permission checks are common and the evaluation of a permission should therefore be highly optimized and preferably not cause additional security checks on the same thread. A mutable condition is system code, it must be designed to work in a constrained environment. The isSatisfied() method should be designed to quickly return. It should normally base its decision on variables and limit its side effects.

However, side effects are sometimes necessary; a key example is user prompting. As discussed in *Security Manager checkPermission Method* on page 225, the evaluation can be postponed towards the end of the check, where a special version of isSatisfied method is called. The Condition object must always return true for the isPostponed() method to be postponed and it must always return the same value.

Mutable postponed conditions must optimize their evaluation by implementing an instance method isSatisfied(Condition[],Dictionary). This method must only be called with a single element in the array; this element is unrelated to the given instance (except that the class is the same).

The following is the code for a condition that verifies that an action is granted by a network server. This is a postponed condition that groups all requests before it asks the host for authorization. The network code is abstracted in a Host class that is not shown here.

```
public class HostCondition implements Condition {
   String       action;

   public HostCondition( Bundle, ConditionInfo info ) {
      action = info.getArgs()[0];
   }

   public boolean isSatisfied() { return false; }
   public boolean isPostponed() { return true; }
   public boolean isMutable()   { return false; }

   static Host host = new Host();

   public synchronized boolean isSatisfied(
      Condition[] conditions, Dictionary state ) {
      Set   granted = (Set) state.get("granted");
      if ( granted == null ) {
         granted = new TreeSet();
         state.put("granted", granted );
      }
      Set   pending = new TreeSet();
      // There will only be one condition
      for ( int i=0; i<conditions.length; i++ ) {
         String a = ((HostCondition)conditions[i]).action;
         if ( ! granted.contains(a) )
            pending.add( a );
      }
      if ( pending.isEmpty() )
         return true;

      if ( ! host.permits( pending ) )
         return false;

      granted.addAll( pending );
      return true;
   }
}
```

The Host Condition has the following Condition Info representation:

```
[ HostCondition "payment" ]
```

The majority of the code is in the isSatisfiedmethod which takes an array of Condition. The constructor only stores the action.

This isSatisfied method first gets the set of granted permissions. The first time the method is called this set does not exist. It is then created and stored in the state dictionary for use in later invocations.

Next, a temporary set pending is created to hold all the actions of the conditions that are checked, minus any conditions that were already granted during this invocation of the Security Manager checkPermission method. If the pending list turns out to be empty because all actions were already granted, the method returns true. Otherwise it asks the host. If the host allows the actions, the pending actions are added to the granted set in the state dictionary.

9.9 Standard Conditions

This specification provides a number of standard conditions. These conditions are explained in the following sections.

9.9.1 Bundle Signer Condition

A Bundle Signer Condition is satisfied when the related bundle is signed with a certificate that matches its argument. That is, this condition can be used to assign permissions to bundles that are signed by certain principals.

The Bundle Signer Condition must be created through its static getCondition(Bundle, ConditionInfo) method. The first string argument is a matching Distinguished Name as defined in *Certificate Matching* on page 17. The second argument is optional, if used, it must be an exclamation mark ("!"). The exclamation mark indicates that the result for this condition must be reversed. For example:

```
[ ...BundleSignerCondition "* ;cn=S&V, o=Tweety Inc., c=US"]
[ ...BundleSignerCondition "* ;cn=S&V" "!"]
```

The Bundle Signer Condition is immutable and can be completely evaluated during the getCondition method.

9.9.2 Bundle Location Condition

The Bundle Location Condition matches its argument against the location string of the bundle argument. Bundle location matching provides many of the advantages of signing without the overhead. However, using locations as the authenticator requires that the download locations are secured and cannot be spoofed. For example, an Operator could permit Enterprises by forcing them to download their bundles from specific locations. To make this reasonable secure, at least the HTTPS protocol should be used. The Operator can then use the location to assign permissions.

```
https://www.acme.com/download/*       Apps from ACME
https://www.operator.com/download/*   Operator apps
```

The Bundle Location Condition must be created through its static getCondition(Bundle, ConditionInfo) method. The first string argument is a location string with possible wildcards ('*'). Wildcards are matched using Filter string matching. The second argument is optional, if used, it must be an exclamation mark ("!"). The exclamation mark indicates that the result for this condition must be reversed. For example:

```
..BundleLocationCondition "http://www.acme.com/*"
..BundleLocationCondition "*://www.acme.com/*"
```

The Bundle Location Condition is satisfied when its argument can be matched with the actual location.

The Bundle Location Condition is immutable and can be completely evaluated during the getCondition method.

9.10 Bundle Permission Resource

Bundles can convey their local permissions using the file OSGI-INF/permissions.perm. This must be a UTF-8 encoded file. The format of the file is line based; lines are not limited in length but must be readable with the BufferedReader readLine method:

```
permissions.perm ::= line *
line             ::= ( comment | pinfo ) ('\r\n'| '\n' )
comment          ::= ( '#' | '//' )
pinfo            ::= '(' qname ( quoted-string
                                ( quoted-string )? )? ')'
// See 1.3.2
```

Each permission must be listed on its own line using the encoded form of Permission Info. Comment lines are allowed. They consist of lines starting with a # or //, where leading spaces must be ignored. Multiple spaces outside quotes must be treated as a single space.

For example (.. must be replaced with the appropriate package prefix.):

```
# Friday, Feb 24 2005
# ACME, chess game
( ..ServicePermission "..log.LogService" "GET" )
( ..PackagePermission "..log" "IMPORT" )
( ..ServicePermission "..cm.ManagedService" "REGISTER" )
( ..PackagePermission "..cm" "IMPORT" )
( ..ServicePermission "..useradmin.UserAdmin" "GET" )
( ..PackagePermission "com.acme.chess" "IMPORT,EXPORTONLY" )
( ..PackagePermission "com.acme.score" "IMPORT" )
```

If this resource is present in the Bundle JAR, it will set the local permissions. If it is not present, the local permissions must be All Permission.

9.10.1 Removing the Bundle Permission Resource

An attacker could circumvent the local permission by simply removing the permissions.perm file from the bundle. This would remove any local permissions that were required by a signer of the bundle. To prevent this type of attack the Conditional Permission Admin must detect that the permissions.perm resource was signed, that is, present in the Manifest, but that it is not in the JAR. If the bundle is being installed when this condition is detected, the install must fail with a Bundle Exception.

9.11 Relation to Permission Admin

If the framework provides a Conditional Permission Admin service and a Permission Admin service then a bundle A will receive its permissions according to the following steps:

1 If the Permission Admin defines the permissions for bundle A (location is set), then these permissions override any Conditional Permission Admin information.
2 If the Conditional Permission Admin has a non-empty table, then this table is used to calculate the permissions for bundle A.
3 If the default permissions are set in Permission Admin, then these are given to bundle A.
4 All Permission is given to bundle A.

The Permission Admin defines a concept of *Default Permissions*, which is not supported by Conditional Permission Admin. Default permissions are now modeled with an empty set of conditions. Empty sets of conditions apply to *all bundles*, this in addition to any more specific conditions. This is very different from the Permission Admin service where the default permissions only apply when there is no location bound permission for that bundle. The default conditions of Permission Admin are therefore never used when Conditional Permission Admin is present and its table is non-empty.

New applications should use the Conditional Permission Admin service. The Permission Admin service will be deprecated in a future release.

9.12 Implementation Issues

9.12.1 Optimizing Immutable Conditions

There is a subtle interaction between mutability and postponement. An immutable postponed condition must be treated as a postponed conditions. This first result can then be cached. The following table shows the interaction between mutability and postponement.The *Direct* column indicates the steps during the permission check, the *After* column indicates the step when all the permissions are checked and found to allow the requested action.

isMutable	isPostponed	Direct	After
false	false	isSatisfied() / cache	
false	true	use cache if exists	isSatisfied(Condition[], Dictionary) / cache
true	false	isSatisfied()	
true	true	postpone	isSatisfied(Condition[], Dictionary) (grouped)

This significant optimization is leveraged by the provided BundleLocationCondition and BundleSignerCondition classes. The Protection Domain will never have to consider conditional permissions that do not match the protection domain's bundle. However, a Condition object can also start as a mutable condition and later become immutable. For example, a user prompt could have the following states:

- *Prompt* – The user must be prompted to get the answer, the Conditional Permission Admin will evaluate the answer to detect if it is satisfied.
- *Blanket* – The user, during an earlier prompt, has indicated it approves or denies access for that remainder of the lifetime of the bundle. In this state, the Condition object has become immutable.

This specification provides a number of condition classes to bind permission sets to specific bundles. However, custom code can also provide conditions. See *Implementing Conditions* on page 233 for more information about custom conditions.

9.12.2   **Optimizing the Permission Check**

Theoretically, every checkPermission method must evaluate every condition for every bundle on the call stack. That is, the Framework Security Manager must iterate through all bundles on the stack, run through the instantiated policy table of that bundle, evaluate all the conditions, test the permissions, until it finds a permission that is implied. This model would be prohibitively expensive.

Implementations are therefore urged to optimize the evaluation of the permission checks as much as possible. They are free to change the algorithms described in this specification as long as the external effect remains the same.

One optimization is pruning the instantiated policy table. A Condition object can be pruned if it is immutable.

If an immutable Condition object is satisfied, it can be removed from the policy's Condition objects because it cannot influence the evaluation anymore. If it is not satisfied, the corresponding policy can be completely discarded because one of the Condition objects is not satisfied, making it impossible for the policy to be used.

For example, assume the following policy table:

```
ALLOW {
    [ ...BundleLocationCondition
        "http://www.acme.com/*" ]
    ( ...SocketPermission "www.acme.com" "connect,accept" )
}
ALLOW {
    [ ...BundleLocationCondition
        "http://www.et.com/*" ]
    [ ...Prompt "Phone home?" ]
    ( ...SocketPermission "www.et.com" "connect,accept" )
}
```

Assume this table is instantiated for a bundle with a location of http://www.acme.com/bundle.jar. The first policy's permissions can be placed in a the special Permission Collection because the Bundle Location condition is immutable and in this case satisfied.

The second policy can be discarded for this bundle because it is immutable and not satisfied for the bundle's location. Any condition that is not satisfied and immutable makes the policy ignorable.

9.12.3   **Using Permission Checks in Conditions**

If there is a chance that permissions will be checked in code being called by isSatisfied, the implementer of the Condition should use the AccessController doPrivileged to ensure needed permissions. For example, a User Prompt Condition has the potential to cause many permission checks as it interacts with the UI.

However, the same Condition object must not be evaluated recursively. The Framework must detect the recursive evaluation of a Condition object and act as if the second invocation returns an unsatisfied, not postponed Condition object.

For example, if a User Prompt Condition is evaluated and this evaluation accesses the UI, which in its turn checks a permission that causes the evaluation of the same User Prompt Condition, then this second evaluation must not take place and be treated as not postponed and false.

9.12.4 Concurrency

A Condition implementation is guaranteed that all evaluations necessary for a single checkPermission invocation are carried out on the same thread. However, multiple permission checks can take place on different threads. It is the responsibility of the Condition class implementers to handle these synchronization issues.

9.12.5 Class Loading

All conditions must come from the boot class path or from the Framework class loader. This is due to security reasons as well as to prevent the case that there are multiple versions of the implementation packages present. Conditions can still be downloaded with bundles by using a Framework extension bundle, see *Extension Bundles* on page 66.

9.12.6 Condition Life Cycle

Condition objects will get instantiated when the framework is restarted or the Bundle Protection Domain is created. Framework implementations can also use optimizations that cause Condition objects to be created and destroyed multiple times within the lifetime of an instance of a Bundle Protection Domain. An implementation of a Condition class must not make any assumptions about its creation or dereferencing.

9.13 Security

9.13.1 Service Registry Security

9.13.1.1 Conditional Permission Admin Service

The Conditional Permission Admin service should be part of the Framework and therefore has All Permission.

9.13.1.2 Client

```
ServicePermission    ..ConditionalPermissionAdmin  GET
PackagePermission    ..condpermadmin               IMPORT
AllPermission
```

Clients of the Conditional Permission Admin service that set permissions must themselves have All Permission because they can give All Permission to any bundle.

9.14 Changes

- Changed the priority of establishing the permissions for a bundle when both the Permission Admin and Conditional Permission Admin are present. See *Relation to Permission Admin* on page 236.
- Clarified through the text the relation between isSatisfied methods and mutability and postponement.
- Added ALLOW/DENY conditional permissions, significant modification of the algorithm
- Changed the incremental management API to the commit based update API
- Deprecated the old incremental way of updating the policy table and provided a new atomic update facility.

9.15 org.osgi.service.condpermadmin

Conditional Permission Admin Package Version 1.1.

Bundles wishing to use this package must list the package in the Import-Package header of the bundle's manifest. For example:

```
Import-Package: org.osgi.service.condpermadmin; version="[1.1,2.0)"
```

9.15.1   Summary

- BundleLocationCondition - Condition to test if the location of a bundle matches or does not match a pattern.
- BundleSignerCondition - Condition to test if the signer of a bundle matches or does not match a pattern.
- Condition - The interface implemented by a Condition.
- ConditionalPermissionAdmin - Framework service to administer Conditional Permissions.
- ConditionalPermissionInfo - A list of Permissions guarded by a list of conditions with an access decision.
- ConditionalPermissionUpdate - Update the Conditional Permission Table.
- ConditionInfo - Condition representation used by the Conditional Permission Admin service.

9.15.2   public class BundleLocationCondition

Condition to test if the location of a bundle matches or does not match a pattern. Since the bundle's location cannot be changed, this condition is immutable.

Pattern matching is done according to the filter string matching rules.

Concurrency   Thread-safe

9.15.2.1   public static Condition getCondition(Bundle bundle, ConditionInfo info)

bundle   The Bundle being evaluated.

info   The ConditionInfo from which to construct the condition. The ConditionInfo must specify one or two arguments. The first argument of the ConditionInfo specifies the location pattern against which to match the bundle location. Matching is done according to the filter string matching rules. Any '*' characters in the first argument are used as wildcards when matching bundle locations unless they are escaped with a '\'character. The Condition is satisfied if the bundle location matches the pattern. The second argument of the ConditionInfo is optional. If a second argument is present and equal to "!", then the satisfaction of the Condition is negated. That is, the Condition is satisfied if the bundle location does NOT match the pattern. If the second argument is present but does not equal "!", then the second argument is ignored.

□   Constructs a condition that tries to match the passed Bundle's location to the location pattern.

Returns   Condition object for the requested condition.

9.15.3   public class BundleSignerCondition

Condition to test if the signer of a bundle matches or does not match a pattern. Since the bundle's signer can only change when the bundle is updated, this condition is immutable.

The condition expressed using a single String that specifies a Distinguished Name (DN) chain to match bundle signers against. DN's are encoded using IETF RFC 2253. Usually signers use certificates that are issued by certificate authorities, which also have a corresponding DN and certificate. The certificate authorities can form a chain of trust where the last DN and certificate is known by the framework. The signer of a bundle is expressed as signers DN followed by the DN of its issuer followed by the DN of the next issuer until the DN of the root certificate authority. Each DN is separated by a semicolon.

A bundle can satisfy this condition if one of its signers has a DN chain that matches the DN chain used to construct this condition. Wildcards (*') can be used to allow greater flexibility in specifying the DN chains. Wildcards can be used in place of DNs, RDNs, or the value in an RDN. If a wildcard is used for a value of an RDN, the value must be exactly "*" and will match any value for the corresponding type in that RDN. If a wildcard is used for a RDN, it must be the first RDN and will match any number of RDNs (including zero RDNs).

Concurrency Thread-safe

9.15.3.1   **public static Condition getCondition(Bundle bundle, ConditionInfo info)**

bundle The Bundle being evaluated.

info The ConditionInfo from which to construct the condition. The ConditionInfo must specify one or two arguments. The first argument of the ConditionInfo specifies the chain of distinguished names pattern to match against the signer of the bundle. The Condition is satisfied if the signer of the bundle matches the pattern. The second argument of the ConditionInfo is optional. If a second argument is present and equal to "!", then the satisfaction of the Condition is negated. That is, the Condition is satisfied if the signer of the bundle does NOT match the pattern. If the second argument is present but does not equal "!", then the second argument is ignored.

□ Constructs a Condition that tries to match the passed Bundle's location to the location pattern.

Returns A Condition which checks the signers of the specified bundle.

9.15.4   **public interface Condition**

The interface implemented by a Condition. Conditions are bound to Permissions using Conditional Permission Info. The Permissions of a ConditionalPermission Info can only be used if the associated Conditions are satisfied.

Concurrency Thread-safe

9.15.4.1   **public static final Condition FALSE**

A Condition object that will always evaluate to false and that is never postponed.

9.15.4.2   **public static final Condition TRUE**

A Condition object that will always evaluate to true and that is never postponed.

9.15.4.3   **public boolean isMutable( )**

□ Returns whether the Condition is mutable. A Condition can go from mutable (true) to immutable (false) over time but never from immutable (false) to mutable (true).

Returns trueisSatisfied() can change. Otherwise, false if the value returned by isSatisfied() will not change for this condition.

9.15.4.4   **public boolean isPostponed( )**

□ Returns whether the evaluation must be postponed until the end of the permission check. If this method returns false (or this Condition is immutable), then this Condition must be able to directly answer the isSatisfied() method. In other words, isSatisfied() will return very quickly since no external sources, such as for example users or networks, need to be consulted.
This method must always return the same value whenever it is called so that the Conditional Permission Admin can cache its result.

Returns true to indicate the evaluation must be postponed. Otherwise, false if the evaluation can be performed immediately.

9.15.4.5   **public boolean isSatisfied( )**

☐   Returns whether the Condition is satisfied. This method is only called for immediate Condition objects or immutable postponed conditions, and must always be called inside a permission check. Mutable postponed Condition objects will be called with the grouped version isSatisfied(Condition[],Dictionary) at the end of the permission check.

Returns   true to indicate the Conditions is satisfied. Otherwise, false if the Condition is not satisfied.

9.15.4.6   **public boolean isSatisfied(Condition[] conditions, Dictionary context)**

conditions   The array of Condition objects, which must all be of the same class and mutable. The receiver must be one of those Condition objects.

context   A Dictionary object that implementors can use to track state. If this method is invoked multiple times in the same permission check, the same Dictionary will be passed multiple times. The SecurityManager treats this Dictionary as an opaque object and simply creates an empty dictionary and passes it to subsequent invocations if multiple invocations are needed.

☐   Returns whether a the set of Condition objects are satisfied. Although this method is not static, it must be implemented as if it were static. All of the passed Condition objects will be of the same type and will correspond to the class type of the object on which this method is invoked.This method must be called inside a permission check only.

Returns   true if all the Condition objects are satisfied. Otherwise, false if one of the Condition objects is not satisfied.

9.15.5   public interface ConditionalPermissionAdmin

Framework service to administer Conditional Permissions. Conditional Permissions can be added to, retrieved from, and removed from the framework. Conditional Permissions are conceptually managed in an ordered table called the Conditional Permission Table.

Concurrency   Thread-safe

9.15.5.1   **public ConditionalPermissionInfo addConditionalPermissionInfo(ConditionInfo[] conditions, PermissionInfo[] permissions)**

conditions   The conditions that need to be satisfied to enable the specified permissions. This argument can be null or an empty array indicating the specified permissions are not guarded by any conditions.

permissions   The permissions that are enabled when the specified conditions, if any, are satisfied. This argument must not be null and must specify at least one permission.

☐   Create a new Conditional Permission Info in the Conditional Permission Table.

The Conditional Permission Info will be given a unique, never reused name. This entry will be added at the beginning of the Conditional Permission Table with an access decision of ALLOW.

Since this method changes the Conditional Permission Table any ConditionalPermissionUpdates that were created prior to calling this method can no longer be committed.

Returns   The ConditionalPermissionInfo for the specified Conditions and Permissions.

Throws   IllegalArgumentException – If no permissions are specified.

SecurityException – If the caller does not have AllPermission.

Deprecated   Since 1.1. Use newConditionalPermissionUpdate() instead.

9.15.5.2   **public AccessControlContext getAccessControlContext(String[] signers)**

signers   The signers for which to return an Access Control Context.

    ☐ Returns the Access Control Context that corresponds to the specified signers. The returned Access Control Context must act as if its protection domain came from a bundle that has the following characteristics:

- It is signed by all of the given signers
- It has a bundle id of -1
- Its location is the empty string
- Its state is UNINSTALLED
- It has no headers
- It has the empty version (0.0.0)
- Its last modified time=0
- Many methods will throw IllegalStateException because the state is UNINSTALLED
- All other methods return a null

Returns An AccessControlContext that has the Permissions associated with the signer.

9.15.5.3 public ConditionalPermissionInfo getConditionalPermissionInfo(String name)

name The name of the Conditional Permission Info to be returned.

    ☐ Return the Conditional Permission Info with the specified name.

Returns The Conditional Permission Info with the specified name or null if no Conditional Permission Info with the specified name exists in the Conditional Permission Table.

Deprecated Since 1.1. Use newConditionalPermissionUpdate() instead.

9.15.5.4 public Enumeration getConditionalPermissionInfos( )

    ☐ Returns the Conditional Permission Infos from the Conditional Permission Table.

The returned Enumeration will return elements in the order they are kept in the Conditional Permission Table.

The Enumeration returned is based on a copy of the Conditional Permission Table and therefore will not throw exceptions if the Conditional Permission Table is changed during the course of reading elements from the Enumeration.

Returns An enumeration of the Conditional Permission Infos that are currently in the Conditional Permission Table.

Deprecated Since 1.1. Use newConditionalPermissionUpdate() instead.

9.15.5.5 public ConditionalPermissionInfo newConditionalPermissionInfo(String name, ConditionInfo[] conditions, PermissionInfo[] permissions, String access)

name The name of the created ConditionalPermissionInfo or null to have a unique name generated when the returned ConditionalPermissionInfo is committed in an update to the Conditional Permission Table.

conditions The conditions that need to be satisfied to enable the specified permissions. This argument can be null or an empty array indicating the specified permissions are not guarded by any conditions.

permissions The permissions that are enabled when the specified conditions, if any, are satisfied. This argument must not be null and must specify at least one permission.

access Access decision. Must be one of the following values:
allow
deny The specified access decision value must be evaluated case insensitively.

    ☐ Creates a new ConditionalPermissionInfo with the specified fields suitable for insertion into a ConditionalPermissionUpdate. The delete method on ConditionalPermissionInfo objects created with this method must throw UnsupportedOperationException.

Returns A ConditionalPermissionInfo object suitable for insertion into a ConditionalPermissionUpdate.

Throws   IllegalArgumentException – If no permissions are specified or if the specified access decision is not a valid value.

Since   1.1

9.15.5.6   **public ConditionalPermissionInfo newConditionalPermissionInfo(String encodedConditionalPermissionInfo)**

*encodedConditionalPermissionInfo*The encoded ConditionalPermissionInfo. White space in the encoded ConditionalPermissionInfo is ignored. The access decision value in the encoded ConditionalPermissionInfo must be evaluated case insensitively. If the encoded ConditionalPermissionInfo does not contain the optional name, null must be used for the name and a unique name will be generated when the returned ConditionalPermissionInfo is committed in an update to the Conditional Permission Table.

   ☐   Creates a new ConditionalPermissionInfo from the specified encoded ConditionalPermissionInfo string suitable for insertion into a ConditionalPermissionUpdate. The delete method on ConditionalPermissionInfo objects created with this method must throw UnsupportedOperationException.

Returns   A ConditionalPermissionInfo object suitable for insertion into a ConditionalPermissionUpdate.

Throws   IllegalArgumentException – If the specified encodedConditionalPermissionInfo is not properly formatted.

See Also   ConditionalPermissionInfo. getEncoded

Since   1.1

9.15.5.7   **public ConditionalPermissionUpdate newConditionalPermissionUpdate( )**

   ☐   Creates a new update for the Conditional Permission Table. The update is a working copy of the current Conditional Permission Table. If the running Conditional Permission Table is modified before commit is called on the returned update, then the call to commit on the returned update will fail. That is, the commit method will return false and no change will be made to the running Conditional Permission Table. There is no requirement that commit is eventually called on the returned update.

Returns   A new update for the Conditional Permission Table.

Since   1.1

9.15.5.8   **public ConditionalPermissionInfo setConditionalPermissionInfo(String name, ConditionInfo[] conditions, PermissionInfo[] permissions)**

name   The name of the Conditional Permission Info, or null.

conditions   The conditions that need to be satisfied to enable the specified permissions. This argument can be null or an empty array indicating the specified permissions are not guarded by any conditions.

permissions   The permissions that are enabled when the specified conditions, if any, are satisfied. This argument must not be null and must specify at least one permission.

   ☐   Set or create a Conditional Permission Info with a specified name in the Conditional Permission Table.

   If the specified name is null, a new Conditional Permission Info must be created and will be given a unique, never reused name. If there is currently no Conditional Permission Info with the specified name, a new Conditional Permission Info must be created with the specified name. Otherwise, the Conditional Permission Info with the specified name must be updated with the specified Conditions and Permissions. If a new entry was created in the Conditional Permission Table it will be added at the beginning of the table with an access decision of ALLOW.

   Since this method changes the underlying permission table any ConditionalPermissionUpdates that were created prior to calling this method can no longer be committed.

Returns   The ConditionalPermissionInfo for the specified name, Conditions and Permissions.

Throws IllegalArgumentException – If no permissions are specified.

SecurityException – If the caller does not have AllPermission.

Deprecated Since 1.1. Use newConditionalPermissionUpdate() instead.

9.15.6   public interface ConditionalPermissionInfo

A list of Permissions guarded by a list of conditions with an access decision. Instances of this interface are obtained from the Conditional Permission Admin service.

Concurrency Immutable

9.15.6.1   public static final String ALLOW = "allow"

This string is used to indicate that a row in the Conditional Permission Table should return an access decision of "allow" if the conditions are all satisfied and at least one of the permissions is implied.

Since 1.1

9.15.6.2   public static final String DENY = "deny"

This string is used to indicate that a row in the Conditional Permission Table should return an access decision of "deny" if the conditions are all satisfied and at least one of the permissions is implied.

Since 1.1

9.15.6.3   public void delete( )

☐ Removes this Conditional Permission Info from the Conditional Permission Table.

Since this method changes the underlying permission table, any ConditionalPermissionUpdates that were created prior to calling this method can no longer be committed.

Throws UnsupportedOperationException – If this object was created by ConditionalPermissionAdmin.newConditionalPermissionInfo or obtained from a ConditionalPermissionUpdate. This method only functions if this object was obtained from one of the ConditionalPermissionAdmin methods deprecated in version 1.1.

SecurityException – If the caller does not have AllPermission.

Deprecated Since 1.1. Use ConditionalPermissionAdmin.newConditionalPermissionUpdate() instead to manage the Conditional Permissions.

9.15.6.4   public boolean equals(Object obj)

obj The object to test for equality with this ConditionalPermissionInfo object.

☐ Determines the equality of two ConditionalPermissionInfo objects. This method checks that specified object has the same access decision, conditions, permissions and name as this ConditionalPermissionInfo object.

Returns true if obj is a ConditionalPermissionInfo, and has the same access decision, conditions, permissions and name as this ConditionalPermissionInfo object; false otherwise.

Since 1.1

9.15.6.5   public String getAccessDecision( )

☐ Returns the access decision for this Conditional Permission Info.

Returns One of the following values:
allow - The access decision is "allow".
deny - The access decision is "deny".

Since 1.1

9.15.6.6   **public ConditionInfo[] getConditionInfos( )**

☐ Returns the Condition Infos for the Conditions that must be satisfied to enable the Permissions.

Returns The Condition Infos for the Conditions in this Conditional Permission Info.

9.15.6.7   **public String getEncoded( )**

☐ Returns the string encoding of this ConditionalPermissionInfo in a form suitable for restoring this ConditionalPermissionInfo.

The encoded format is:

```
access {conditions permissions} name
```

where *access* is the access decision, *conditions* is zero or more encoded conditions, *permissions* is one or more encoded permissions and *name* is the name of the ConditionalPermissionInfo.

name is optional. If *name* is present in the encoded string, it must quoted, beginning and ending with ". The *name* value must be encoded for proper parsing. Specifically, the ", \, carriage return, and line feed characters must be escaped using \", \\, \r, and \n, respectively.

The encoded string contains no leading or trailing whitespace characters. A single space character is used between *access* and { and between } and *name*, if *name* is present. All encoded conditions and permissions are separated by a single space character.

Returns The string encoding of this ConditionalPermissionInfo.

Since 1.1

9.15.6.8   **public String getName( )**

☐ Returns the name of this Conditional Permission Info.

Returns The name of this Conditional Permission Info. This can be null if this Conditional Permission Info was created without a name.

9.15.6.9   **public PermissionInfo[] getPermissionInfos( )**

☐ Returns the Permission Infos for the Permissions in this Conditional Permission Info.

Returns The Permission Infos for the Permissions in this Conditional Permission Info.

9.15.6.10   **public int hashCode( )**

☐ Returns the hash code value for this object.

Returns A hash code value for this object.

Since 1.1

9.15.6.11   **public String toString( )**

☐ Returns the string representation of this ConditionalPermissionInfo. The string is created by calling the getEncoded method on this ConditionalPermissionInfo.

Returns The string representation of this ConditionalPermissionInfo.

Since 1.1

9.15.7   **public interface ConditionalPermissionUpdate**

Update the Conditional Permission Table. There may be many update objects in the system at one time. If commit is called and the Conditional Permission Table has been modified since this update was created, then the call to commit will fail and this object should be discarded.

Since 1.1

Concurrency   Thread-safe

9.15.7.1   **public boolean commit( )**

☐   Commit this update. If no changes have been made to the Conditional Permission Table since this update was created, then this method will replace the Conditional Permission Table with this update's Conditional Permissions. This method may only be successfully called once on this object.

If any of the ConditionalPermissionInfos in the update list has null as a name it will be replaced with a new ConditionalPermissionInfo object that has a generated name which is unique within the list.

No two entries in this update's Conditional Permissions may have the same name. Other consistency checks may also be performed. If this update's Conditional Permissions are determined to be inconsistent in some way then an IllegalStateException will be thrown.

This method returns false if the commit did not occur because the Conditional Permission Table has been modified since the creation of this update.

Returns   true if the commit was successful. false if the commit did not occur because the Conditional Permission Table has been modified since the creation of this update.

Throws   SecurityException – If the caller does not have AllPermission.

IllegalStateException – If this update's Conditional Permissions are not valid or inconsistent. For example, this update has two Conditional Permissions in it with the same name.

9.15.7.2   **public List getConditionalPermissionInfos( )**

☐   This method returns the list of ConditionalPermissionInfos for this update. This list is originally based on the Conditional Permission Table at the time this update was created. The list returned by this method will be replace the Conditional Permission Table if commit is called and is successful.

The delete method of the ConditionalPermissionInfos in the list must throw UnsupportedOperationException.

The list returned by this method is ordered and the most significant table entry is the first entry in the list.

Returns   A List of the ConditionalPermissionInfos which represent the Conditional Permissions maintained by this update. Modifications to this list will not affect the Conditional Permission Table until successfully committed. The list may be empty if the Conditional Permission Table was empty when this update was created.

9.15.8   public class ConditionInfo

Condition representation used by the Conditional Permission Admin service.

This class encapsulates two pieces of information: a Condition *type* (class name), which must implement Condition, and the arguments passed to its constructor.

In order for a Condition represented by a ConditionInfo to be instantiated and considered during a permission check, its Condition class must be available from the system classpath.

The Condition class must either:

- Declare a public static getCondition method that takes a Bundle object and a ConditionInfo object as arguments. That method must return an object that implements the Condition interface.
- Implement the Condition interface and define a public constructor that takes a Bundle object and a ConditionInfo object as arguments.

Concurrency   Immutable

9.15.8.1   **public ConditionInfo(String type, String[] args)**

type The fully qualified class name of the Condition represented by this ConditionInfo.

args The arguments for the Condition. These arguments are available to the newly created Condition by calling the getArgs() method.

☐ Constructs a ConditionInfo from the specified type and args.

Throws NullPointerException – If type is null.

9.15.8.2   **public ConditionInfo(String encodedCondition)**

encodedCondition The encoded ConditionInfo.

☐ Constructs a ConditionInfo object from the specified encoded ConditionInfo string. White space in the encoded ConditionInfo string is ignored.

Throws IllegalArgumentException – If the specified encodedCondition is not properly formatted.

See Also getEncoded

9.15.8.3   **public boolean equals(Object obj)**

obj The object to test for equality with this ConditionInfo object.

☐ Determines the equality of two ConditionInfo objects. This method checks that specified object has the same type and args as this ConditionInfo object.

Returns true if obj is a ConditionInfo, and has the same type and args as this ConditionInfo object; false otherwise.

9.15.8.4   **public final String[] getArgs( )**

☐ Returns arguments of this ConditionInfo.

Returns The arguments of this ConditionInfo. An empty array is returned if the ConditionInfo has no arguments.

9.15.8.5   **public final String getEncoded( )**

☐ Returns the string encoding of this ConditionInfo in a form suitable for restoring this ConditionInfo.

The encoded format is:

```
[type "arg0" "arg1" ...]
```

where *argN* are strings that must be encoded for proper parsing. Specifically, the ", \, carriage return, and line feed characters must be escaped using \", \\, \r, and \n, respectively.

The encoded string contains no leading or trailing whitespace characters. A single space character is used between type and "*arg0*" and between the arguments.

Returns The string encoding of this ConditionInfo.

9.15.8.6   **public final String getType( )**

☐ Returns the fully qualified class name of the condition represented by this ConditionInfo.

Returns The fully qualified class name of the condition represented by this ConditionInfo.

9.15.8.7   **public int hashCode( )**

☐ Returns the hash code value for this object.

Returns A hash code value for this object.

9.15.8.8   **public String toString( )**

☐   Returns the string representation of this ConditionInfo. The string is created by calling the getEncoded method on this ConditionInfo.

Returns   The string representation of this ConditionInfo.

9.16   References

[53]   *Java 1.3*
http://java.sun.com/j2se/1.3

10 Permission Admin Service Specification

Version 1.2

10.1 Introduction

Note: The Permission Admin has been superseded by the Conditional Permission admin. See *Conditional Permission Admin Specification* on page 213.

In the Framework, a bundle can have a single set of permissions. These permissions are used to verify that a bundle is authorized to execute privileged code. For example, a FilePermission defines what files can be used and in what way.

The policy of providing the permissions to the bundle should be delegated to a Management Agent. For this reason, the Framework provides the Permission Admin service so that a Management Agent can administrate the permissions of a bundle and provide defaults for all bundles.

Related mechanisms of the Framework are discussed in *Security Overview* on page 9.

10.1.1 Essentials

- *Status information* – The Permission Admin Service must provide status information about the current permissions of a bundle.
- *Administrative* – The Permission Admin Service must allow a Management Agent to set the permissions before, during, or after a bundle is installed.
- *Defaults* – The Permission Admin Service must provide control over default permissions. These are the permissions for a bundle with no specific permissions set.

10.1.2 Entities

- PermissionAdmin – The service that provides access to the permission repository of the Framework.
- PermissionInfo – An object that holds the information needed to construct a Permission object.
- *Bundle location* – The string that specifies the bundle location. This is described in *Bundle Identifiers* on page 83.

Figure 10.57   Class Diagram org.osgi.service.permissionadmin.

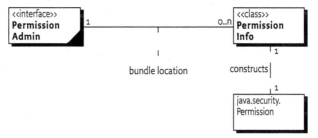

10.1.3   Operation

The Framework maintains a repository of permissions. These permissions are stored under the bundle location string. Using the bundle location allows the permissions to be set *before* a bundle is downloaded. The Framework must consult this repository when it needs the permissions of a bundle. When no specific permissions are set, the bundle must use the default permissions. If no default is set, the bundle must use java.security.AllPermission. If the default permissions are changed, a bundle with no specific permissions must immediately start using the new default permissions.

The Permission Admin service is registered by the Framework's system bundle under the org.osgi.service.permissionadmin.PermissionAdmin interface. This is an optional singleton service, so at most one Permission Admin service is registered at any moment in time.

The Permission Admin service provides access to the permission repository. A Management Agent can get, set, update, and delete permissions from this repository. A Management Agent can also use a SynchronousBundleListener object to set the permissions during the installation or updating of a bundle.

10.2   Permission Admin service

The Permission Admin service needs to manipulate the default permissions and the permissions associated with a specific bundle. The default permissions and the bundle-specific permissions are stored persistently. It is possible to set a bundle's permissions before the bundle is installed in the Framework because the bundle's location is used to set the bundle's permissions.

The manipulation of a bundle's permissions, however, may also be done in real time when a bundle is downloaded or just before the bundle is downloaded. To support this flexibility, a SynchronousBundleListener object may be used by a Management Agent to detect the installation or update of a bundle, and set the required permissions before the installation completes.

Permissions are activated before the first time a permission check for a bundle is performed. This means that if a bundle has opened a file, this file must remain usable even if the permission to open that file is removed at a later time.

Permission information is *not* specified using java.security.Permission objects. The reason for this approach is the relationship between the required persistence of the information across Framework restarts and the concept of class loaders in the Framework. Actual Permission classes must be subclasses of Permission and may be exported from any bundle. The Framework can access these permissions as long as they are exported, but the Management Agent would have to import all possible packages that contain permissions. This requirement would severely limit permission types. Therefore, the Permission Admin service uses the PermissionInfo class to specify permission information. Objects of this class are used by the Framework to create Permission objects.

PermissionInfo objects restrict the possible Permission objects that can be used. A Permission subclass can only be described by a PermissionInfo object when it has the following characteristics:

- It must be a subclass of java.security.Permission.
- It must use the two-argument public constructor type(name,actions).
- The class must be available to the Framework code from the system class path or from any exported package so it can be loaded by the Framework.
- The class must be public.

If any of these conditions is not met, the PermissionInfo object must be ignored and an error message should be logged.

The permissions are always set as an array of PermissionInfo objects to make the assignment of all permissions atomic.

The PermissionAdmin interface provides the following methods:

- getLocations() – Returns a list of locations that have permissions assigned to them. This method allows a Management Agent to examine the current set of permissions.
- getPermissions(String) – Returns a list of PermissionInfo objects that are set for that location, or returns null if no permissions are set.
- setPermissions(String,PermissionInfo[]) – Associates permissions with a specific location, or returns null when the permissions should be removed.
- getDefaultPermissions() – This method returns the list of default permissions.
- setDefaultPermissions(PermissionInfo[]) – This method sets the default permissions.

10.2.1 File Permission for Relative Path Names

A java.io.FilePermission assigned to a bundle via the setPermissions method must receive special treatment if the path argument for the FilePermission is a relative path name. A relative path name is one that is not absolute. See the java.io.File.isAbsolute method for more information on absolute path names.

When a bundle is assigned a FilePermission for a relative path name, the path name is taken to be relative to the bundle's persistent storage area. This allows additional permissions, such as **execute**, to be assigned to files in the bundle's persistent storage area. For example:

```
java.io.FilePermission "-" "execute"
```

can be used to allow a bundle to execute any file in the bundle's persistent storage area.

This only applies to FilePermission objects assigned to a bundle via the setPermission method. This does not apply to default permissions. A FilePermission for a relative path name assigned via the setDefaultPermission method must be ignored.

10.3 Security

The Permission Admin service is a system service that can be abused. A bundle that can access and use the Permission Admin service has full control over the OSGi Service Platform. However, many bundles can have ServicePermission[PermissionAdmin,GET] because all methods that change the state of the Framework require AdminPermission.

No bundle must have ServicePermission[PermissionAdmin,REGISTER] for this service because only the Framework should provide this service.

10.4 org.osgi.service.permissionadmin

Permission Admin Package Version 1.2.

Bundles wishing to use this package must list the package in the Import-Package header of the bundle's manifest. For example:

```
Import-Package: org.osgi.service.permissionadmin; version="[1.2,2.0)"
```

10.4.1 Summary

- PermissionAdmin - The Permission Admin service allows management agents to manage the permissions of bundles.
- PermissionInfo - Permission representation used by the Permission Admin service.

10.4.2	**public interface PermissionAdmin**

The Permission Admin service allows management agents to manage the permissions of bundles. There is at most one Permission Admin service present in the OSGi environment.

Access to the Permission Admin service is protected by corresponding ServicePermission. In addition AdminPermission is required to actually set permissions.

Bundle permissions are managed using a permission table. A bundle's location serves as the key into this permission table. The value of a table entry is the set of permissions (of type Permission-Info) granted to the bundle named by the given location. A bundle may have an entry in the permission table prior to being installed in the Framework.

The permissions specified in setDefaultPermissions are used as the default permissions which are granted to all bundles that do not have an entry in the permission table.

Any changes to a bundle's permissions in the permission table will take effect no later than when bundle's java.security.ProtectionDomain is next involved in a permission check, and will be made persistent.

Only permission classes on the system classpath or from an exported package are considered during a permission check. Additionally, only permission classes that are subclasses of java.security.Permission and define a 2-argument constructor that takes a *name* string and an *actions* string can be used.

Permissions implicitly granted by the Framework (for example, a bundle's permission to access its persistent storage area) cannot be changed, and are not reflected in the permissions returned by get-Permissions and getDefaultPermissions.

Concurrency   Thread-safe

10.4.2.1   **public PermissionInfo[] getDefaultPermissions( )**

□   Gets the default permissions.

These are the permissions granted to any bundle that does not have permissions assigned to its location.

Returns   The default permissions, or null if no default permissions are set.

10.4.2.2   **public String[] getLocations( )**

□   Returns the bundle locations that have permissions assigned to them, that is, bundle locations for which an entry exists in the permission table.

Returns   The locations of bundles that have been assigned any permissions, or null if the permission table is empty.

10.4.2.3   **public PermissionInfo[] getPermissions(String location)**

location   The location of the bundle whose permissions are to be returned.

□   Gets the permissions assigned to the bundle with the specified location.

Returns   The permissions assigned to the bundle with the specified location, or null if that bundle has not been assigned any permissions.

10.4.2.4   **public void setDefaultPermissions(PermissionInfo[] permissions)**

permissions   The default permissions, or null if the default permissions are to be removed from the permission table.

□   Sets the default permissions.

These are the permissions granted to any bundle that does not have permissions assigned to its location.

Throws   SecurityException – If the caller does not have AllPermission.

10.4.2.5   **public void setPermissions(String location, PermissionInfo[] permissions)**

location   The location of the bundle that will be assigned the permissions.

permissions   The permissions to be assigned, or null if the specified location is to be removed from the permission table.

☐   Assigns the specified permissions to the bundle with the specified location.

Throws   SecurityException – If the caller does not have AllPermission.

10.4.3   public class PermissionInfo

Permission representation used by the Permission Admin service.

This class encapsulates three pieces of information: a Permission *type* (class name), which must be a subclass of java.security.Permission, and the *name* and *actions* arguments passed to its constructor.

In order for a permission represented by a PermissionInfo to be instantiated and considered during a permission check, its Permission class must be available from the system classpath or an exported package. This means that the instantiation of a permission represented by a PermissionInfo may be delayed until the package containing its Permission class has been exported by a bundle.

Concurrency   Immutable

10.4.3.1   **public PermissionInfo(String type, String name, String actions)**

type   The fully qualified class name of the permission represented by this PermissionInfo. The class must be a subclass of java.security.Permission and must define a 2-argument constructor that takes a *name* string and an *actions* string.

name   The permission name that will be passed as the first argument to the constructor of the Permission class identified by type.

actions   The permission actions that will be passed as the second argument to the constructor of the Permission class identified by type.

☐   Constructs a PermissionInfo from the specified type, name, and actions.

Throws   NullPointerException – If type is null.

IllegalArgumentException – If action is not null and name is null.

10.4.3.2   **public PermissionInfo(String encodedPermission)**

encodedPermission   The encoded PermissionInfo.

☐   Constructs a PermissionInfo object from the specified encoded PermissionInfo string. White space in the encoded PermissionInfo string is ignored.

Throws   IllegalArgumentException – If the specified encodedPermission is not properly formatted.

See Also   getEncoded

10.4.3.3   **public boolean equals(Object obj)**

obj   The object to test for equality with this PermissionInfo object.

☐   Determines the equality of two PermissionInfo objects. This method checks that specified object has the same type, name and actions as this PermissionInfo object.

Returns   true if obj is a PermissionInfo, and has the same type, name and actions as this PermissionInfo object; false otherwise.

10.4.3.4   **public final String getActions( )**

☐   Returns the actions of the permission represented by this PermissionInfo.

Returns   The actions of the permission represented by this PermissionInfo, or null if the permission does not have any actions associated with it.

10.4.3.5   **public final String getEncoded( )**

□   Returns the string encoding of this PermissionInfo in a form suitable for restoring this Permission-Info.

The encoded format is:

   (type)

or

   (type "name")

or

   (type "name" "actions")

where *name* and *actions* are strings that must be encoded for proper parsing. Specifically, the ",\, carriage return, and line feed characters must be escaped using \", \\,\r, and \n, respectively.

The encoded string contains no leading or trailing whitespace characters. A single space character is used between *type* and "*name*" and between "*name*" and "*actions*".

Returns   The string encoding of this PermissionInfo.

10.4.3.6   **public final String getName( )**

□   Returns the name of the permission represented by this PermissionInfo.

Returns   The name of the permission represented by this PermissionInfo, or null if the permission does not have a name.

10.4.3.7   **public final String getType( )**

□   Returns the fully qualified class name of the permission represented by this PermissionInfo.

Returns   The fully qualified class name of the permission represented by this PermissionInfo.

10.4.3.8   **public int hashCode( )**

□   Returns the hash code value for this object.

Returns   A hash code value for this object.

10.4.3.9   **public String toString( )**

□   Returns the string representation of this PermissionInfo. The string is created by calling the getEncoded method on this PermissionInfo.

Returns   The string representation of this PermissionInfo.

11 URL Handlers Service Specification

Version 1.0

11.1 Introduction

This specification standardizes the mechanism to extend the Java run-time with new URL schemes and content handlers through bundles. Dynamically extending the URL schemes that are supported in an OSGi Service Platform is a powerful concept.

This specification is necessary because the standard Java mechanisms for extending the URL class with new schemes and different content types is not compatible with the dynamic aspects of an OSGi Service Platform. The registration of a new scheme or content type is a one time only action in Java, and once registered, a scheme or content type can never be revoked. This singleton approach to registration makes the provided mechanism impossible to use by different, independent bundles. Therefore, it is necessary for OSGi Framework implementations to hide this mechanism and provide an alternative mechanism that can be used.

The Release 4 specifications has also standardized a Connector service that has similar capabilities. See the *IO Connector Service Specification* on page 223.

11.1.1 Essentials

- *Multiple Access* – Multiple bundles should be allowed to register ContentHandler objects and URLStreamHandler objects.
- *Existing Schemes Availability* – Existing schemes in an OSGi Service Platform should not be overridden.
- *life cycle Monitored* – The life cycle of bundles must be supported. Scheme handlers and content type handlers must become unavailable when the registering bundle is stopped.
- *Simplicity* – Minimal effort should be required for a bundle to provide a new URL scheme or content type handler.

11.1.2 Entities

- *Scheme* – An identifier for a specific protocol. For example, "http" is a scheme for the Hyper Text Transfer Protocol. A scheme is implemented in a java.net.URLStreamHandler sub-class.
- *Content Type* – An identifier for the type of the content. Content types are usually referred to as MIME types. A content type handler is implemented as a java.net.ContentHandler sub-class.
- *Uniform Resource Locator (URL)* – An instance of the java.net.URL class that holds the name of a scheme with enough parameters to identify a resource for that scheme.
- *Factory* – An object that creates other objects. The purpose is to hide the implementation types (that may vary) from the caller. The created objects are a subclass/implementation of a specific type.
- *Proxy* – The object that is registered with Java and that forwards all calls to the real implementation that is registered with the service registry.
- *java.net.URLStreamHandler* – An instance of the java.net.URLStreamHandler class that can create URLConnection objects that represent a connection for a specific protocol.
- *Singleton Operation* – An operation that can only be executed once.

- *URLStreamHandlerService* – An OSGi service interface that contains the methods of the URLStreamHandler class with public visibility so they can be called from the Framework.
- *AbstractURLStreamHandlerService* – An implementation of the URLStreamHandlerService interface that implements the interface's methods by calling the implementation of the super class (java.net.url.URLStreamHandler). This class also handles the setting of the java.net.URL object via the java.net.URLStreamHandlerSetter interface.
- *URLStreamHandlerSetter* – An interface needed to abstract the setting of the java.net.URL object. This interface is related to the use of a proxy and security checking.
- *java.net.URLStreamHandlerFactory* – A factory, registered with the java.net.URL class, that is used to find java.net.URLStreamHandler objects implementing schemes that are not implemented by the Java environment. Only one java.net.URLStreamHandlerFactory object can be registered with Java.
- *java.net.URLConnection* – A connection for a specific, scheme-based protocol. A java.net.URLConnection object is created by a java.net.URLStreamHandler object when the java.net.URL.openConnection method is invoked.
- *java.net.ContentHandler* – An object that can convert a stream of bytes to a Java object. The class of this Java object depends on the MIME type of the byte stream.
- *java.net.ContentHandlerFactory* – A factory that can extend the set of java.net.ContentHandler objects provided by the java.net.URLConnection class, by creating new ones on demand. Only one java.net.ContentHandlerFactory object can be registered with the java.net.URLConnection class.
- *MIME Type* – A name space for byte stream formats. See [56] *MIME Multipurpose Internet Mail Extension.*

The following class diagram is surprisingly complex due to the complicated strategy that Java uses to implement extendable stream handlers and content handlers.

Figure 11.58   Class Diagram, java.net (URL and associated classes)

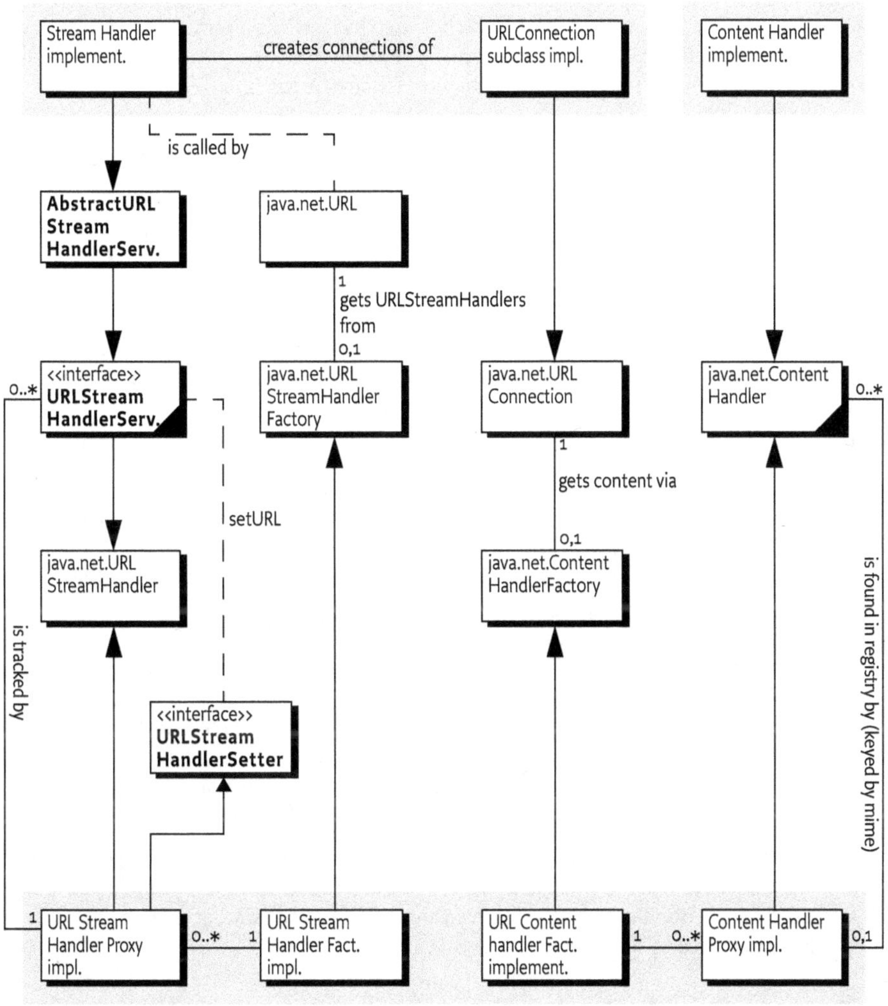

11.1.3   Operation

A bundle that can implement a new URL scheme should register a service object under the URLStreamHandlerService interface with the OSGi Framework. This interface contains public versions of the java.net.URLStreamHandler class methods, so that these methods can be called by the *proxy* (the object that is actually registered with the Java run-time).

The OSGi Framework implementation must make this service object available to the underlying java.net implementation. This must be supported by the OSGi Framework implementation because the java.net.URL.setStreamHandlerFactory method can only be called *once*, making it impossible to use by bundles that come and go.

Bundles that can convert a content-typed stream should register a service object under the name java.net.ContentHandler. These objects should be made available by the OSGi Framework to the java.net.URLConnection class.

11.2   Factories in java.net

Java provides the java.net.URL class which is used by the OSGi Framework and many of the bundles that run on the OSGi Service Platform. A key benefit of using the URL class is the ease with which a URL string is translated into a request for a resource.

The extensibility of the java.net.URL class allows new schemes (protocols) and content types to be added dynamically using java.net.URLStreamHandlerFactory objects. These new handlers allow existing applications to use new schemes and content types in the same way as the handlers provided by the Java run-time environment. This mechanism is described in the Javadoc for the URLStreamHandler and ContentHandler class, see [54] *Java*.

For example, the URL http://www.osgi.org/sample.txt addresses a file on the OSGi web server that is obtained with the HTTP scheme (usually a scheme provided by the Java run-time). A URL such as rsh://www.acme.com/agent.zip is addressing a ZIP file that can be obtained with the non-built-in RSH scheme. A java.net.URLStreamHandlerFactory object must be registered with the java.net.URL class prior to the successful use of an RSH scheme.

There are several problems with using only the existing Java facilities for extending the handlers used by the java.net.URL class:

* *Factories Are Singleton Operations* – One java.net.URLStreamHandlerFactory object can be registered *once* with the java.net.URL class. Similarly, one java.net.ContentHandlerFactory object can be registered once with the java.net.URLConnection class. It is impossible to undo the registration of a factory or register a replacement factory.
* *Caching Of Schemes* – When a previously unused scheme is first used by the java.net.URL class, the java.net.URL class requests a java.net.URLStreamHandler object for that specific scheme from the currently registered java.net.URLStreamHandlerFactory object. A returned java.net.URLStreamHandler object is cached and subsequent requests for that scheme use the same java.net.URLStreamHandler object. This means that once a handler has been constructed for a specific scheme, this handler can no longer be removed, nor replaced, by a new handler for that scheme. This caching is likewise done for java.net.ContentHandler objects.

Both problems impact the OSGi operating model, which allows a bundle to go through different life cycle stages that involve exposing services, removing services, updating code, replacing services provided by one bundle with services from another, etc. The existing Java mechanisms are not compatible when used by bundles.

11.3   Framework Procedures

The OSGi Framework must register a java.net.URLStreamHandlerFactory object and a java.net.ContentHandlerFactory object with the java.net.URL.setURLStreamHandlerFactory and java.net.URLConnection.setContentHandlerFactory methods, respectively.

When these two factories are registered, the OSGi Framework service registry must be tracked for the registration of URLStreamHandlerService services and java.net.ContentHandler services.

A URL Stream Handler Service must be associated with a service registration property named URL_HANDLER_PROTOCOL. The value of this url.handler.protocol property must be an array of scheme names (String[] or String).

A Content Handler service must be associated with a service registration property named URL_CONTENT_MIMETYPE. The value of the URL_CONTENT_MIMETYPE property must be an array of MIME types names (String[] or String) in the form type/subtype. See [56] *MIME Multipurpose Internet Mail Extension.*

11.3.1   Constructing a Proxy and Handler

When a URL is used with a previously unused scheme, it must query the registered java.net.URLStreamHandlerFactory object (that should have been registered by the OSGi Framework). The OSGi Framework must then search the service registry for services that are registered under URLStreamHandlerService and that match the requested scheme.

If one or more service objects are found, a proxy object must be constructed. A proxy object is necessary because the service object that provides the implementation of the java.net.URLStreamHandler object can become unregistered and Java does not provide a mechanism to withdraw a java.net.URLStreamHandler object once it is returned from a java.net.URLStreamHandlerFactory object.

Once the proxy is created, it must track the service registry for registrations and unregistrations of services matching its associated scheme. The proxy must be associated with the service that matches the scheme and has the highest value for the org.osgi.framework.Constants.SERVICE_RANKING service registration property (see *Service Properties* on page 109) at any moment in time. If a proxy is associated with a URL Stream Handler Service, it must change the associated handler to a newly registered service when that service has a higher value for the ranking property.

The proxy object must forward all method requests to the associated URL Stream Handler Service until this service object becomes unregistered.

Once a proxy is created, it cannot be withdrawn because it is cached by the Java run-time. However, service objects can be withdrawn and it is possible for a proxy to exist without an associated URLStreamHandlerService/java.net.ContentHandler object.

In this case, the proxy must handle subsequent requests until another appropriate service is registered. When this happens, the proxy class must handle the error.

In the case of a URL Stream Handler proxy, it must throw a java.net.MalformedURLException exception if the signature of a method allows throwing this exception. Otherwise, a java.lang.IllegalStateException exception is thrown.

In the case of a Content Handler proxy, it must return InputStream to the data.

Bundles must ensure that their URLStreamHandlerService or java.net.ContentHandler service objects throw these exceptions also when they have become unregistered.

Proxies for Content Handler services operate slightly differently from URL Stream Handler Service proxies. In the case that null is returned from the registered ContentHandlerFactory object, the factory will not get another chance to provide a ContentHandler object for that content-type. Thus, if there is no built-in handler, nor a registered handler for this content-type, a ContentHandler proxy must be constructed that returns the InputStream object from the URLConnection object as the content object until a handler is registered.

11.3.2   Built-in Handlers

Implementations of Java provide a number of sub-classes of java.net.URLStreamHandler classes that can handle protocols like HTTP, FTP, NEWS etc. Most Java implementations provide a mechanism to add new handlers that can be found on the class path through class name construction.

If a registered java.net.URLStreamHandlerFactory object returns null for a built-in handler (or one that is available through the class name construction mechanism), it will never be called again for that specific scheme because the Java implementation will use its built-in handler or uses the class name construction.

As a result, even though it is not forbidden for URL Handlers Service implementations to override built-in handlers, it is not possible to guarantee that a registered URLStreamHandlerService object will be used when it is overriding a built-in handler. For consistency reasons, it is therefore recommended to never override built-in handlers.

The Content Handler Factory is implemented using a similar technique and has therefore the same problems.

To facilitate the discovery of built-in handlers that are available through the name construction, the method described in the next section must be used by the Framework before any handlers are searched for in the service registry.

11.3.3   Finding Built-in Handlers

If the system properties java.protocol.handler.pkgs or java.content.handler.pkgs are defined, they must be used to locate built-in handlers. Each property must be defined as a list of package names that are separated by a vertical bar ('|', \u007C) and that are searched in the left-to-right order (the names must *not* end in a period). For example:

```
org.osgi.impl.handlers | com.acme.url
```

The package names are the prefixes that are put in front of a scheme or content type to form a class name that can handle the scheme or content-type.

A URL Stream Handler name for a scheme is formed by appending the string ".Handler" to the scheme name. Using the packages in the previous example, the rsh scheme handler class is searched by the following names:

```
org.osgi.impl.handlers.rsh.Handler
com.acme.url.rsh.Handler
```

MIME type names contain the '/' character and can contain other characters that must not be part of a Java class name. A MIME type name must be processed as follows before it can be converted to a class name:

1. First, all slashes in the MIME name must be converted to a period ('.' \u002E). All other characters that are not allowed in a Java class name must be converted to an underscore ('_' or \u005F).

```
application/zip          application.zip
text/uri-list            text.uri_list
image/vnd.dwg            image.vnd_dwg
```

2. After this conversion, the name is appended to the list of packages specified in java.content.handler.pkgs. For example, if the content type is application/zip, and the packages are defined as in the previous example, then the following classes are searched:

```
org.osgi.impl.handlers.application.zip
com.acme.url.application.zip
```

The Java run-time specific packages should be listed in the appropriate properties so that implementations of the URL Stream Handler Factory and Content Handler Factory can be made aware of these packages.

11.3.4   Protected Methods and Proxy

Implementations of java.net.URLStreamHandler class cannot be registered in the service registry for use by the proxy because the methods of the URLStreamHandler class are protected and thus not available to the proxy implementation. Also, the URLStreamHandler class checks that only the URLStreamHandler object that was returned from the URLStreamHandlerFactory object can invoke the setURL method. This means that URLStreamHandler objects in the service registry would be unable to invoke the setURL method. Invoking this method is necessary when implementing the parseURL method.

Therefore, the URLStreamHandlerService and URLStreamHandlerSetter interfaces were created. The URLStreamHandlerService interface provides public versions of the URLStreamHandler methods, except that the setURL method is missing and the parseURL method has a new first argument of type URLStreamHandlerSetter. In general, sub-classes of the URLStreamHandler class can be converted to URLStreamHandlerService classes with minimal code changes. Apart from making the relevant methods public, the parseURL method needs to be changed to invoke the setURL method on the URLStreamHandlerSetter object that the URLStreamHandlerService object was passed, rather then the setURL method of URLStreamHandler class.

Figure 11.59   Proxy Issues

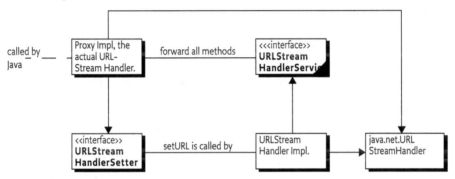

To aid in the conversion of URLStreamHandler implementation classes, the AbstractURLStreamHandlerService has been provided. Apart from making the relevant methods public, the AbstractURLStreamHandlerService stores the URLStreamHandlerSetter object in a private variable. To make the setURL method work properly, it overrides the setURL method to invoke the setURL method on the saved URLStreamHandlerSetter object rather then the URLStreamHandler.setURL method. This means that a subclass of URLStreamHandler should be changed to become a sub-class of the AbstractURLStreamHandlerService class and be recompiled.

Normally, the parseURL method will have the following form:

```
class URLStreamHandlerImpl {
    ...
    protected URLStreamHandlerSetter realHandler;
    ...
    public void parseURL(
        URLStreamHandlerSetter realHandler,
            URL u, String spec, int start, int limit) {
            this.realHandler = realHandler;
            parseURL(u, spec, start, limit);
    }
    protected void setURL(URL u,
        String protocol, String host,
        int port, String authority,
```

```
            String userInfo, String path,
            String query,String ref) {
        realHandler.setURL(u, protocol, host,
            port, authority, userInfo, path,
            query, ref);
    }
    ...
}
```

The URLStreamHandler.parseURL method will call the setURL method which must be invoked on the proxy rather than this. That is why the setURL method is overridden to delegate to the URLStreamHandlerSetter object in realHandler as opposed to super.

11.3.5 Stream Handlers that use java.net.Proxy

Java 1.5 introduced a new method on the URLStreamHandler class: URLConnection openConnection(URL,Proxy). Adding this method to the URL Stream Handler service poses the following problems:

· It would have broken all existing implementations.
· The references to the java.net.Proxy class would make the API dependent on Java 1.5

Therefore, scheme providers can optionally implement the openConnection(URL,Proxy) method as a public method. If the scheme provider implements this method, then the framework must call it (using reflection). If this method is not implemented in the URL Stream Handler service an Unsupported Operation Exception must be thrown.

Framework implementations should be careful not to create unwanted dependencies on Java 1.5. This will require two different implementation classes for the URLStreamHandler class that is used to proxy the URL Stream Handler services.

11.4 Providing a New Scheme

The following example provides a scheme that returns the path part of the URL. The first class that is implemented is the URLStreamHandlerService. When it is started, it registers itself with the OSGi Framework. The OSGi Framework calls the openConnection method when a new java.net.URLConnection must be created. In this example, a DataConnection object is returned.

```
public class DataProtocol
    extends AbstractURLStreamHandlerService
    implements BundleActivator {
    public void start( BundleContext context ) {
        Hashtable  properties = new Hashtable();
        properties.put( URLConstants.URL_HANDLER_PROTOCOL,
            new String[] { "data" } );
        context.registerService(
            URLStreamHandlerService.class.getName(),
            this, properties );
    }
    public void stop( BundleContext context ) {}

    public URLConnection openConnection( URL url ) {
        return new DataConnection(url);
    }
}
```

The following example DataConnection class extends java.net.URLConnection and overrides the constructor so that it can provide the URL object to the super class, the connect method, and the getInputStream method. This last method returns the path part of the URL as an java.io.InputStream object.

```
class DataConnection extends java.net.URLConnection {
   DataConnection( URL url ) {super(url);}
   public void connect() {}

   public InputStream getInputStream() throws IOException {
      String s = getURL().getPath();
      byte [] buf = s.getBytes();
      return new ByteArrayInputStream(buf,1,buf.length-1);
   }
   public String getContentType() {
      return "text/plain";
   }
}
```

11.5 Providing a Content Handler

A Content Handler should extend the java.net.ContentHandler class and implement the getContent method. This method must get the InputStream object from the java.net.URLConnection parameter object and convert the bytes from this stream to the applicable type. In this example, the MIME type is text/plain and the return object is a String object.

```
public class TextPlainHandler extends ContentHandler
   implements BundleActivator {

   public void start( BundleContext context ) {
      Hashtableproperties = new Hashtable();
      properties.put( URLConstants.URL_CONTENT_MIMETYPE,
         new String[] { "text/plain" } );
      context.registerService(
         ContentHandler.class.getName(),
         this, properties );
   }
   public void stop( BundleContext context ) {}

   public Object getContent( URLConnection conn )
         throws IOException {
      InputStream in = conn.getInputStream();
      InputStreamReader r = new InputStreamReader( in );
      StringBuffer sb = new StringBuffer();
      int c;
      while ( (c=r.read()) >= 0 )
         sb.append( (char) c );
      r.close(); in.close();
      return sb.toString();
   }
}
```

11.6 Security Considerations

The ability to specify a protocol and add content handlers makes it possible to directly affect the behavior of a core Java VM class. The java.net.URL class is widely used by network applications and can be used by the OSGi Framework itself.

Therefore, care must be taken when providing the ability to register handlers. The two types of supported handlers are URLStreamHandlerService and java.net.ContentHandler. Only trusted bundles should be allowed to register these services and have ServicePermission[URLStreamHandlerService|ContentHandler, REGISTER] for these classes. Since these services are made available to other bundles through the java.net.URL class and java.net.URLConnection class, it is advisable to deny the use of these services (ServicePermission[<name>, GET]) to all, so that only the Framework can get them. This prevents the circumvention of the permission checks done by the java.net.URL class by using the URLStreamHandlerServices service objects directly.

11.7 Changes

* Built-in URL handlers now should take priority instead of must. This allows frameworks to override existing handlers if so desired. See *Built-in Handlers* on page 261.

11.8 org.osgi.service.url

URL Stream and Content Handlers Package Version 1.0.

Bundles wishing to use this package must list the package in the Import-Package header of the bundle's manifest. For example:

```
Import-Package: org.osgi.service.url; version="[1.0,2.0)"
```

11.8.1 Summary

* AbstractURLStreamHandlerService - Abstract implementation of the URLStreamHandlerService interface.
* URLConstants - Defines standard names for property keys associated with URLStreamHandlerService and java.net.ContentHandler services.
* URLStreamHandlerService - Service interface with public versions of the protected java.net.URLStreamHandler methods.
* URLStreamHandlerSetter - Interface used by URLStreamHandlerService objects to call the setURL method on the proxy URLStreamHandler object.

11.8.2 public abstract class AbstractURLStreamHandlerService extends URLStreamHandler implements URLStreamHandlerService

Abstract implementation of the URLStreamHandlerService interface. All the methods simply invoke the corresponding methods on java.net.URLStreamHandler except for parseURL and setURL, which use the URLStreamHandlerSetter parameter. Subclasses of this abstract class should not need to override the setURL and parseURL(URLStreamHandlerSetter,...) methods.

Concurrency Thread-safe

11.8.2.1 protected volatile URLStreamHandlerSetter realHandler

The URLStreamHandlerSetter object passed to the parseURL method.

11.8.2.2 **public AbstractURLStreamHandlerService( )**

11.8.2.3 **public boolean equals(URL u1, URL u2)**

☐ This method calls super.equals(URL,URL).

See Also java.net.URLStreamHandler.equals(URL,URL)

11.8.2.4 **public int getDefaultPort( )**

☐ This method calls super.getDefaultPort.

See Also java.net.URLStreamHandler.getDefaultPort

11.8.2.5 **public InetAddress getHostAddress(URL u)**

☐ This method calls super.getHostAddress.

See Also java.net.URLStreamHandler.getHostAddress

11.8.2.6 **public int hashCode(URL u)**

☐ This method calls super.hashCode(URL).

See Also java.net.URLStreamHandler.hashCode(URL)

11.8.2.7 **public boolean hostsEqual(URL u1, URL u2)**

☐ This method calls super.hostsEqual.

See Also java.net.URLStreamHandler.hostsEqual

11.8.2.8 **public abstract URLConnection openConnection(URL u) throws IOException**

See Also java.net.URLStreamHandler.openConnection

11.8.2.9 **public void parseURL(URLStreamHandlerSetter realHandler, URL u, String spec, int start, int limit)**

realHandler The object on which the setURL method must be invoked for the specified URL.

☐ Parse a URL using the URLStreamHandlerSetter object. This method sets the realHandler field with the specified URLStreamHandlerSetter object and then calls parseURL(URL,String,int,int).

See Also java.net.URLStreamHandler.parseURL

11.8.2.10 **public boolean sameFile(URL u1, URL u2)**

☐ This method calls super.sameFile.

See Also java.net.URLStreamHandler.sameFile

11.8.2.11 **protected void setURL(URL u, String proto, String host, int port, String file, String ref)**

☐ This method calls realHandler.setURL(URL,String,String,int,String,String).

See Also java.net.URLStreamHandler.setURL(URL,String,String,int,String,String)

Deprecated This method is only for compatibility with handlers written for JDK 1.1.

11.8.2.12 **protected void setURL(URL u, String proto, String host, int port, String auth, String user, String path, String query, String ref)**

☐ This method calls realHandler.setURL(URL,String,String,int,String,String,String,String).

See Also java.net.URLStreamHandler.setURL(URL,String,String,int,String,String,String, String)

11.8.2.13 **public String toExternalForm(URL u)**

☐ This method calls super.toExternalForm.

See Also   `java.net.URLStreamHandler.toExternalForm`

11.8.3   public interface URLConstants

Defines standard names for property keys associated with URLStreamHandlerService and java.net.ContentHandler services.

The values associated with these keys are of type java.lang.String[] or java.lang.String, unless otherwise indicated.

11.8.3.1   public static final String URL_CONTENT_MIMETYPE = "url.content.mimetype"

Service property naming the MIME types serviced by a java.net.ContentHandler. The property's value is a MIME type or an array of MIME types.

11.8.3.2   public static final String URL_HANDLER_PROTOCOL = "url.handler.protocol"

Service property naming the protocols serviced by a URLStreamHandlerService. The property's value is a protocol name or an array of protocol names.

11.8.4   public interface URLStreamHandlerService

Service interface with public versions of the protected java.net.URLStreamHandler methods.

The important differences between this interface and the URLStreamHandler class are that the set-URL method is absent and the parseURL method takes a URLStreamHandlerSetter object as the first argument. Classes implementing this interface must call the setURL method on the URL-StreamHandlerSetter object received in the parseURL method instead of URLStreamHandler.set-URL to avoid a SecurityException.

See Also   `AbstractURLStreamHandlerService`

Concurrency   Thread-safe

11.8.4.1   public boolean equals(URL u1, URL u2)

See Also   `java.net.URLStreamHandler.equals(URL, URL)`

11.8.4.2   public int getDefaultPort( )

See Also   `java.net.URLStreamHandler.getDefaultPort`

11.8.4.3   public InetAddress getHostAddress(URL u)

See Also   `java.net.URLStreamHandler.getHostAddress`

11.8.4.4   public int hashCode(URL u)

See Also   `java.net.URLStreamHandler.hashCode(URL)`

11.8.4.5   public boolean hostsEqual(URL u1, URL u2)

See Also   `java.net.URLStreamHandler.hostsEqual`

11.8.4.6   public URLConnection openConnection(URL u) throws IOException

See Also   `java.net.URLStreamHandler.openConnection`

11.8.4.7   public void parseURL(URLStreamHandlerSetter realHandler, URL u, String spec, int start, int limit)

realHandler   The object on which setURL must be invoked for this URL.

☐   Parse a URL. This method is called by the URLStreamHandler proxy, instead of java.net.URLStream-Handler.parseURL, passing a URLStreamHandlerSetter object.

See Also   `java.net.URLStreamHandler.parseURL`

11.8.4.8   **public boolean sameFile(URL u1, URL u2)**

See Also   java.net.URLStreamHandler.sameFile

11.8.4.9   **public String toExternalForm(URL u)**

See Also   java.net.URLStreamHandler.toExternalForm

11.8.5   public interface URLStreamHandlerSetter

Interface used by URLStreamHandlerService objects to call the setURL method on the proxy URL-StreamHandler object.

Objects of this type are passed to the URLStreamHandlerService.parseURL method. Invoking the setURL method on the URLStreamHandlerSetter object will invoke the setURL method on the proxy URLStreamHandler object that is actually registered with java.net.URL for the protocol.

Concurrency   Thread-safe

11.8.5.1   **public void setURL(URL u, String protocol, String host, int port, String file, String ref)**

See Also   java.net.URLStreamHandler.setURL(URL,String,String,int,String,String)

Deprecated   This method is only for compatibility with handlers written for JDK 1.1.

11.8.5.2   **public void setURL(URL u, String protocol, String host, int port, String authority, String userInfo, String path, String query, String ref)**

See Also   java.net.URLStreamHandler.setURL(URL,String,String,int,String,String,String, String)

11.9   References

[54]   *Java*
http://java.sun.com/j2se/1.4/docs/api/java/net/package-summary.html

[55]   *URLs*
http://www.ietf.org/rfc/rfc1738.txt

[56]   *MIME Multipurpose Internet Mail Extension*
http://www.nacs.uci.edu/indiv/ehood/MIME/MIME.html

[57]   *Assigned MIME Media Types*
http://www.iana.org/assignments/media-types

12 Service Hooks Specification

Version 1.0

12.1 Introduction

The OSGi framework has built-in support for the normal service primitives: *publish, find,* and *bind.* Despite their simplicity, these primitives are surprisingly powerful and have become quite popular. However, these primitives operate on information that is not completely visible to the bundles. For example, it is impossible to find out what services are being waited upon by other bundles. This information can be useful to provide a service just in time to that bundle. Additionally, it is also not possible to allow bundles functionality that interacts with the service engine. For example, a bundle could proxy another service but to do this transparently, it is required to hide the original service and offer the proxy only to a specific bundle. With the current primitives this is also not possible.

Therefore, this service hook specification provides a number of new mechanisms that closely interact with the service engine. These interactions are *not* intended for use by application bundles. The service primitives appear simple but require surprisingly complex code to make them appear simple to the bundle developer. Modifying the behavior of the service engine requires developers to closely follow the semantics of the OSGi service model and this is often hard, requiring a significant amount of code.

However, the service hooks provide a more symmetric model for service based programming that can act as a multiplier for the framework. The basic framework provides a powerful service engine and this specification allows a bundle to interact with this service engine

12.1.1 Essentials

- *Robust* – The service primitives are very simple and work reliably in many scenarios. The specified hooks interact with this robust service engine. This interaction must not cause disruption of the normal operations.
- *Find listeners* – Provide information about the services specific bundles are interested in.
- *Control visibility* – Provide a mechanism to hide the visibility of a service to one or more bundles.
- *Intercept finds* – Provide a mechanism to detect the searches of a bundle in the service registry and restrict the set of found service references.
- *Whiteboard based* – Use the whiteboard to simplify the writing of the interceptors.

12.1.2 Entities

- *Client* – The bundle that finds services, gets services, and/or receives events about services.
- *Handler* – The bundle that registers a hook service and uses this to view or modify the state.
- *Target* – A client bundle being targeted by a Handler.
- *Publisher* – A client bundle that publishes services.
- *Consumer* – A client bundle that consumes services.
- *Service Engine* – The internal framework machinery that makes the service registry work.
- *Event Hook* – An event hook intercepts service events before they are delivered to the client. The hook can select to remove events for specific bundles, which effective allows the hook to hide service events from a bundle.
- *Find Hook* – A find hook intercepts the getServiceReference(s) call just before it is returns the result to the client. The result can be influenced by removing service entries. The find hook can be used to hide specific services for specific bundles.

- *Listener Hook* – The listener hook provides insight into what services are being waited for in the system. It gets updated as service listeners are added and removed from the service registry.

Figure 12.1   *Foreign Applications, org.osgi.application package*

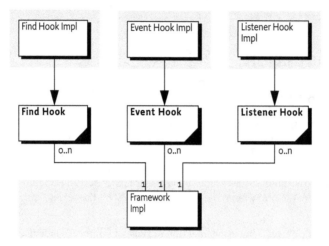

12.1.3   Synopsis

A bundle that needs to hide service references from other bundles, or wants to be informed about the service events another bundle sees, can register a *find* and *event* hook by registering a Find Hook service and an Event Hook service with the framework. If a service event is generated, it will pass this event to the hook. The event hook method can then inspect the arguments and optionally remove bundles from the event delivery list.

When a bundle uses the Bundle Context getServiceReference or getServiceReferences method, the Find Hook is notified with the list of discovered services. The hook can then remove any service references it wants to hide for the target bundle.

A bundle that wants to be aware of the services bundles are waiting for to be registered can register a Listener Hook. The framework will notify such hooks of all existing listeners as well as any changes in this list. The interceptor can use the filter information registered with the listener to detect the services that are being listened for.

12.2   Service Hooks

Service hooks provide an interaction with the service engine. This service engine provides the following primitives to the bundle:

- Register a service under an interface/class name with a set of properties
- Modify the set of properties of a service
- Unregister a service
- Find services based on their interface class name and/or property values
- Listen for the life cycle events of a service

Figure 12.2   *Service Primitives*

These primitives provide the cornerstone for *service oriented programming*. Service oriented programming consists of a code base that is decoupled from the outside world through *services*. It can provide services to other bundles and it can consume services from other bundles. In the OSGi variation of service oriented programming, a service is a plain Java object that can be registered and unregistered in runtime.

The dynamics of OSGi services forces bundles to consider the absence, presence, and arrival of services. The cause of these dynamics can be external events, the result of an update, a bundle that is stopped, or the disappearance of a dependent service. A number of support libraries have been developed to minimize the amount of work for the developer that these dynamics can bring. The dynamic nature of services have made them an excellent tool to handle a wide array of dependency scenarios. Services can easily model a real world concept that a bundle depends upon. The features of the service model combined with support libraries like iPOJO, Declarative Services, Spring DM, and others have made the OSGi service model easy to use and very powerful.

A key aspect of the service model is the centrality of the OSGi framework. The service model acts as a guard between bundles. All service primitives pass through the framework and bundles can not intercept the result of other bundles interacting with the service registry. This design was intentional because it creates a boundary between bundles that increases robustness and security. However, the success of the service model also means that it becomes very attractive to interact with the service engine because all inter-bundle communication runs through this engine.

For complexity reasons, this specification does not introduce any ordering dependencies between the handlers and the client bundles.

12.3   Usage Scenarios

The service hooks are general mechanisms but they were designed for some specific use cases. The following sections detail some of those use cases.

12.3.1   Proxying

In an OSGi system, all communication is normally tunneled through services. This makes it a very interesting place for a handler to intercept the service communications. These handlers can provide facilities like proxying, extra security, authentication, and other functions completely transparent to the parties that interact through services.

Proxying an existing service for a specific bundle requires the following steps:

- Hide the existing service X
- Register a proxy X' with the same properties as X

Registering a proxy service X' is trivial with the OSGi API, there are no special requirements on the service. As long as it implements the listed interfaces and provides the same attributes then it can pose as service X.

Hiding service X can be implemented with a combination of the Event Hook and the Find Hook. The Event Hook can be used to hide any service events from the target bundle and the Find Hook can be used to remove X from the delivered results of the getServiceReference(s) methods.

In the following figure the difference between a normal service interaction and a proxied interaction is depicted. In the normal case, Bundle A directly uses Service X, in the proxying case, the Proxy Bundle hides the original and provides an alternative.

Figure 12.3   *Normal and proxied service interaction*

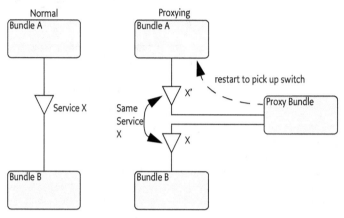

However, there is one complication with the service hiding: what is the observing state of the target bundle when proxying begins? The Event Hook must be registered to act as a filter on the service events. Just after this registration it can not determine what events have been seen by the target bundle. If it has already checked out X, the hook has no possibility to make the target bundle unget the service. A solution is to transiently stop the target bundle before the hook is registered and then transiently started it again, if the bundle is active. It is usually not advised to start/stop other bundles but this seems to be the only reliable solution. The problem can be alleviated when the start level is used to start the proxying handler bundle before the target bundles, in that case the target bundle is not started when the proxy is created. Though this optimizes the normal case, stopping the target bundle remains necessary because any of the bundles can be updated or stopped at any moment in time.

The following example shows how to hide a specific Service Reference from a specific bundle.

```
public class Hide implements EventHook, FindHook {
    final Bundle            bundle;
    final ServiceReference  reference;
    final BundleContext     context;
    ServiceRegistration      reg;

    Hide(BundleContext context,
        ServiceReference reference,
        Bundle bundle) {
        this.context = context;
        this.bundle = bundle;
        this.reference = reference;
    }

    void open() {
        boolean active =
            bundle.getBundleState() == Bundle.ACTIVE;
        if ( active )
            bundle.stop(Bundle.STOP_TRANSIENTLY);
        reg = context.registerService(
```

```
            new String[] {
                FindHook.class.getName(),
                EventHook.class.getName() }, this, null);
        if ( active )
            bundle.start(Bundle.START_TRANSIENTLY);
    }

    public void close() { reg.unregister();}
```

The Hide class registers a Event Hook and Find Hook service in the open method. Once registered, these services will receive their event callbacks. In the find hook, the target Service Reference is removed from the results if the bundle that called the getServiceReference(s) method is the target bundle.

```
    public void find(BundleContext ctx,
        String name, String filter,
        boolean allServices, Collection refs) {
        if (ctx.getBundle() == bundle) {
            refs.remove(reference);
        }
    }
```

The event method is the opposite of the find method. In this method, the target bundle is removed from the event destinations if the related Service Reference is the target Service Reference.

```
    public void event(ServiceEvent event,
        Collection bundles) {
        if (event.getServiceReference().equals(
            reference))
            bundles.remove(bundle);
    }
}
```

Once the Hide class is working, a proxy can be registered. For example:

```
void startProxy(ServiceReference ref,Bundle for,
        Object proxy ) {
    Hide hide = new Hide(ctx, ref, for);
    hide.open();
    ServiceRegistration reg = ctx.registerService(
        (String[]) ref.getProperty("objectClass"),
        proxy,
        makeProperties(ref)  // copy the properties
    );
}
...
```

12.3.2   Providing a Service on Demand

The Listener Hook provides information about services that bundles are listening for. This makes it possible to look outside the OSGi framework to see if a listened for service could be provided in another way. For example, this service could come from Jini, SLP, or through some other means.

A Listener Hook receives events every time a bundle adds or removes a Service Listener. The Listener Hook is called with an added and removed method that take a collection of ListenerInfo objects. These objects provide the identity of the bundle that added a Service Listener and the optional filter string. The Listener Hook can use this filter string to look for specific properties, for example the objectClass property to determine the type that is being sought. Extracting the property from this filter string is non-trivial though regular expressions can in general be used to extract the needed information.

The following class uses an unexplained Track object to do the low level details. The example only shows how the Listener Hook can interact with these track objects.

```
public class OnDemand implements ListenerHook {
    final BundleContext context;
    final Map          tracked = HashMap();
    ServiceRegistrationreg;
```

The constructor saves the Bundle Context. The registration is done in an open method.

```
public OnDemand(BundleContext context) {
    this.context = context; }
public void open() {
    reg = context.registerService(
        ListenerHook.class.getName(), this, null); }
```

The Listener Hook has added and removed methods that take collections. It is easier to handle the concurrency per object.

```
public void added(Collection listeners) {
    for (Iterator i=listeners.iterator(); i.hasNext();) {
        add((ListenerHook.ListenerInfo) i.next());
} }
public void removed(Collection listeners) {
    for (Iterator i=listeners.iterator(); i.hasNext();) {
        remove((ListenerHook.ListenerInfo) i.next());
} }
```

In the add hook, a ListenerInfo object provides the information about the Service Listener. In this example, a Track object is created for each active listener and associated with the given info object. This requires proper synchronization and should handle the rare case that the events are delivered out of order. The ListenerInfo object contains an isRemoved method that provides this information. If it is true, the corresponding removed event has already been called or will be called very soon. In that case, it is safe to discard the added event. For proper cleanup, the reg field is tested to see if it is set, if not, this call is during closing and should be ignored.

```
synchronized void add(ListenerHook.ListenerInfo info) {
    if ( reg == null || info.isRemoved() )
        return;

    Track t = new Track(info);
    tracked.put(info, t);
    t.open();
}
```

To remove a Track object it is necessary to consult the tracked map. If the track object is in the map, it must be closed. If not, there is an out of order delivery and this event can be ignored, the add method will ignore the corresponding ListenerInfo object because the isRemoved flag will be set. For proper closing, the reg field is tested for null.

```
synchronized void remove(ListenerHook.ListenerInfo info){
    if ( reg == null )
        return;
    Track t = tracked.remove(info);
    if ( t != null )
```

```
        t.close();
    }
```

The close method is straightforward. The hook services are unregistered and all the remaining Track objects are closed. The reg field is used to make sure the event methods are ignoring any outstanding calls by setting it to null. After the synchronized block, any incoming event is ignored.

```
public void close() {
    reg.unregister();
    synchronized(this) { reg = null; }
    for ( Track t : tracked.values() ) { t.close(); }
    tracked.clear();}  }
```

12.4 Event Hook

To intercept events being delivered to bundles, a handler must register an EventHook object as a service with the framework. The framework must then send a service events to all the registered hooks. The calling order of the hooks is defined by the reversed compareTo ordering of their Service Reference objects. That is, the service with the highest ranking number is called first. Event hooks are called *after* the event is generated but *before* they are filtered by the optional filter expressions of the service listeners. Before the return, the handler can remove bundles from the given list. This allows an event hook to hide service events for specific bundles. Event hooks are not exposed to service events related to any of the service hooks.

The model is depicted in the Figure 12.4. A target bundle listens for service events but these events can be filtered by the handler because it has registered an Event Hook service that is accepted by the Framework.

Figure 12.4   *Event Hook Interaction*

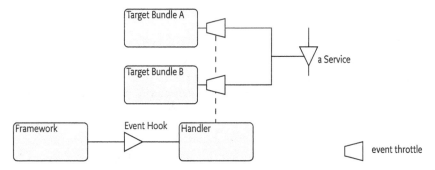

An event hook receives all events, REGISTERED, MODIFIED, UNREGISTERING, and MODIFIED_ENDMATCH, that are to be delivered to all Service Listener objects registered with the framework, regardless of the presence of a service listener filter.

The EventHook class has a single method:

- event(ServiceEvent,Collection) – A service event has been generated. The implementer of this method can optionally shrink the given collection of target bundles.

One of the parameters of the event method is a collection of target bundles. The handler can shrink this list by removing bundles. The collection and its iterator must therefore implement the remove method.

Removing a bundle from the list of target bundles will effectively hide the service event from the target bundle. The target bundle can still get the service, though the Find Hook can be used to block this access to the service.

Implementers of the Event Hook must ensure that target bundles continue to see a consistent set of service events. Service events are normally used in a state machine. Such state machines can get confused if some events are missed. For example, if a Service Tracker sees a REGISTERED event but is hidden from the corresponding UNREGISTERING event then the service will never be released. A simple solution is to stop the target bundle when the filter is put in place. However, when the bundle that implements the event hook is stopped, it will of course no longer be able to filter events and the target bundle might see an service events for services it was not aware of.

12.5   Find Hook

The Find Hook is called when a target bundle searches the service registry with the getServiceReference or getServiceReferences methods. A registered Find Hook service gets a chance to inspect the returned set of service references and can optionally shrink the set of returned services. The order in which the find hooks are called is the reverse compareTo ordering of their Service References. That is, the service with the highest ranking number must be called first.

• find(BundleContext,String,String,boolean,Collection) – The callback when a bundle calls the getServiceReference, getServiceReferences, or getAllServiceReferences method. As parameters, it gets the bundle context of the calling bundle, the service name, the filter name, the flag that indicates that all services are considered or only the ones that are class compatible with the target bundle. The last parameter is the set of service references that will be returned. This list can be shortened by removing service references form the given list.

The purpose of the Find Hook is to limit the visibility of services to selected target bundles. For this reason, the hook implementation can remove selected service references from the result collection.

12.6   Listener Hook

The Framework API provides extensive insight in the registration, modification, and unregistration of services. However, it does not provide the information about what services bundles are waiting for. It is a common pattern that a bundle waits for a service to arrive before it is able to perform its function, having the knowledge what bundles are waiting for, allows a number of interesting scenarios.

The Listener Hook is a white-board service that is informed about the coming and going of all service listeners. When a Listener Hook service is registered with the Framework, the Framework will inform this service of all existing listeners and keep it updated of all removed and newly registered service listeners. The events are dispatched in order of the Listener Hook service registration.

In the following figure, it is depicted how the interceptor can find out about target bundles listening for services. It *listens* to registration and unregistration of Service Listeners.

Figure 12.5   *Listener Hook Interaction*

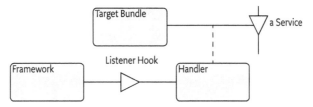

The ListenerHook interface is composed of the following methods:

- added(Collection) – Inform the hook of the registered listeners. The collection is immutable and contains ListenerInfo objects. These objects identify a unique ServiceListener object registration with the framework. They provide the registering bundle as well as the optional filter. The ListenerInfo class is nested class of the ListenerHook class.
- removed(Collection) –Inform the hook of listeners that have been removed because the bundle is stopped or the bundle implementation has unregistered a listener. The ListenerInfo objects are equal to their corresponding Info Listener object during the addition.

The ListenerHook.ListenerInfo class provides the following methods:

- getBundleContext() – The Bundle Context of the bundle that registered the service listener.
- getFilter() – The filter used in the registration.
- isRemoved() – Provides information if this Listener Info is still valid.

A ListenerInfo object is related to the registration of a ServiceListener with the Framework. The Framework maintains only one registration for a specific, identity based, Service Listener object. That is, registering the same object again, even with a different filter, will automatically unregister the previous registration. This will be visible as a removed - added pair of calls.

The equality and hashCode method of a ListenerInfo object must guarantee that the hook can place the Listener Info objects in hashed collections, such that an ListenerInfo object received in the added method's collection parameter matches its corresponding ListenerInfo object in the removed method's collection parameter. This is trivially met by the identity equals and hashCode methods if the same objects are used in both methods.

The reason the Listener Hook provides methods that take collection instead of a single ListenerInfo object is because of performance optimization. When a Listener Hook service gets registered, there can already be a large number of Service Listeners available. Similarly, when a bundle gets stopped, it could have registered a number of service listeners that then need to be unregistered. Being able to provide all changes in a batch improves performance.

The framework must report each registration of a Service Listener with the Bundle Context with a new ListenerInfo object that is unequal to any other ListenerInfo object. If the same Service Listener object is registered multiple times, each previous registration must be removed before the listener is added again.

The event method in a Listener Hook is called synchronously with the registration of the Service Listener to minimize the overhead for the framework. However, this does not imply that delivery is always ordered. There are rare cases where a removal is reported before the corresponding addition. Handling this case is simplified by the isRemoved method. If the removed and added methods are synchronized, then the isRemoved method can be used in the added method to detect the out of order delivery. A simple strategy is to ignore removed events without corresponding added events and ignore added events where the ListenerInfo object is already removed.

The following code shows a skeleton of how the Listener Hook methods can be implemented.

```
final HashMap tracked = new HashMap();
```

```
public void added( Collection lis ) {
  for ( Iterator li = lis.iterator(); li.hasNext(); ) {
    ListenerHook.ListenerInfo li =
      (ListenerHook.ListenerInfo) li.next();
    synchronized(tracked) {
      if ( li.isRemoved() )
        return;
      ... create some object t
      tracked.put( li, t );
    }
  }
}
public void removed( Collection lis ) {
  for ( Iterator li = lis.iterator(); li.hasNext(); ) {
    ListenerHook.ListenerInfo li =
      (ListenerHook.ListenerInfo) li.next();
    synchronized(tracked) {
      Object t =  tracked.remove( li );
      if ( t != null )
        ... dispose object t
    }
  }
}
```

12.6.1   Filter

A key concept in the Listener Hook is the filter. When a bundle is interested in a specific set of services, it registers a service listener with a filter. This filter is an indication of what services are interesting to the target bundle. The objectclass property holds the names of the interfaces and classes. However, just searching for this property with a regular expression is not guaranteed to return a usable value. The form of the sub-expressions can make the property part of an and or even negate. For example, looking for the objectclass in the following expression gives a result that is the opposite of what is searched.

(!(objectclass=org.osgi.service.cm.ConfigurationAdmin))

However, understanding a full filter expression is quite difficult. An acceptable strategy is to look for the object classes in the filter string with a regular expression but evaluate the filter against any conclusions that are being drawn. That is, testing a Configuration Admin service against the filter in the previous example will not match.

Realistically, many scenarios that are enabled by the Listener Hook will require the filters to have a simple structure.

12.7   Architectural Notes

12.7.1   Remove Only

The Event Hook and Find Hook both allow the interceptor to remove elements from a collection and not add elements. The reason is that adding almost inevitably violates framework invariants that can trip the receivers. These invariants are very important to keep the programming model for the bundle developers simple.

12.7.2 Ordinary Services

All service hooks are treated as ordinary services. If the framework uses them, their Service References will show that the system bundle is using them, and if a hook is a Service Factory, then the actual instance will be properly created.

The only speciality of the service hooks is that the framework must not use them for the hooks themselves. That is, the Event and Find Hooks can not be used to hide the services from the framework.

12.7.3 Ordering

The hooks are very sensitive to ordering because they modify the basic behavior of the OSGi Framework. Before a hook is registered, a client bundle interacts with the framework directly. However, ordering in an OSGi Framework can never be relied upon from an programmer's perspective. It is bad practice to rely on start level ordering in a program because updates and other disturbances will inevitably break this ordering. Start level ordering is a tool for deployers to smoothen initialization problems, not to handle ordering dependencies.

Implementers of the hooks must therefore be intricately aware that they can be started before or after their target bundles are started.

12.7.4 Providing the Service Object

Many scenarios for the hooks specified here could be simplified by being able to intercept the getService call of the target bundle. This design was investigated and rejected because it created a dependency graph (registering bundle, proxying bundle, and target bundle) that could not be properly managed in a dynamic OSGi system. For example, if a proxying bundle provides an alternative implementation for a service, how does the receiving bundle know that it should stop using this service? It has no knowledge that the proxying bundle even exists. Instead of creating a much more complex service registry, it was decided to keep the model simple and reuse the existing primitives. This puts the complexity at implementing the hooks, but leaves the overall service model simple.

12.7.5 Multi Threading

All hooks in this specification must be thread safe because the hooks can be called any time. All hook methods must be re-entrant, the framework can enter them at any time, and in rare cases in the wrong order. Most methods will be called synchronously with framework activities. It is fully allowed to call the framework from any of the hook methods. However, even more than usual, it is highly recommended to not hold any locks while calling the framework.

12.8 Security

All hooks described in this specification are highly complex facilities that require great care in their implementation to maintain the Framework invariants concerning the service registry. It is therefore important that in a secure system the permission to register these hooks is only given to privileged bundles.

In this case, the user of the hook services is the framework. Therefore, there is never a need to provide:

- ServicePermission[..EventHook,GET],
- ServicePermission[..FindHook,GET], or
- ServicePermission[..ListenerHook,GET]

Implementers of these hooks must have:

- ServicePermission[..EventHook,REGISTER] for Event Hook services.
- ServicePermission[..FindHook,REGISTER] for Find Hook services
- ServicePermission[..ListenerHook,REGISTER] for Listener Hook services

12.9 org.osgi.framework.hooks.service

Framework Service Hooks Package Version 1.0.

Bundles wishing to use this package must list the package in the Import-Package header of the bundle's manifest. For example:

Import-Package: org.osgi.framework.hooks.service;version="[1.0,2.0)"

12.9.1 Summary

- EventHook - OSGi Framework Service Event Hook Service.
- FindHook - OSGi Framework Service Find Hook Service.
- ListenerHook - OSGi Framework Service Listener Hook Service.
- ListenerHook.ListenerInfo - Information about a Service Listener.

12.9.2 public interface EventHook

OSGi Framework Service Event Hook Service.

Bundles registering this service will be called during framework service (register, modify, and unregister service) operations.

Concurrency Thread-safe

12.9.2.1 public void event(ServiceEvent event, Collection contexts)

event The service event to be delivered.

contexts A Collection of Bundle Contexts for bundles which have listeners to which the specified event will be delivered. The implementation of this method may remove bundle contexts from the collection to prevent the event from being delivered to the associated bundles. The collection supports all the optional Collection operations except add and addAll. Attempting to add to the collection will result in an UnsupportedOperationException. The collection is not synchronized.

□ Event hook method. This method is called prior to service event delivery when a publishing bundle registers, modifies or unregisters a service. This method can filter the bundles which receive the event.

12.9.3 public interface FindHook

OSGi Framework Service Find Hook Service.

Bundles registering this service will be called during framework service find (get service references) operations.

Concurrency Thread-safe

12.9.3.1 public void find(BundleContext context, String name, String filter, boolean allServices, Collection references)

context The bundle context of the bundle performing the find operation.

name The class name of the services to find or null to find all services.

filter The filter criteria of the services to find or null for no filter criteria.

allServices true if the find operation is the result of a call to BundleContext.getAllServiceReferences(String, String)

references A Collection of Service References to be returned as a result of the find operation. The implementation of this method may remove service references from the collection to prevent the references from being returned to the bundle performing the find operation. The collection supports all the optional Collection operations except add and addAll. Attempting to add to the collection will result in an UnsupportedOperationException. The collection is not synchronized.

☐ Find hook method. This method is called during the service find operation (for example, Bundle-Context.getServiceReferences(String, String)). This method can filter the result of the find operation.

12.9.4   public interface ListenerHook

OSGi Framework Service Listener Hook Service.

Bundles registering this service will be called during service listener addition and removal.

Concurrency Thread-safe

12.9.4.1   public void added(Collection listeners)

listeners A Collection of ListenerInfos for newly added service listeners which are now listening to service events. Attempting to add to or remove from the collection will result in an UnsupportedOperation-Exception. The collection is not synchronized.

☐ Added listeners hook method. This method is called to provide the hook implementation with information on newly added service listeners. This method will be called as service listeners are added while this hook is registered. Also, immediately after registration of this hook, this method will be called to provide the current collection of service listeners which had been added prior to the hook being registered.

12.9.4.2   public void removed(Collection listeners)

listeners A Collection of ListenerInfos for newly removed service listeners which are no longer listening to service events. Attempting to add to or remove from the collection will result in an UnsupportedOp-erationException. The collection is not synchronized.

☐ Removed listeners hook method. This method is called to provide the hook implementation with information on newly removed service listeners. This method will be called as service listeners are removed while this hook is registered.

12.9.5   public static interface ListenerHook.ListenerInfo

Information about a Service Listener. This interface describes the bundle which added the Service Listener and the filter with which it was added.

Concurrency Thread-safe

12.9.5.1   public boolean equals(Object obj)

obj The object to compare against this ListenerInfo.

☐ Compares this ListenerInfo to another ListenerInfo. Two ListenerInfos are equals if they refer to the same listener for a given addition and removal life cycle. If the same listener is added again, it must have a different ListenerInfo which is not equal to this ListenerInfo.

Returns true if the other object is a ListenerInfo object and both objects refer to the same listener for a given addition and removal life cycle.

12.9.5.2   **public BundleContext getBundleContext( )**

☐ Return the context of the bundle which added the listener.

Returns The context of the bundle which added the listener.

12.9.5.3   **public String getFilter( )**

☐ Return the filter string with which the listener was added.

Returns The filter string with which the listener was added. This may be null if the listener was added without a filter.

12.9.5.4   **public int hashCode( )**

☐ Returns the hash code for this ListenerInfo.

Returns The hash code of this ListenerInfo.

12.9.5.5   **public boolean isRemoved( )**

☐ Return the state of the listener for this addition and removal life cycle. Initially this method will return false indicating the listener has been added but has not been removed. After the listener has been removed, this method must always return true.

There is an extremely rare case in which removed notification to ListenerHooks can be made before added notification if two threads are racing to add and remove the same service listener. Because ListenerHooks are called synchronously during service listener addition and removal, the Framework cannot guarantee in-order delivery of added and removed notification for a given service listener. This method can be used to detect this rare occurrence.

Returns false if the listener has not been been removed, true otherwise.

End Of Document

www.ingramcontent.com/pod-product-compliance
Lightning Source LLC
LaVergne TN
LVHW062308060326
832902LV00013B/2107